Politics: Last Act of Defiance: Volume II

(Strategic Campaign)

Author: Scott Bolinger

Copyright 2024 by

Scott Bolinger of
Alliance Nebraska

Dedication: I would like to dedicate this book to my wife Marilyn and my kids Angela, Cris, Brandy, Waylon, and Jennifer for their support and patience in my political pursuits.

Published by:

Scott Bolinger
Email: LB@LarryBolinger.com
Website: www.ScottBolinger.website
Website: www.LarryBolinger.com
Facebook: https://www.facebook.com/groups/larrybolinger%20
Twitter: @Bolinger_Larry

3

Content

Introduction

Larry Bolinger for Attorney General

This manual will cover Larry's campaign for the Nebraska Attorney General seat for the 2022 election period. This will help create some structure to gain knowledge on how to run for public office. Larry had run for public office several times. He ran for City Council, Legislature, Congress, and Attorney General. He wrote a book called "Politics: Last Act of Defiance." That book covered his first campaigns, fighting for property rights, and fighting against corruption in government. This book will focus on his campaign for Attorney General, his strategies, how he pushed policies, and review research analysis to help push those policies, and it will also discuss how he built a campaign team.

Larry's base platform is law reform, trying important cases, and working with programs to reduce recidivism. Law reform is a very wide argument. He had between 20 to 30 policies that he was arguing. Some policies are outdated and he argued accountability to put some pressure on policymakers to recognize the need for change. Some policies conflict with other policies and some don't fit the legal description. Some laws were created that don't fit the crime which creates an overreaching penalty. Some policies may be argued and some policies may conflict with or impede constitutional law. You utilize critical thinking to help create your argument for the changes you think are needed.

The argument for legalization shows an improper Schedule of marijuana and an argument for accountability. There are arguments of Critical Race theory, voting policy reform, meat packing inspector reform, housing market argument, and right to repair. He did a research analysis on environmental issues with the main focus on water. There would be a need to revive the environmental issue as the environmental disaster in Mead Nebraska progresses. There is accountability for the government's failure to act on environmental issues. Some of the accountability should come from an Attorney General. In that position, they are supposed to make sure EPA regulations are imposed. Failing to impose EPA regulations could cost the state significantly. **In campaigning, it is best to stay away from negative campaigns, but when running against an incumbent you may need to argue accountability. If they failed in their job and failed accountability, it could give you enough information to argue negligence.**

Trying important legal cases would need a fair amount of research to create a good argument. The cases being considered are:

1) Issues of fraudulent enrichment practices and business ethics infractions in our banking industries. This would include extortion of funds from contractors and ethics violations in foreclosure practices.
2) Looking into issues of the pharmaceutical companies in price gouging and unethical political activities.
3) Charges against a government that willfully violates Title 18, United States Code, Section 1001. 1) knowingly and willfully; 2) make any materially false, fictitious, or fraudulent statement or representation; 3) in any matter within the jurisdiction of the executive, legislative, or judicial branch of the United States.
4) IRS ethics violations and enrichment violations in their billing practices.
5) The Mead environment disaster and the EPA policy violations. The responsibility of the corporation and the responsibility of the government. The government has the obligation to act when a company does not.

The work that was done in this manual documented Larry's campaign, documenting arguments, and debates. Larry will conduct research analysis which may include literary reviews and article reviews so you will have cited information to help add credibility to the argument. Many of the policies that are argued will be sent to State and Federal representatives to help create the argument for change.

This book can serve as an outline of things you can do for your campaigns. This gives examples of a platform and has some examples of speeches. There are several arguments presented that can be used or cited to help interested people in their argument. The book started as a study guide. It started as just standard notes with items of interest. Then Larry conducted research in those interest areas to expand the data so that he could argue those topics more thoroughly. The book ended up being a study guide and was reviewed before events or debates. But it transformed into a training guide to help others with their campaign strategies.

The key to a successful argument is to conduct an in-depth research analysis on the subject of interest and review it regularly so that you are prepped and ready to give a speech. Talk about something you are educated on and have a passion for. There are several big topics that Larry talked about which have resulted in more than 100 pages of research. One of the problems in campaigns is when politicians argue about what is in the media. They are only educated by watching what is in the media. When they are asked the hard questions, they don't know or they reply with what they heard which may come from a biased outlet or from an outlet that is not credible. Being limited in knowledge shows a lack of interest in a topic that the candidate chose to talk about. Lack of knowledge on a topic you chose, shows that you may lack credibility in your campaign. It is very important to do the research.

The purpose of this manual is to give an outline used for a campaign so that others may follow the examples. In the first chapter, Larry gives a general write-up of why he ran for office along with some of the volunteer work and his history, and then a write-up with his base platform along with a speech.

My suggestion is to write your speech and make several copies. Always have a copy of your speech in your back pocket. You do that so you are ready to talk about your main topics if you get an interview phone call.

One of Larry's primary roles in his campaign for Attorney General was preparing speeches for open forms and debates. Being low budget would put a lot of demands on recruiting. Running for a State office and expecting to win cannot be done alone. That leaves the candidate's major role in preparing for forums and recruiting management teams.

The stakeholders in the AG campaign are the candidate and the leaders of the Party that which the AG is affiliated. In this case, Larry was in the Legal Marijuana Now Party. Other stakeholders would be the management that the AG recruits. The LMN party endorsed the candidate and they helped with the marketing of both the candidate and the party. Setting goals and strategies on how to obtain those goals are the responsibility of the AG candidate and his management team.

Having a winning team means listening to that team. Know when there is a need for change and then set the goals and strategies based on those changes. Larry had run for AG up until the primary without any management team and limited support. Not having managers across the state limited his coverage. For a state office, you have to have good coverage all across the state, with a focus on the major cities. The larger parties have district managers in all Counties across the State. If you can't cover the entire State yourself, then you have to recruit supporters and managers. A manager can work in a specified area, town, or county and not have to worry about the rest of the state. 20 different managers in different parts of the state with staff and volunteers can create significant coverage. The single most influential person for change would be the candidate. But any good candidate will listen to their management team, advisors, and party leaders.

Once elected to office there are several stakeholders. Larry as an Attorney General would be the lead legal official in the state. But, there are several policies that he would need to change. To change any of the policies, he would have to present arguments to the Legislature. Everyone in the Legislature would have a stake in policy changes. Another interested party would be the Nebraska Department of Corrections. As there would be changes presented that would directly affect that department. A recommendation from them to the Legislature could help pass policies.

When selecting new staff, Larry would have to search for people in specialty areas. There is a need to update policies, but there are several legal concerns. To update policies, he would present what needs to be done and then he would have staff specialized in policies to finalize those bills and ready them to be presented to Committee and then to the Legislature or Floor. In legal matters, he would want people who specialize in different fields. The different specialty fields would help tackle discrimination cases, cultural discrimination, consumer rights violations, title 18 violations, international law violations, and environmental policy violations. To make the necessary changes, there needs to be some form of conformity in specialized areas. But to improve and change, those areas need to be hit hard. That will take a coordinator and many specialists. So in this type of election, Larry was looking at both policy changes and structural changes.

When running a campaign you should have your strategy all laid out to help keep any volunteers informed of what is happening. The information Larry put into this manual is information he uses for his campaign. Anytime Larry got a manager or volunteer, he sent them a copy of the manual. Sometimes he sent both Volumes I and II of "Politics: Last Act of Defiance," so they have a full view of why he ran and a full scope of the many policies that he supports.

There are many research analyses to review to help argue policies. If a manager is arguing about one of Larry's policies, they do not have to research anything. Everything is presented in the book including citations. However, people should be to do more research to help educate themselves and add credibility to their argument.

Running a campaign can be a very large coordinated system or strategy. You may end up with a lot of people that want to volunteer or you may have to look for volunteers. You may have to search for campaign managers. To run a statewide campaign successfully, you will need a lot of support. Having managers in many places throughout the state is something that needs to be done as early in the campaign as possible and then continue to try and gather more support throughout the campaign. Having supporting materials is vital to your campaign to help keep the people who support you informed. Keeping everyone informed helps create a well-working machine.

Larry was a "walk-on" for the Primary, so he automatically advanced to the regular election. After the primary, it is crunch time. You have to stay busy on a regular base. And that means working with your team, putting out signs, setting up forums, and knocking on doors. Larry's timeline of speeches after the primary starts on June 4th.

- May 31st: order large campaign signs.
- On June 4th: run a booth at the Pride event in Scottsbluff, Nebraska.
- On June 11th: run a booth at the Pride event in Alliance, Nebraska. Larry will be expected to conduct a speech at the event in Alliance.
- After that, Larry will need to have the entire month of July planned out to be able to have large signs along highways covering most counties. Getting the signs out in the quickest possible time will take the work of driving, mailing signs, coordinating with campaign managers and volunteers, and setting up campaign forums.
- After the June 11th event, Larry will need to have a solid schedule for July with a solid staff in place.
- By June 15th, Larry should have solid sign coverage in the Panhandle. That would cover 8 Counties.
- On roughly July 17th, Larry should be making a Northern run across the state. He will need to have events set up in several different towns along the way.
- The first week of every month, there will need to be a letter to the editor or an article of submission on a topic of interest. Which will cover a topic in this manual as well as relate to a current article in the newspaper.
- 20th of June, Larry expects to have staff management in 20 counties that can help with setting up forums.
- 7 July 2022, have 87,000 signatures to legalize medical marijuana to be eligible to be on the November ballot.
- 8 November 2022, have a minimum of 10,000 LMN registered voters to meet the qualification for the 2024 election.
- 8 November 2022. Election day and the ending date of this manual. Is it a success or failure?

You should set your goals in increments. If you are not meeting your goals, you need to work harder or have more staff meetings to come up with ideas to meet your goals. Running for office is a race. If you slack, you might fall too far behind to catch up. Set your goals, and work hard to meet those goals. Don't just work hard. Work hard to meet your goals. If you're not doing that, step back, re-evaluate, and then adjust your strategy.

Chapter 1

Biography

Campaign for Nebraska Attorney General

2022 campaign for Attorney General pic in Bidgport, NE

The campaign for Congress in 2020 ended up with a loss in the Primaries. Larry's announcement to run for Attorney General was in July 2021, giving him almost a year and a half to campaign for office. In May 2021 the Legal Marijuana Now Party was established as an official party in Nebraska. Many people worked together to gather enough signatures on a petition to make the LMN party legal so people could run on that platform. There was some underhanded politics and a miscount by people who opposed legalization. That led to legal actions being taken to conduct a recount in some Counties.

There have been several political struggles. One was trying to get legalization on the ballot. Supporters acquired more than double what was needed for signatures on a petition to add the policy to the 2020 ballot. But the Governor of Nebraska (Pete Rickets) and the Secretary of State fought it and filed a complaint to the Supreme Court because they did not like how the policy was written, claiming it was illegal. So the policy was not allowed to be voted on in the 2020 election period.

"I am a strong supporter of allowing people their voices to help guide our state." (Bolinger)

In this case, the Governor and Secretary of State refused to allow the people their voice.

When developing the LMN party, there were plenty of votes to get the party registered. But some dirty politics and a miscount caused them to come up short on the signatures. They were only 28 votes short. The LMN party filed charges, got a recount, and magically found the extra votes.

Larry: "When I ran for Congress in 2018 and 2020 I supported the legalization groups and I promoted their agenda. When the LMN party was officially approved, the lead organizers of the party asked if I would take the Chairman position for District 3 and I accepted. I debated what positions to run for. I considered Congress but the party would need at least 100,000 members to have a chance of obtaining that seat. I considered the Clerk of the District Court and the local Sheriff's position. I felt I would do well in either position because I have studied law, court proceedings, and criminology. But the party needed people to run for State office. They suggest the Secretary of State or Attorney General. I felt that the Secretary of State would be the easier of the jobs, but the biggest need was to help our state in law reform which would be the Attorney General's position. So that is what I campaigned for."

Press release from the North Platte Post.

This is the official announcement to run for Attorney General.

Legal Marijuana Now chairman to run for Nebraska AG

Posted Jul 15, 2021, 5:11 AM

By Scott Carlson
North Platte Post
ALLIANCE, Neb.-The grassroots political party in Nebraska Legal Marijuana Now will have a candidate for Nebraska Attorney General on the 2022 ticket.

Larry Bolinger announced his bid for the office on Wednesday.

Bolinger, of Alliance, is the District 3 chairman of the Legal Marijuana Now party and ran for the 3rd Congressional District seat in 2020.

Bolinger said in a news release that he plans to focus his campaign on law reform, reduce penalties for victimless crimes, remove truancy as a status offense, and expand drug courts to help reduce recidivism, as well as the legalization of marijuana in the state.

At age 52, Bolinger earned a Bachelor of Science Degree at the University of Nebraska at Omaha, majoring in Political Science and a Minor in Criminology with a concentration in government affairs and civic engagement.

Bolinger has served on several local commissions, including the Alliance Planning Commission. Attorney General Doug Peterson is currently serving his second term. (Carlson, 2021)

If you are going to run for office, I would suggest volunteering on a political board or volunteering with non-profit organizations to show that you are willing to work for your community. It is best to show what you have done, rather than promise what you are going to do when elected. Promising you are going to do something when elected when you have not contributed to your community is considered an empty promise. A standard political act that few would take seriously. Actions speak louder than words.

One of the projects that Larry worked on over the past few years is a bike-share program. This program is part of Panhandle Health which created the Activate Alliance program. Larry had been working with the Activate Alliance program for a couple of years to help create things to get people more active and to make running around the city safer. The idea that he initially proposed to the organization was to start up a bike-share program. It took a while to get things going but once it started it grew quickly. When Larry initially presented the program to the Activate Alliance group it was met with opposition. One lady was very stern that we did not need this program. She said the city would never support this program and that they would not consider having it because of the liability and that it would cost too much money. So Larry asked her why they would not approve this program and he asked how much it would cost. She started mumbling about something else, so Larry asked her again why the city would not support this program. She had no answer. She was not a person in a position that could make that decision.

As of September 2021, people from the community donated 40 bikes, a workbench, and a bunch of tools. The lady from the meeting said nobody would donate bikes, but our sub-bike group proved her wrong. Several people donated money. In this picture, the Box Butte Health Foundation is presenting an $8000 check to the Activate Alliance program. $3000 of that was put 78uuuuuuuuuuuuuuuutowards the bike program. That was enough to get the bikes repaired and painted, with money left over. (Alliance Times 2021) By 2022 the bike share program had roughly 75 bikes donated. Some of the bikes had to be scrapped and used for parts. But they were left with 54 good running bikes.

The picture was taken on January 17[th.] 2022. The Bike Share Sub-committee is getting ready to launch the bike program that week. There was an article done on NBC Scottsbluff and the Alliance Times-Herald.

5-18-2022

Letter from the Chief of Police in Alliance, NE about the bike program.

"I have seen these bikes in use. I think this is a wonderful program and appreciate what you all are doing to contribute. I was especially touched to see one being ridden to and from Safeway for a person to get to work. Many people don't realize but these subtle changes make an overall difference in crime. Since last year our crime has been dramatically trending downward. I really hope to see Alliance get an "A" rating over the internet for crime. You all have a great day."

Phil

Bike Repair Station Ribbon Cutting (l-r) – Dan Newhoff, Shelbi Pitt, Daylin Libsack, Larry Bolinger, Earl Jones, Shaun Ridgeway, and Janelle Visser. October 2023. Healthy Blue donated $8000 to the bike share program and we had a bike repair station installed in Alliance and in Hemingford.

Reference:

Alliance-Times-Herald. 11 August 2021. BBHF Donates $8,000 To Activate Alliance

https://alliancetimes.com/bbhf-donates-8000-to-activate-alliance/%20

Alvarez, Angel. (January 2022). "New Bike Share Program in Alliance Nebraska." NBC Scottsbluff.
https://www.nbcnebraskascottsbluff.com/2022/01/17/new-bike-share-program-alliance/?fbclid=IwAR033dRdzhbUWLEyN995OBe1QzWMMbAS9C0oJZAVabZi2MfLvtNzo56cFv0

Official Registration Announcement:

1/15/2022

<u>Author: Larry Bolinger</u>

Larry Bolinger of Alliance Nebraska has officially registered as a candidate for Attorney General with the support of the newly formed "Legal Marijuana Now Party."

Bolinger was a candidate for Nebraska's 3rd Congressional District House of Representatives seat in 2018 and 2020.

Bolinger is an author of 16 books and a veteran who served honorably in both the US Air Force and Army National Guards. He is also a volunteer with the Activate Alliance to make communities safer and more active, and the Volunteer In Police Services helping law enforcement when needed. Received a Bachelor of Science degree from the University of Nebraska. Majored in Political Science and Minored in Criminology.

Bolinger states*: "I started in politics more than a decade ago. I started as a Planning Commissioner for a few years. I saw some unethical business practices being conducted by the local City Council when they were forcing landowners to sell their properties to the local government so the local government could flip it and sell the land to a bank. The procedures they conducted did not follow state statutes. I spoke out against it, but the City went after those business owners anyway and took their properties. From that, I decided to run for City Council* *so that there would be at least one person who has the public interest. In the 2006 campaign, both myself and now Senator Fischer had campaigned against the "Substandard and Blighted" program because local governments can force people to sell their properties by utilizing unethical means. I have also spoken out against the change in the tax lien foreclosure law that made it easier for the wealthy to take away property from the less fortunate. Many policies have been created to help the rich get richer at the expense or loss of the poor or less fortunate."*

Larry's public career consists of running for City Council, State Legislature, Congress, and Attorney General. Larry has argued and changed several policies at the local, state, and federal levels. He received a Bachelor of Science degree at UNO with a Major in Political Science and a Minor in Criminology. Larry fought against government officials who committed unlawful actions. Such as: refusing to follow state statutes, refusing to follow judicial procedures, creating fraudulent extorsion practices, refusing to follow police procedures, committing fraud on official documentation, 1st Amendment violations, 8th Amendment violations (over penalizations), and **law violations under** The United States Code Title 18 10001 and the Federal Rules of Civil Procedure 9(b). **Title 18, United States Code, Section 1001,** just to name a few.

Larry's focus for his campaign for Attorney General is reviewing and introducing new policies concerning victimless crimes.

Larry: "Over the past 20 years, our government has been focused on creating harsher penalties and expanding our correctional facilities. This has created an overpopulation in our correctional facilities with a high recidivism rate. I am the only candidate that is focused on law reform. Now is the time to get that done. If we keep on electing career politicians, we'll need to add several more correctional facilities. We need more focus on a rehab program, mediation, drug courts, community service, and intense supervision programs. Those programs have been statistically proven to reduce recidivism by as much as 60%. If we continue the same path we could double the prison population within the next 10 years. We need change."

Larry argued against truancy being labeled as a status offense. Putting kids through juvenile courts has shown to increase worse behaviors and it damages the social development of the child. Charging Parents with misdemeanor charges for their child skipping school is an overreaching and unjust penalty. Unjust penalties create distrust in our legal system. With changes in school procedures due to the Pandemic, there is a need for flexibility and continued procedural improvements.

Larry had initially started pushing for police reform about a decade ago when he ran for Legislature. He pushed for reform after one of the kids that he cared for at the Nebraska Boys Ranch was brutally murdered by the Police Chief in Crawford Nebraska. The Police Chief got away with the murder because the lawyer failed to file the paperwork properly. He made a push to help support the President's Taskforce on 21st-century policing. He wrote a training manual and presented a proper restraint program to many law enforcement agencies in several States to help change from the 1980s era community policing to 21st-century policing to help improve law enforcement procedures and to help reduce recidivism rates.

Larry presented an issue where Marijuana has been knowingly labeled on the wrong Schedule for the past several decades causing hundreds of thousands of people their livelihood. It was proven to have medical use in 1997 by the Institute of Medicine.

Larry had sent policies that showed how the banking institutes were allowed to get away with not paying contractors. He presented a lengthy research analysis on many illegal functions in our banking industry to both our State and Federal representatives with little to no action being done by our elected officials. This concerns thousands of contractors where the banking industry extorted their work for no payout costing contractors hundreds of thousands of dollars. President Bush's policy to make the banks unbreakable should not mean they have the right to steal from American workers.

Larry sent a request to change our meatpacking policies and pointed out how the large packing facilities were manipulating the pricing so that the Ranchers got a lower pay and the consumer had to pay more to allow the packing plants a higher payout. It showed some of the problems in the new state meat inspection program and it showed what policies need to be added so that we can have State Inspectors, USDA Inspectors, and USDA-certified State Inspectors with the cooperative to allow state–to–state trade and international trade.

Larry: "I believe that in many cases when you are passing policies, you need to do in-depth research so there are fewer errors In policies. Review the numbers, review the statistics, and listen to the public so you can come up with the best decision. Sometimes a lack of policies could stop a business from running. In this issue, the state and federal policies would clash and would not allow state-to-state sales or international sales if the policies I presented are not implemented."

During Larry's campaign for Attorney General, he was working on more than 20 different policies on law reform. Many more policies could have been looked at, but it would be far too long to put all the arguments in one article. He wrote a book on most of his arguments in the first 15 years in politics called "Politics: Last Act of Defiance." Volume II is a continuation of that but with a strategic plan for the campaign.

End of Announcement

Larry: *"One thing that I do find appalling is when politicians make baseless or empty promises. When they say they are going to do something when elected for office. If they are not doing anything now, then odds are, they will not do anything if they are elected to office."*

Chapter 2

Campaign Marketing

There are many ways to campaign for office. You get creative and utilize as many assets as you can. Creating a diversified marketing strategy is a key component in running a winning campaign. When Larry ran for city council it was to fight for property rights, which turned into fighting against government criminal behaviors. When Larry ran for the State Legislature, he fought for police reform. When Larry ran for Congress he fought for economic growth. When Larry ran for Attorney General, he had a more diversified platform and promotional strategy. His primary focus was on law reform and diversion programs but he also worked on neutral policies that were agreeable to all Parties. The thing that was missing from those campaigns was a management team. One person cannot do all the work required to get enough promotion and gain name recognition for an entire region or state.

Larry had changed from the Republican party to the Legal Marijuana Now Party with the party endorsement. This was the first "Party" endorsement he had ever received. There were many ways that he tried to promote his campaign. There were several ways that he tried to get donations and endorsements. Working with the LMN party they conducted t-shirt sales for each candidate to help earn funds for each campaign. That created about $50 per candidate. Larry's opponent for Attorney General received over $400,000 in campaign funds. So moneywise, it is just slightly uneven. The LMN party did not want to be a party that panders to corporations or is controlled by corporations or bureaucracies. But, not going out and doing what they can do to gain funds limits marketing abilities. It puts more pressure on candidates to do all the marketing and not much reliance on the party.

Larry: I can also see the reasoning behind not going all out, trying to gain as much endorsement as you can. You gain a certain amount, then you have to register with the Accountability and Disclosure Committee. That can be a bit too much responsibility for a first-year political party. The leaders did not want to put up with the hassle.

When Larry started his campaign he set up media accounts. He created a Facebook account just for campaigns with a group page just for the campaign. He created a Twitter account just for the campaign. He also set up an email account and website. He was able to market all his media information on the website. He conducted several research analyses and then re-wrote those in a speech format, then did several videos and posted those on the website. Every radio interview had links that were posted on his website. I then added a Newsletter that people can sign up for. He also added donation tags to the site. Staying consistent in your marketing strategy helps get your name out on a regular base. Creating good documentation and keeping those documents and videos available creates a way so that you can easily share information with a wide audience within minutes.

Through years of campaigning, Larry had created an email list of businesses and media outlets. So when he wanted to do a letter to the editor or an article of submission, he was able to send out a mass email and obtain good coverage. For some research analysis that he had done, he put it in speech format for a YouTube video and in a letter format to send to media outlets as a Letter to the Editor or Article of Submission. Some newspaper outlets will only allow up to a 400-word letter as a "letter to the editor." If you are over the 400-word mark and unable to get your letter under 400, you can try and submit the letter as an Article of Submission.

Larry: "I believe one of the first things a person should do in their campaign is write up a speech and hit your main topics. Run several copies of that and keep one copy in your pocket at all times. This way you are always ready for an interview. You are less likely to miss your primary points if you have your speech ready at all times. The second thing is to research your topics and make notes that you can refer back to. It is standard practice to cite at least 5 sources for your research to help add credibility. You will also want to do a standard write-up for an open and closing statement when you conduct a debate or open forum. Consider what is best for your campaign. I usually talk about policies that I am working on or issues in policies with solutions to those problems. But I've seen candidates do what I call the bleeding heart open statements. They don't talk about anything specific that pertains to the job. But they give a story as to why they are running to appeal to one's humanity rather than logic. In my many campaigns, people react more toward a bleeding heart story rather than one running on logic and statistics."

Set your goals:

Larry was a "walk-on" for the Primary, so he automatically advanced to the regular election. He slacked a bit in the Primary, but after the Primary, it was crunch time until November for the regular election. You have to stay busy on a regular basis. And that means working with your team, putting out signs, setting up forums, and knocking on doors. Larry's timeline of speeches after the primary starts on June 4th. In this case, the Primary was on May 10th.

- May 31st, order large campaign signs.
- On June 4th run a booth at the Pride event in Scottsbluff, Nebraska.
- On June 11th, run a booth at the Pride event in Alliance, Nebraska. Conduct a speech at the event in Alliance.
- After that, Larry will need to have the entire month of July planned out to be able to have large signs along highways covering most counties. Getting the signs out in the quickest possible time will take the work of driving, mailing signs, coordinating with campaign managers and volunteers, and setting up campaign forums.
- After the June 11th event, he will need to have a solid schedule for July with a solid staff in place.
- By June 15th, he should have solid sign coverage in the Panhandle. That would cover 8 Counties.
- On roughly July 17th, he should be making a Northern run across the state. He will need to have events set up in several different towns along the way.
- The first week of every month, He will need to send out a letter to the editor or an article of submission on a topic of interest. Which will cover a topic in this manual as well as relate to a current article in the newspaper.
- 20th of June, he expects to have staff management in 20 counties that can help with setting up forums.
- 7 July 2022, have 87,000 signatures on the petition to legalize medical marijuana so that it is eligible to be on the November ballot.
- 8 November 2022, have a minimum of 10,000 LMN registered voters to meet the qualification for the 2024 election. Attaining 5% of the votes guarantees a party's existence in the next election.
- 8 November 2022. Election day and the ending date of this manual. Is it a success or failure?

You should set your goals in increments. If you are not meeting your goals, you need to work harder or have more staff meetings to come up with ideas to meet your goals. Running for office is a race. If you slack, you might fall too far behind to catch up. Set your goals, and work hard to meet those goals. Don't just work hard. Work hard to meet your goals. If you're not doing that, step back, re-evaluate, and then adjust your strategy. Larry's main goal which was set on 1 June 2022 is to have 20 managers by June 20th and have 16 signs along highways in 8 counties to create dominant coverage for the Panhandle. If Larry wasn't able to get both done by the 20th, he would have to step back and re-evaluate. In many towns, you are not allowed to place campaign signs in town, but you can place them along the highways. So, you can get signs out early along the highways. In this election, most cities ignored the city code on sign placement. In-town sign placement in many towns starts 60 days before the election. Many people who ran for state and federal office put their signs out before that. Larry's primary focus before the Primary was placing signs along the highway. There was a focus on gaining business support. When it came close to the 60-day mark, he focused on door-to-door knocking and residential sign placement. City government seems to be more strict on sign placements for people running for local office.

Creating Interests Groups:
Many interest groups were created to help gain political support. A legal PAC is a registered organization with the Secretary of State. You would pick a topic or area of focus and recruit people to that program to support the PAC and the policies they are trying to enforce. Some political parties created a dozen PACs and recruited people into those groups based on interests and then utilized those groups to push a political agenda.

Example #1:

> "Nebraska for 21st Century Policing and Procedures" to support police reform. Or ensuring change in Policing and Procedures. ICPP for short or Insuring 21st Century Policing and Procedures (ICPP)

Note: one of the areas that would help in support of the 21st-century policy is working on procedural changes in our court system so that the county court system supports the policing efforts. Such as training for judges, county attorneys, prosecuting attorneys, and county defense attorneys on 21st-century policing. So that they are utilizing the city's assets to help people who need counseling or drug or alcohol rehabilitation. This would include introducing a drug court system.

Example #2:
> People Over Taxation (POT for short): to argue taxation laws.

<u>Taxation Argument</u>

Is Taxation Theft? : Some say it is so. ☺
 Larry: "I would like to see a policy in place that limits taxation. I would start off limits that the total tax that could be collected from the local, state, and federal government cannot exceed 15% of one's income. Over-taxation puts people's businesses and homes at risk. It increases unemployment rates. When unemployment rates go up, the poverty rates go up, which increases criminal activities. This results in the fight or flight mode to survive."

 A list of questionable taxes that should be argued:

- *Death tax*
- *Motel tax*
- *Consumption tax*
- *Landline tax (to help keep landline companies afloat)*
- *Overinflated land tax*
- *Infrastructure tax (economy tax): (taxes are already used for infrastructure, there is no need for an additional tax for this)*
- *Overinflated federal tax*
- *Unethical IRS penalties*

Example campaign speech:

<u>2022 Candidate for Attorney General</u>

Larry Bolinger

I am the best choice for Attorney General because I am the only candidate who is willing to update our legal system for the 21st century. I am the only candidate that is willing to conduct law reform.

I have stayed fairly busy in politics for more than 15 years. I have run for local, State, and Federal offices and have argued many policies. I am a Veteran of both the Airforce and Army National Guards. I earned a Bachelor of Science Degree at the University of Nebraska at Omaha.

Major in Political Science and Minor in Criminology with a concentration in government affairs and civic engagement. I studied law, constitutional law, international law, and police procedures. I am working on a Master's degree in Public Administration at Bellevue University.

Public services and community activities:

- Was on the City of Alliance Planning Commission for several years
- Chairman for LMN Party of Nebraska District 3
- I helped raise funds for Nebraska Boys Ranch, YMCA, ABATE, and the DAVA for disabled veterans.
- Volunteer on the Activate Alliance Initiative. One of the programs I worked on was to create a bicycle share program for the city of Alliance.
- Gave free rental space for the BBC tower to allow internet access for the local government in Alliance, NE.
- Volunteer In Police Services (VIPS). This organization helps local law enforcement where needed voluntarily.
- Donated training materials to several police departments and law enforcement academies.

My focus is on Law Reform, Working on Serious Legal Issues, and working with programs that reduce recidivism.

I expect to try all important cases. There will not be cases approved based solely on political affiliation. Cases are based on what is a constitutional infraction or a possible infraction. Some examples of cases I would try are:

1) issues of fraudulent enrichment practices and business ethics infractions in our banking industries. This would include extortion of funds from contractors and ethics violations in foreclosure practices.
2) I would look into issues of the pharmaceutical companies in price gouging and unethical political activities.
3) I would press charges against a government that willfully violates Title 18, United States Code, Section 1001. 1) knowingly and willfully; 2) make any materially false, fictitious, or fraudulent statement or representation; 3) in any matter within the jurisdiction of the executive, legislative, or judicial branch of the United States.
4) IRS ethics violations and enrichment violations in their billing practices.
5) I would look further into the Mead environment disaster and the EPA policy violations. I would look into the responsibility of the corporation and the responsibility of the government. The government has the obligation to act when a company does not.

- **Law enforcement reform.** Continue the education on the Presidential taskforce on 21st Community policing
- **Bail Reform:** There is a problem in our bail system where if you are wealthy you're able to post bail and not see any jail time while if you are poor you go to jail. We need a better program that treats the poor and wealthy as equals when there is a crime committed.
- **Reform to reduce recidivism:** I would support diversion programs.

We need an Attorney General who will fight for the people because the government certainly is unwilling to do that. The Constitution was created to protect the people and limit the government's reach over the people. The law is there to govern the people, but the Constitution is there to limit the government's power.

Some things on the table that are of interest:

- **Right to Repair:** to argue against the Digital Millennium Copyright Act and restore consumer protection.
- **Law reform with a focus on victimless crimes.** When possession of marijuana has a higher penalty than rape, that tells me my government doesn't value women as much as it should.
- **Remove Truancy as a status offense.** Using Mediation between Social Services, the child, parent, and schools has cut recidivism by as much as 40% while the Juvenile court system has increased recidivism resulting in other criminal activities)
- **Reduce marijuana possession penalties.** I will try and push to reduce penalties until marijuana is legalized.
- **I would want to make sure the policies are done right for the state meatpacker inspectors to allow state-to-state and international sales.** There were issues in other states that lacked policies and were denied state-to-state sales and international sales until they were USDA-qualified. I want to make sure our business is not stopped because of this. And if the state inspectors are USDA qualified a grant can pay half the cost of the inspector.
- **I would like to see marijuana removed as a Schedule 1 drug.** The Institute of Medicine presented proof of a medical need decades ago, but politicians refuse to listen

to those professionals. A government knowingly giving a false description could be considered a violation of US Code Title 18, section 1001 of the Federal Rules of Civil Procedure.

- **Remove the policy for paraphernalia.** It is an empty charge. Anything can be considered paraphernalia depending on how creative you are. Most times it ends up being what I would consider a double charge of possession.
- **Remove the charge of losing your license if in possession of marijuana.** The charge should fit the crime. If someone was driving while under the influence, a license suspension would be a fitting penalty. But for simple possession, a license suspension penalty does not fit the crime. It is an overreaching penalty that could be a violation of the 8th Amendment.
- **Support expansions of drug courts and rehab programs**. (Research analysis has shown that this has cut down recidivism by as much as 60%)
- **We need proper policies prepared and introduced for legalization.**
- **Harsh penalties for cybercrimes.** (as new technology is created so are online criminal activities). Some cybercrimes are from other Nations and there should be charges filed in international court and hold those countries liable.
- **Protect property rights.** Many policies need to be reviewed and argued that were created to give more power to the government and banks to allow more property takeovers. Such as the Substandard and Blighted program, the changes in the tax lien program, and the newly presented LB695.
- I'd like to see higher penalties for scams that have been created to extort money from Seniors.
- **Environment concerns:** Many issues have developed where there has been illegal dumping of chemicals that leaked into our water supplies. The companies and the government need to be held accountable for those actions and be held accountable to clean up the toxins and reimburse for any losses. I am also a supporter of the "Laws of the Sea" and the London Dumping Convention which focuses on clean water and stopping the dumping of garbage into our sea.

Larry Bolinger
2022 Attorney General Candidate
Email: lb@larrybolinger.com
www.LarryBolinger.com
https://legalmarijuananowpartyofnebraska.com/index.html

Example of Note Cards for a speech:

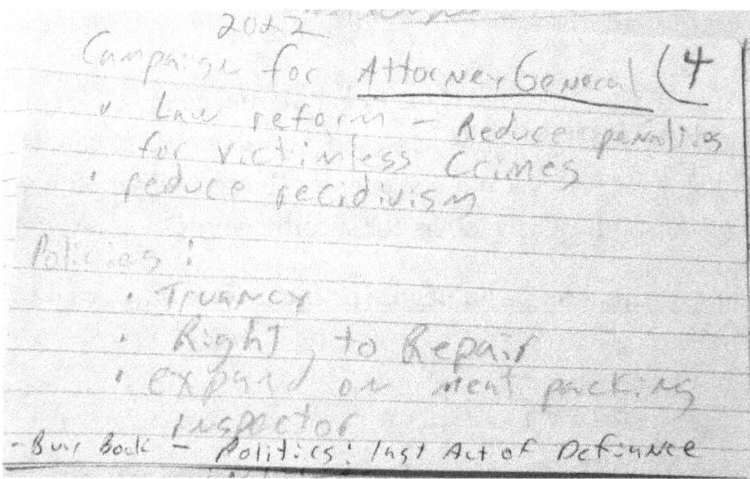

Closing statement:

When selecting your next Attorney General, I ask that you consider who is going to take us forward and who is going to hold us back. Do we want decisions made based on facts or fiction?

I left the Republican Party because of too many misinformation campaigns. Misinformation campaigns are disrespectful. When a leader runs a campaign based on misinformation is an insult to every Nebraskan. They feed you bad information in hopes you will follow. Nebraskan deserves better than what we have today.

I ask that you consider our status. Do we want to continue pushing the conservative movement, which has kept us from progressing, or do we move forward? Nebraska has the highest per capita prison population in the nation. While other states' recidivism rates are going down, Nebraska's recidivism rate is going up. Do we want to move forward or standstill?

Notes: In the first speech, Larry talked about several topics of interest. It is too big for an opener for a debate. The second speech that utilizes the cards is far better as an opener for debate. In the first speech, each topic would need a research analysis so that you can conduct educated arguments on each topic. The first speech is what you would want to keep in your pocket for radio interviews. The second one can be utilized in debates or open forums. However, the closing statement I used created significant controversies during a debate. You need to have a good introduction statement and a good closing statement.

Endorsement Requests. The party Larry represents is the Legal Marijuana Now Party, so he focused on contacting Hemp cultivators and vape businesses to gain support and endorsements. When Larry first sent out mailers, the request was not personable. The second set of mailers was more direct to the business or person. With BOLD letters for specific words to draw attention.

<u>Example #1: endorsement request with a focus on people or businesses interested in the legalization of marijuana:</u>

Larry Bolinger
For Attorney General

To:

I am writing you to contribute to my election campaign for Nebraska Attorney General so I can continue to fight for common-sense legislation, constitutional rights, and procedural law. I am a Veteran with a Bachelor of Science degree from the University of Nebraska.

For more than a decade, I have fought for our civil rights, **property rights**, police procedural and philosophy reform, and supporting policies that will help the **farming and ranching** community.

As a representative of the **Legal Marijuana Now Party**, I am committed to law reform, **legalization** of marijuana, legalization of medical marijuana, removing marijuana as a **Schedule 1 drug**, changing the THC level in hemp/CBD from .3% to 1%, removing policy that bans paraphernalia, remove the policy that allows the government to take away your drivers license if you are caught in possession, and **expunging records** for possession. I am also trying to push policies to utilize more diversion programs over jail. Diversion programs have been statistically proven to reduce recidivism by as much as 60%.

My base platform is to work on **law reform**, try important cases, and work on programs that reduce recidivism. This is a very big job and it is not going to be an easy task. As a Veteran and Business owner, I know what it takes to get the job done.

I need your support so that I can get into office to pass these policies and continue the support that I've been doing for the past several years.

Please contribute whatever you can afford. Contributions don't need to be in the thousands. Enough people contributing $25, $50, or $100 can help my campaign significantly. You can donate online by going to www.LarryBolinger.com or you can send a check by mail to Larry Bolinger, 507

<u>Example #2: endorsement request with a focus on the farming and ranching community:</u>

Larry Bolinger
For Attorney General

To:

I am writing you to contribute to my election campaign for Nebraska Attorney General so I can continue to fight for common-sense legislation, constitutional rights, and procedural law. I am a Veteran with a Bachelor of Science degree from the University of Nebraska.

For more than a decade, I have fought for our civil rights, **property rights**, police procedural and philosophy reform, and supporting policies that will help the **farming and ranching** community.

I have supported the **Farm Bill** and **SNAP** programs to help feed people in need and to help provide a consistent customer base for our farmers and ranchers. I fought to get approval for the **Prime Act** and the state meat packing inspector program when I ran for Congress in 2018 and 2020. I do support the label of origin. I do believe that there needs to be a review of government overreach concerning issues of the Packers and Stockyard Act as well as the Wholesome Meals Act. I will fight to preserve your right to run your business.

As a candidate running for Attorney General, I have continued to support the **State Meat Packing** inspector program. I am trying to make sure there are policies in place to allow state-to-state sales and international trade. I am fighting for a **Right to Repair** policy to allow farmers and ranchers to repair the machinery they bought. I am trying to get the Digital Millennium Act repealed as a Consumer Rights violation.

I need your support so that I can get into office to pass these policies and continue the support that I've been doing for the past several years.

Please contribute whatever you can afford. Contributions don't need to be in the thousands. Enough people contributing $25, $50, or $100 can help my campaign significantly. You can donate online by going to www.LarryBolinger.com or you can send a check by mail to Larry Bolinger, 507 Niobrara Avenue, Alliance, Nebraska 69301.

Sincerely

Larry Bolinger

Phone: ___________. Email: Lb@LarryBolinger.com. Website: www.LarryBolinger.com

<u>Example #3: endorsement request with no target area:</u>

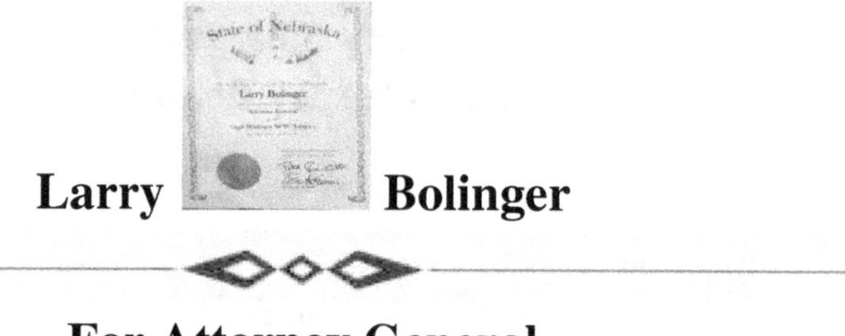

Larry Bolinger

---◇◇◇---

For Attorney General

Larry Bolinger
507 Niobrara
Alliance, Nebraska 69301

I am writing you to contribute to my election campaign for Nebraska Attorney General so I can continue to fight for common-sense legislation, constitutional rights, procedural law, and holding our government accountable. I am a **Veteran** with a Bachelor of Science degree from the University of Nebraska.

For more than a decade, I have fought for our civil rights, **property rights**, police procedures, police philosophy reform, and weeding out corruption in our government.

- The lack of accountability has caused the worst environmental disaster in Nebraska's history. The disaster in Mead Nebraska has been going on for 12 years and our representatives have done little to nothing to get things cleaned up.
- The Lack of accountability has created the highest per capita prison over populations in the nation. While each state's recidivism rates are going down, Nebraska's is going up. That shows a complete failure in policies.

My base platform is to work on **law reform**, try important cases, and work on programs that **reduce recidivism**. This is a very big job and it is not going to be an easy task. As a Veteran and Business owner, I know what it takes to get the job done. Law reform and diversion programs have shown to **reduce crime** by as much as 40% and it has shown to reduce recidivism by as much as 60%. My program works. My program will save Nebraskan's millions. We need to be tough on crime, but smart on reform.

I need your support so that I can get into office and bring our legal system into the 21st century. Please contribute whatever you can afford. Enough people contributing $25, $50, or $100 can help my campaign significantly. My first goal is to raise $50,000 so that I can have solid coverage throughout the state. You can donate online by going to www.LarryBolinger.com or you can send a check by mail to Larry Bolinger, 507 Niobrara Avenue, Alliance, Nebraska 69301. You can donate anonymously or publicly to help promote your campaign or business.

Sincerely

Larry Bolinger

Phone: _______________. Email: Lb@LarryBolinger.com. Website: www.LarryBolinger.com

<u>**Example 4: Endorsement request**</u>

Larry Bolinger

For Attorney General

I am writing you to contribute to my election campaign for Nebraska Attorney General so I can continue to fight for common-sense legislation, constitutional rights, procedural law, and holding our government accountable. I am a **Veteran** with a Bachelor of Science degree from the University of Nebraska with continuing education in Public Administration at Bellevue University.

For more than a decade, I have fought for our civil rights, **property rights**, police procedures, police philosophy reform, and weeding out corruption in our government. Your donation will help me improve our policing efforts and improve law policies, help improve policies to protect property rights, and help address and fix environmental concerns.

- **Improve policies in Community Policing and Law:** For over 15 years I have worked on continuing education for law enforcement. In 2015 the need to change community policy started due to profiling issues when departments utilized 1980's era community policing. Updating policing tactics and law reform to bring it into the 21st Century has reduced crime by as much as 40% while reducing recidivism by as much as 60%.

- **Protect Property Rights:** 2 areas of property rights I will change are; 1) address issues of violations of section 18 US code 1001 to stop unethical government land grabs, 2) change tax liens from 1 month, back to 4 years before a 3rd party investor is able to buy back-taxes. The goal is to reduce tax lien foreclosures by 40%.

- **Environment Concerns:** One of the Attorney Generals' jobs is to understand EPA regulations and make sure our government follows those guidelines. I will make sure our government is utilizing these policies in the best interest of the people to preserve our health and our land. There were a lot of policies ignored or overlooked that resulted in the environmental disaster in **Mead Nebraska**. The people's voices were ignored when our government approved dumping fracking water into Nebraska. I will put the people's needs first.

- **Protect parental rights:** Establish and support parents' rights, the child's rights, and welfare, and review concerns of procedural policies.
    - ➤ Parents should not have to fear that their children will be taken away if they ask the government for help.
    - ➤ Parents should not have to fear that their child will be taken away when they take their child to the hospital for an injury.

> Children should not have to go through the Juvenile system over truancy issues.
> There are over 400,000 children in foster care. Being poor should never be a reason a child is taken away from their parent.
> Establish reunification procedures.
> Establish policies to be utilized locally that allow parents the ability to appeal. Keep issues local rather than controlled by the state.

My base platform is to work on **law reform**, try important cases, and work on programs that **reduce recidivism**. This is a very big job and it is not going to be an easy task. We need to be tough on crime, but smart on reform. As a Veteran and Business owner, I know what it takes to get the job done. The improvements I will make will save Nebraska millions of dollars and open the door to decreasing taxes.

I need your support so that I can bring our legal system into the 21st century. Please contribute whatever you can afford. Enough people contributing $25, $50, or $100 can help my campaign significantly. My first goal is to raise $50,000 so that I can have solid coverage throughout the state. You can donate online by going to www.LarryBolinger.com or you can send a check by mail to Larry Bolinger, 507 Niobrara Avenue, Alliance, Nebraska 69301. You can donate anonymously or publicly to help promote your campaign or business. The Accountability and Disclosure Commission has my campaign business listed as "Larry Bolinger for Attorney General."

Thank You for Your Support.

Sincerely

Larry Bolinger

Contact Info:
Larry Bolinger
Address:
Email: LB@LarryBolinger.com
Website: www.LarryBolinger.com

The numbers at the primary were not what Larry expected. The primary was not open voting. Larry did get all the LMN votes. But donations were very low. He received $160 in donations, and spent around $5000, while the opponent received more than $400,000 in donations. He received a lot of verbal support from the Democrat Party and Libertarians, but zero official endorsements from either party. His opponent was Senator Hilgars who is the Speaker of the House for Nebraska's Legislation and he is terming out this election period from the legislatures, so he already has an "iron triangle." He received endorsements from the governor, the current Attorney General, the past Governor, several Senators, and the Farm Bureau.

At this time as per the 2022 primary, Larry had exhausted what he was able to do for his campaign. Now it is time to reorganize and add to the management. Larry started some random recruiting for campaign managers and then he looked at all the candidates that lost in the primary who had similar interests. He told those people that would work together on their policies in his campaign. Larry quickly got managers in the 2 major cities in Nebraska. In June he participated in 2 Pride events and ran a booth for the LMN party to help promote both the LMN party and his campaign. The focus is to add management and set and achieve goals. The major focus points are Omaha, Lincoln, and the Tri-state area. That is the largest population, so that should be the primary focal point. Early in the election period, the goal would be to install 2 large signs along highways in each County and conduct interviews in media outlets in those areas. There is a need to get volunteers, and donations, and utilize those in the best way possible to gain name recognition.

Areas to improve on:

The primary focus is expanding management. Create pods in the largest cities. Recruit running mates for specialty areas such as Native Law, consumer rights laws, and laws on discrimination, and recruit for the Assistance to the Attorney General positions from Senators that are termed out. Rather than trying to gain support, pushing to gain management or leaders would give a much wider support line with people who have roles in a specific campaign.

Don't get pulled into an argument that doesn't pertain to your platform. A rule of thumb is that you can argue some crazy off-topic policies before the primary or after the regular election but tone it down between the primary and regular election. Put more focus on your platform rather than political entanglements. Staying focused and on topic will help with public acceptance. Recruiting managers, termed-out Senators, and specialized staff can give you the professional appearance and council that is needed for a winning campaign.

In any campaign strategy, you use as many tools as you can to help market and promote your campaign and the name of the person who is running. Larry's primary support came from Democrats. In the 2022 election, he received 188,000 votes for his campaign for Attorney General. Below is his memo to the Nebraska Democrat Party to help them in the 2024 election year.

To: The DNC Chair

From: Larry Bolinger

Communication Strategy Recommendation to the DNC Memo

Over the past several years marketing strategies for public office have changed. In this past election period, the Democrat party missed several State offices by a very narrow margin. I have several recommendations that may help create a more effective communication strategy or add to what you already are doing.

I ran for public office several times. My last campaign was for the Attorney General. I received a significant amount of support from the Democrat party. That resulted in 188,000 votes. To gain those numbers I had to utilize several different styles of marketing strategies and external communications. I majored in Political Science and working on a Master's in Public Administration. I did pay attention to what each party was doing in their campaign and used that to try to better what I was doing in my campaign. There was a need to try and engage a wider audience and build relations with several different groups. "Research found that 80% of the population are registered on social networks and 90% of 14-65year-olds use the internet." (Benhardt, 2020) These numbers assure the demand to make a bigger push to utilize the internet to expand your base support. Utilizing newer technologies can help expand your voter base and help get people's support based on interest support rather than looking at just the Party. Voter bias is usually at the State and Federal levels. You can gain unbias support if there is more focus on unicameral Legislation. Focusing on unbiased or nonpartisan legislation will help gain support based on areas of interest. When you gain interest support, you will naturally obtain Party support.

When Covid hit in 2020, it shut down traditional campaign strategies of running events and the traditional door-to-door campaign. Covid disrupted campaigning strategies, businesses, and schools. That led to utilizing online interaction. One of the main programs that were utilized was Zoom. With that program, you can have interactive meetings online. During the 2022 election, this was used by individual candidates and Party managers to promote both the party, candidates, and training. I would encourage monthly zoom meetings for training and a monthly meeting to discuss political strategies. While each candidate should have regular zoom meetings for their districts. District chairs should be helping out to make sure meetings stay consistent. The DNC does utilize zoom in some of its activities, but it is something that could be utilized more often for several different things. One of the issues that I have seen in the DNC zoom meetings is that the link to the meeting does not kick out in a mass email as it should. So many people who would like to go to the meeting don't get the required invite. There should be some focus on training on how to campaign for State Legislature so that you can increase your overall voter base.

Another strategy that was widely used was creating several interest groups and getting them registered with the State. Create an online presence in several instant messenger programs such as Facebook and Twitter. You can create a dozen interest groups for specific policy categories and gain unilateral interest. Then when it gets closer to the election period, those groups can endorse the DNC candidate. You create the PAC without party affiliation to gain interest in the specific category that way the interest group recruits based on a biased party outlook. You gain support because of the interest in that subject. If they feel the subject is of great importance, they will support the people running for office who support that policy. If you create 10 PACs, that will give you 10 interest groups. You can conduct fundraisers, promotions, and lobby policies through those PACs. So, instead of one revenue stream for that party, you have 11. When it gets built up, you then endorse your candidates. One of the things that would need to happen is media exposure to the PAC or PAC topic. This is where you could do a video and a write-up as a "letter to the editor" so that you can send information out to newspapers, radio stations, TV stations, and online outlets. Each category should have a research analysis with cited information to educate the primary speaker so there is proper representation.

A third strategy is to create videos to share online. A traditional way to gain media exposure is through television ads, radio ads, and the Newspaper. But, many people cannot afford those media programs. When I ran for Attorney General, I received a quote of $14,000 for a newspaper ad for the Lincoln paper. Prices seem to increase because media outlets assume you receive a significant amount of donations. Most candidates do not receive large donations and are on a limited budget. What I would suggest is having each candidate commit to creating 5 videos on 5 different topics. One of those topics is an introduction and why they are running for office. Then load those videos to YouTube. That way, they will be able to add the links to websites and share them with media outlets. People will be able to put a face to the name. Repetition in media exposure gains name recognition.

Conclusion:

As technology advances so should our strategies. Utilizing as many assets as you can, can create a higher rate of success. In these three different areas, there is a need to create positions that can educate and coordinate each category. I would highly recommend a coordinator for each area as well as a research analysis group that can provide the needed research to be able to argue each category. Creating a more diverse online presence can help create more civic engagement as you are expanding your target area, which can expand your voter base.

Sincerely:
Larry Bolinger
<u>Larry Bolinger Date: 12/12/2022</u>

Resources:

Benhardt, Robert. Denhardt, Janet. Aristigueta, Maria. Rawlings, Kelly. (2020). *"Managing Human Behavior in Public and Nonprofit Organization 5th edition."* Sage Publications LTD. Pages 429 - 464

Bolinger, Scott. (2022) *"Politics: Last Act of Defiance. Volume II"*

Bolinger, Scott. (2022) *"Politics: Last Act of Defiance. Volume I"*

Chapter 3

Preparing Policies

When running for office there is a need to understand how a policy is developed, and processed, and how to present the policy. Anyone can write a policy, but creating a policy or a policy change request would be more acceptable if it is presented in a professional form. You will also need to know the correct procedures on how to file a policy. If you are presenting a bill to your local government you file it with the City Clerk and you would be added to the agenda for the City Council. If it is a County policy, you would file with the County Clerk and then you would be added to the agenda for the County Commissioner. If you want to file for a state issue, that would have to file and go to your state representative, and if you gain support on the bill it would be sent to the Clerk of the Legislature and assigned to the proper legislative Committee. If approved by Committee it would be added as an agenda item in the next session of the Legislative body. If the bill is passed in Legislation, the bill goes to the Governor. If your state has a two-house system the bill would go to the Committee, then to the Lower House, then to the higher House Committee, then then the Higher House agenda, similar to how Congress is run. If it is federal policy, your Congressional representative would sponsor the bill and then take the policy before a House Committee, if approved would be argued in the House of Representatives. How it gets on the agenda is a representative sponsors the bills and then gives it to the clerk, then the Speaker of the House assigns the bill to the committee to be argued, and if approved at the Committee it gets put on the House Agenda. If approved at the House, it goes to a Senate Committee and goes through similar transactions at the House. If approved by the Committee, it gets put on the Senate agenda. If approved by the Senate the bill goes to the President for final approval.

In this chapter, there will be a standard outline of how to present a policy. There are several ways to address a policy. You can do a standard write-up and send it to your representative, or address the bill in a speech and/or the news. My suggestion is to address the bill to your representative first. Unless you're running for office and it's an election year. In that case, you build up your platform. This manual outlines the campaign strategy for Larry Bolinger's campaign for Attorney General in 2022. Several policies were argued that are posted in several separate chapters. Many of those policies were argued in a debate, presented at speaking events, written as a letter to the editor, and sent to State Legislature and Congressional representatives.

Your primary goal of any bill is creating the idea and presenting that idea through the proper channels. You are there to create the idea. You do not have to put a policy into legal form, each Legislative body has people that can put the proposal into legal form and they have people that can conduct a research analysis. Using some sort of form makes your proposal look professional. If your proposal looks professional it will be given serious consideration.

Outside of writing your standard proposal or speech, you will want to conduct a research analysis. You can create a research analysis, and then create your policy form or speech based on what is in the research. This will help prepare you to argue your policy. By having your research already done, you will have the extra materials that you can send to the representative who is sponsoring your bill.

Policy Proposal Template:

    I.   Title
    II.   State the purpose of the bill.
    III.   State who the bill will affect and how the bill will affect them.
    IV.   State what you want to accomplish
    V.   State how you want to accomplish your goal
    VI.   Conclusion: This may be the area where you state the consequences of not acting and the benefits of acting to approve the bill.

Example:

I.   Title
Addressing the opioid addiction crises

II.   State the purpose of the bill.
The requested support is to help with adding necessary detox rehab centers in Nebraska to have proper support throughout the state.

III.   State who the bill will affect and how the bill will affect them.
This will help address the drug addiction problem in our state. Addressing addiction will reduce drug-related repeat offenses which will reduce crime and reduce the population in our prisons.

     This will help reduce transporting people hundreds of miles to rehab. This will also secure rooms and stability in the rehab process. Transporting a patient 300 miles without a secured room is not a stable process.

IV.   State what you want to accomplish
What I want to accomplish is to gain support for the rehab/detox center that is proposed to be built in Alliance, Nebraska. There is not a detox center within 300 miles of Alliance. Many clinics were defunded and shut down more than 4 years ago, so addictions are not properly addressed.

     The person who is putting together this detox center may only have 8 units. I would like to see this expanded to 30 units so that it can support the region.

V.   State how you want to accomplish your goal
     I would like to see the state use some of the funds from the opioid drug rehab policy to help fund the rehab center in Alliance. I would like to see some ideas of other areas where we can gain more funds so that the program is a regional program rather than just small-area support.

VI.   Conclusion: This may be the area where you state the consequences of not acting and the benefits of acting to approve the bill.
     The Alliance police department has made major changes in how they conduct law reform and implement diversion programs that have reduced crime by 20%. An area that we lack, in the entire region is addressing drug addiction. A big part of diversion programs is

utilizing rehab, council, and mediation programs. Most areas, when they make big changes to utilize diversion programs can see a reduction of 40%, without the programs, you limit your success. 20% is a great accomplishment. With a proper detox/rehab center, we should see another 20% drop in crime according to the statistics. Going by the numbers, you would see on average a 60% decrease in recidivism and a 40% reduction in crime. With a big enough center, you will see a reduction in drug-related crime in the entire region. Without it, we will continue packing our prison systems and expecting our prisons to fix our drug addiction crises.

Contact info:
Larry Bolinger.
Lb@LarryBoligner.com
www.LarryBolinger.com

In some cases you might write a policy or category of a policy followed by several sub-policies and a standard format would look something like this:

I.   Title
      A) Sub-title:
      State the purpose of the bill.
      State who the bill will affect and how the bill will affect them.
      State what you want to accomplish
      B) Sub-title:
      State the purpose of the bill.
      State who the bill will affect and how the bill will affect them.
      State what you want to accomplish
      C) Sub-title:
      State the purpose of the bill.
      State who the bill will affect and how the bill will affect them.
      State what you want to accomplish
II.   State how you want to accomplish your goal
III.   Conclusion: This may be the area where you state the consequences of not acting and the benefits of acting to approve the bill.

Another tinplate for using several sub-policies is:

I.   Title
II.   State the purpose of the bill.
III.   State who the bill will affect and how the bill will affect them.
IV.   State what you want to accomplish
      a)

       b)

       c)

V.   State how you want to accomplish your goal

VI.   Conclusion: This may be the area where you state the consequences of not acting and the benefits of acting to approve the bill.

Grouping multiple policies under one category can help get several policies approved in one swoop or may look to be overreaching and denied.

Speech Template:

Introduction

1) Attention getter with a general introduction
2) Importance: Describe the important factors
3) Credibility: Describe why you are a credible source.
4) Preview: Let people know what items you will be reviewing. (it is standard to try and hit 3 topic areas)

Body:

I)   Topic #1
        A) Review
        B) Review

Transition:

II)   Topic #2
        A) Review

Transition:

III)   Topic #3
        A) Review
        B) Review
        C) Review

Conclusion:

Sign Post and Summary:

Importance:

Memorable Ending:

Research Analysis Template:

Introduction to Thesis

Hypothesis

Literature Review or article review: This can be researched by reviewing articles in newspapers, magazines, scholarly papers, books… etc. It is best not to use information from a biased source. Bias sources reduce the credibility of the information you provide. Conduct a minimum of 5 article reviews

Methodology: Explain how you collected the data and how the data you collected is credible. Such as using questionnaires, polls, statistics, and experimentation…. Etc. How you will collect data to prove the hypothesis. Explains how the experiment was done and how the data was analyzed.

DATA: Standard collected data. If there are policies or law reviews, this would be a place for a specific date to refer to those policies or specific laws.

Conclusion: A summary of what you found. What you have concluded from your findings in your research.

Budget: What is the budget to implement your program or to continue research on this topic?

References: List the source of the materials you used to create credibility in your research.

Chapter 4

Law Reform:

Larry Bolinger ran for Attorney General in 2022 and part of his platform was on "Law Reform." This chapter will be on arguing policies that he had argued. This will show some of the research that was done and create arguments in structured forms to help continue the argument. Larry lost in the regular election but continued to push for policy changes addressing the new leaders in office.

I. **Title**

Addressing "law reform" and "Diversion Programs."

II. **State the purpose of the bill.**

The purpose of the bill is to make some changes in law and procedures to reduce the repeat offender rate in our prison system. By reducing repeat offending we will see a crime reduction.

III. **State who the bill will affect and how the bill will affect them.**

This policy would help law enforcement by giving them tools to use to help decrease the population in our prison system, reduce repeat offenses, and reduce drug addictions.

IV. **State what you want to accomplish**

- Change THC allowable levels in CBD oil: Change from .3% to 1% THC.
- Possession charge state statute 28.416 (19): Remove the penalty "diver license suspension." To get a suspended driver's license, there needs to be an issue of driving while under the influence (DUI).
- Marijuana possession penalty: change the penalty for possession of 1 pound or less of marijuana to an infraction.
- Marijuana possession penalty: change the penalty for possession of more than 1 pound of marijuana to a class III misdemeanor. This would change this from a felony to a misdemeanor.
- Truancy: Remove truancy as a status offense and put more focus on diversion programs.
- Marijuana Schedule 1 drug change: Change marijuana from a schedule 1 drug to a schedule 5 drug.
- Drug paraphernalia: Dissolve the state statute 28-144 for drug paraphernalia. This is a double penalty for possession. A higher penalty or double penalty has not resulted in increased crime.
- Additional rehab: For each drug offense, there should be rehab included in each offense or repeated offense.

V. **State how you want to accomplish your goal.**

Most of these policies can be changed if argued in the State Legislature, so there would be a need to have someone from the State Legislature sponsor one or all of these ideas. To add diversion programs would include changing the policing philosophy. That would need the support of the States Attorney General. Ending truancy as a status offense and utilizing diversion programs would take a coordinated effort between law enforcement, parents, schools, resource officers, county prosecutors, judges, and local community support.

VI. **Conclusion: This may be the area where you state the consequences of not acting and the benefits of acting to approve the bill.**

Statistics show that utilizing diversion programs with youths reduces recidivism rates by 40% and that putting kids through the Juvenile system increases criminal behavior that goes into adulthood. Diversion programs will reduce criminal activities. Reducing penalties for victimless crimes and using diversion programs will help decrease drug addiction and repeat offending. If our system is not updated we will continue to see increases in criminal behaviors.

Law Reform and Diversion Programs

Research Analysis

Introduction:

Law reform and supportive diversion programs will help bring our legal system into the 21st century. But mass change needs to be a coordinated effort. This means going out and gathering information from the communities that would be impacted and seeing what is needed. Mass changes without talking to the communities would be irresponsible.

- Law reform will be a large issue to tackle. That would mean going through every policy that creates a penalty for victimless crimes. Then present the policy to the community to be argued, and then make proposals to the legislatures to remove or change those policies. To date, Larry has already sent in a research analysis with a request to remove truancy as a status offense. This would replace sending kids to a juvenile court by utilizing mediation and rehab programs. A study has shown a drop of 40% when utilizing mediation such as a social service mediator that works with the child, parents, and school. Implementing such changes would need community support. Diversion programs utilize a town's assets. You would have to make sure the towns are ready for change and provide information and training if need be.
- Some victimless crimes are issues concerning drugs or possession. This would not include toxins such as fentanyl. One item that needs to be argued would be removing the Schedule 1 classification for Marijuana and reclassifying it as having medical uses. The Institute of Medicine has presented information to Congress several times with research that shows several medical needs, with 38 states already approving its medical needs. Larry had done a research analysis and sent that information to both Congress and the State Legislature for review early in 2022.

Many victimless crime penalties need to be reviewed. They will need to be presented to the population and argued. At one point these items were not illegal to do, some were infractions, and some had increased penalties from an infraction to a misdemeanor or felony. Many laws and penalty increases for those law violations were done without the general population's input. It is best to fix policies with the general population's input. Many victimless crimes need to be looked at that have overreaching penalties.

A combination of law reform and training on diversion programs may be the mixture we need to improve our system of government. Utilizing diversion programs in an adult setting has been shown to reduce recidivism by as much as 60%. That can make a significant impact on the overpopulation in our prisons which can save taxpayer money.

Larry: "An Attorney General is the top legal officer in the State. They advise and represent the Legislature and State agencies and act as the "People's Lawyer." Everything I have done in politics over the past 15 years has been to fight for what is right for the people and I will continue to do that as the Next Attorney General."

Literature Review

I reviewed research by Angela Dills called "The Effects of State Marijuana Legalization" which was just updated in 2021. In her research, she states that Colorado and Washington were the two first states to approve legalization in 2012. As of 2021, eleven States are legalized and four States will have legalization on the ballot in 2022. 33 states have legalized marijuana for medical purposes. (Dills, 2021)

There were many reasons given for and against legalization. One claim was that it would create more criminal activities. But a 2014 report by Denver Police Chief Robert White showed that there was a 9% decrease in crime.

In 1971 Marijuana was classified as a Schedule I drug because they claimed there was no acceptable medical use and there was a high potential for abuse. But in the 1990's it was used to help treat chronic pain, glaucoma, Alzheimer's, Parkinson's, epilepsy, and other medical needs.

Studies do show that there was an increase in Marijuana usage after legalization. But I would question the results. How accurate would the numbers be before and after legalization? It would be tough to get an accurate number before legalization because you could not accurately count sales. After legalization, there would be a transition period where people would stop using dealers and start buying at stores.

There are some claims that marijuana is an effective treatment for bipolar disorder, depression, and other mood disorders. There are also research claims that marijuana may increase the risk of depression, schizophrenia, unhealthy drug abuse, and anxiety. However, the research did not conclude that marijuana created a mental disorder or that a person with a mental disorder happened to use marijuana. But Dills states that "the link between medical marijuana and lower suicide rates may stem partly from the fact that medical marijuana can substitute for the more dangerous pain killers and opiates." (Dills, 2021)

There had been concerns that legalization could increase criminal activity. The study had shown that there was no significant increase or decrease in violent crimes. There were concerns about a possible increase in traffic violations. In Colorado, there was a 4% increase in vehicle fatalities. In California, there was no increase. Another study said there was no change in any legalized state.

The legalization in the different states made significant increases in the state budget. Colorado collected 20 million dollars a month and in 2015 Colorado collected $135 million in taxes.

Yu-Wei Luke Chu wrote a research analysis called "Do Medical Marijuana Laws Increase Hard-Drug Use." Chu analyzed the date on drug arrests and treatment admissions. His data shows that "marijuana consumption increased by 10 to 15%. But no evidence that hard drugs like cocaine or heroin increased. The arrest date shows a decrease of 10 to 15 percent in arrests for cocaine and heroin. From the treatment date, it showed a 20 percent decrease in admissions for heroin-related treatment." (Chu,2015)

Research analysis by Stephanie Lake, Thomas Kerr, & Julio Montaner called "Prescribing medical cannabis in Canada: Are we being too cautious" was published in the Canadian Journal of Public Health. In this review, it stated that the California Medical Association acknowledged the therapeutic role of cannabis. They stated that it helps with pain, nausea, and vomiting caused by chemotherapy, spasticity, and anorexia associated with aids. In a PubMed review, it showed that there was significant neuropathic pain relief associated with cannabis treatment. (Stephanie Lake, Thomas Kerr, & Julio Montaner., 2015)

An article in USA Today reported statements by Nebraska Governor Ricketts. Ricketts states that if you legalize marijuana, you are gonna kill your kids. He claims that is what the data shows. When asked about the data, he said " the two studies found an increase in marijuana use among teens who died by suicide. He said that two cases where young men who died by suicide had eaten cannabis edibles. Rickets stated that marijuana is a Schedule I classified drug which makes it as dangerous as heroin and LSD. He also states that it has no currently accepted medical use. Rickets made claims that marijuana would increase emergency room visits, vehicle fatality accidents, the risk to mental health, develop schizophrenia, more suicide, and aggravate social anxiety and bipolar disorder. (Cummings, 2021)

I am the only person running for the Attorney General's position who is preparing policies to help fix this problem. There are many policies concerning victimless crimes that could be reduced. Many laws that are victimless crimes could be removed as crimes. Studies do show that when utilizing Drug Courts and mediation, recidivism is reduced by as much as 60%. I would utilize more drug courts, counseling, mediation, community services, intensive supervision, and up-to-date law enforcement agencies to utilize 21st-century community policing tactics. Many areas of Nebraska have been updated, but we need to continue to update. Instead of trying to spend 400 million for a new correctional facility, we should be putting more money into education, higher education for law enforcement, drug courts, and rehab programs.

Methodology

In arguing for reducing victimless crime penalties and in some cases arguing to dissolve some of the policies I would argue some of the penalties on drug possessions. State statute 28-144 is a policy that I would want to dissolve. This is a class III misdemeanor for advertising drug paraphernalia. Drug paraphernalia is defined as anything sold with the intent to be used with a controlled substance. This policy could be used to assume unlawful use when there is no intent. I received a bong as a present. People could assume that I smoke Marijuana. But I don't. I thought it was a nice gift. Ultimately you could make a smoking device out of almost anything. Such as corn cob, pop cans, apples, and potatoes. If someone was busted with weed and an apple we could assume that the apple is paraphernalia and create two charges. The war on drugs should just focus on the actual drug and not be focused on creating penalties for having a vase or apple or pop can as those things are not a narcotic. That would be the same as busting a person for drunk driving because they had keys in their pocket. They can assume the intent was there when there was obviously none.

To further research diversion programs and our increase in crime, you would want to start with the statistics in 2000 and do a 25-year study to show the change from utilizing youth centers and HHS to changing the focus on mediation to making using the Juvenile Courts and the primary deterrent. Then continue the study in each town as they implement diversion programs and make changes from using Juvenile Courts to using mediation and diversion programs. You would want to add a comparison study of repeat offenders who were put through the Drug Courts and rehab and compare that to drug offenders who went straight to jail to review the recidivism rates. Conduct a review of 5 years, to now, then another review in 5 years after there has been a push on diversion programs to help show the direction and legal system should pursue.

Data:

Under the Nebraska State Statute, possession could be a class II felony under state statute 28-416.

- Anyone in possession of more than one ounce but not more than one pound shall be guilty of a Class III misdemeanor.
- Any person that has more than one pound of Marijuana shall be guilty of a Class IV felony.
- Less than one-ounce first offense in an infraction and fined $300 and may be required to attend a drug course.
- 2nd office under one ounce is a class IV misdemeanor and fined four hundred dollars and jail time up to five days.

- A 3rd offense of less than one ounce is a class IIIA misdemeanor and fined five hundred dollars and imprisoned not to exceed seven days.

- Schedule 1 drug is defined as a drug that does not have a medical purpose. It is also looked at from its addictive nature. This has been knowingly labeled wrong for decades. Marijuana has been used for medical purposes for years. Marijuana was used to treat neuralgia, tetanus, typhus, tonsillitis, dysentery, insanity, excessive ministration, and uterine bleeding. It was used as a useful drug until the creation of the Marijuana Tax Act of 1937. How can something have medical use until the government creates a tax?

- The Narcotic Control Act of 1951 created the drug classification and labeled Marijuana as a Schedule 1 drug. A Schedule 1 drug is said to have a high potential for abuse, no medical use, and is not safe even under medical supervision.

- In 1997, the Institute of Medicine (IOM) conducted a study of marijuana's medical use. Their findings were that it is a safe effective medicine and patients should have access.

- In a political arena, one could argue that any drug offense pertaining to Marijuana could push for record expungement. The IOM proved that it does have medical value but the government refused its findings. That is putting politics over science. This could be argued under The United States Code Title 18 10001 and the Federal Rules of Civil Procedure 9(b). Title 18, United States Code, Section 1001 makes it a crime to 1) knowingly and willfully; 2) make any materially false, fictitious, or fraudulent statement or representation; 3) in any matter within the jurisdiction of the executive, legislative, or judicial branch of the United States.

- In 1971 Marijuana was argued and classified again as a Schedule I drug because they claimed there was no acceptable medical use and there was a high potential for abuse. But in the 1990s it was used to help treat chronic pain, glaucoma, Alzheimer's, Parkinson's, epilepsy, and other medical needs. As of 2022, 36 States allow medical marijuana. More than half of the States in the US agree that Marijuana has a medical purpose.

Conclusion:

Governor Rickets is a conservative. His statement on marijuana medical use contradicts Larry's research that has viable resources. So we can only assume that Rickets motivation is only political. In 38 states they allow medical use. Rickets says there is no medical use but 38 states disagree. So there is no acceptable reason to classify marijuana as a Schedule 1 drug as there are many credible types of research done that have proven medical use.

Proposed Changes:

The requested change is if someone had one pound or less of Marijuana, it is considered an infraction. More than one pound is considered distributed as a class III misdemeanor. Each time there is an infraction of the law on possession or distribution there will be an availability of drug reform. Statistics do show that when a drug offender goes through drug court and rehab there is a 60% reduction in recidivism. Marijuana is classified as a Schedule I drug and by that is considered not to have any accepted medical use. However, Larry's research shows that there are several accepted medical uses for marijuana.

State statute 28-416 (19) adds additional penalties. The penalty is if a person is convicted of being in possession, may have their driver's license suspended for 30 days to 12 months. What I would do is change this penalty. The only time this policy should be used is if the person was driving while under the influence. If there was no driving while under the influence or in possession with the intent of distributing then there is no driving violation. The penalty itself does not fit the crime and is therefore unjust. Taking people's licenses away could create an issue of them not being able to go to work which creates economic problems. Economic problems can occur when we create laws that deter people from working.

With the push for the legalization of Marijuana and several states already legalizing both medical and private use, eventually, every state will be legalized. Nebraska is a mostly Republican-conservative state. Being too conservative slows down progress. As of today (13 Sept. 2021), there are two petitions to add two policies concerning marijuana. One is to legalize medical marijuana and one is to create a committee so that there is responsible legislation. Petitions have been done before. In the 2020 election, there were enough signatures on a petition to allow the policy to be added to the ballot. But the Secretary of State did not like how it was written so he filed a complaint that went to the Supreme Court and they found it an unlawful policy and refused to allow it on the ballot. If an illegal act is made legal then it is no longer illegal. That is the whole point of changing a law. But if we have the same people looking at the new petition, they could reject the petition again. So there should be arguments on two fronts. One argument would be for legalization and the other for decreasing penalties. If marijuana gets legalized then the penalties are dropped. If legalization is rejected again, they can still review and decrease penalties to help prepare for the eventual legalization.

Reference:

Dills, Angela, et al. *The Effect of State Marijuana Legalizations: 2021 Update*. Cato Institute, 2021, http://www.jstor.org/stable/resrep30177.

Chu, Y.-W. L. (2015). Do Medical Marijuana Laws Increase Hard-Drug Use? *The Journal of Law & Economics*, *58*(2), 481–517. https://doi.org/10.1086/684043

Stephanie Lake, Thomas Kerr, & Julio Montaner. (2015). Prescribing medical cannabis in Canada: Are we being too cautious? *Canadian Journal of Public Health / Revue Canadienne de Santé Publique*, *106*(5), e328–e330. http://www.jstor.org/stable/canajpublheal.106.5.e328

Commings, Willams. (2021) "Nebraska Gov.Ricketts warns: If you legalize marijuana, You're going to kill your kids." USA Today.

https://www.usatoday.com/story/news/politics/2021/03/12/nebraska-gov-pete-ricketts-legal-marijuana-kill-your-kids/4663466001/

Bolinger, Scott. (2022). *"Politics Last Act of Defiance."* Volume I. Chapter 26

News channel Nebraska. (6 January 2022). *"Report long sentences a factor in Nebraska prison crowding?"* https://southeast.newschannelnebraska.com/story/45600495/report-long-sentences-a-factor-in-nebraska-prison-crowding?fbclid=IwAR3j-5g380REK32c1KYgitml9mEfHaQLE7qmtzCZTpd5hwk6cqUObxCiupw

Marijuana Schedule 1 Campaign

Letter sent to the Health and Human Services Committee (12 December 2021):

Hello
My name is Larry Bolinger.

I have a policy change that I would like presented.
I would like to have the Health and Human Service Committee look into the issue of Marijuana being labeled as a Schedule 1 drug.

In 1971 Marijuana was classified as a Schedule I drug because they claimed there was no acceptable medical use and there
was a high potential for abuse. But in the 1990's it was used to help treat chronic pain, glaucoma, Alzheimer's, Parkinson's, epilepsy
, and other medical needs.

I would like to know how I can get this in front of a committee to be argued. I believe that this would be a starting point to allow
medical use.

The drugs and the different Schedules:
- Schedule 1: marijuana, heroin, LSD, ecstasy, and magic mushrooms
- Schedule 2: cocaine, meth, oxycodone, Adderall, Ritalin, and Vicodin
- Schedule 3: Tylenol with codeine, ketamine, anabolic steroids, and testosterone
- Schedule 4: Xanax, Soma, Darvocet, Valium, and Ambien
- Schedule 5: Robitussin AC, Lomotil, Motofen, Lyrica, and Parepectolin

I would propose to move marijuana from Schedule 1 and reclassify it as a Schedule 5 drug.

Larry: "I decided to restructure my letter and then sent it to every State Legislature in Nebraska, to some DEA management, FDA management, and a Nebraska ACLU representative. The DEA, FDA, and ACLU can not change policies but they could be a big help if they endorse the policy change or make a recommendation to change the policy."

Letter:

Hello
My name is Larry Bolinger.

I have a policy change that I would like presented.
I would like to have a committee look into the issue of Marijuana being labeled as a Schedule 1 drug.

In 1971 Marijuana was classified as a Schedule I drug because they claimed there was no acceptable medical use and there was a high potential for abuse. But in the 1990's it was used to help treat chronic pain, glaucoma, Alzheimer's, Parkinson's, epilepsy, and other medical needs. At the moment, 36 States allow medical marijuana. More than half of the States in the US agree that Marijuana has a medical purpose.

I am requesting help to bring this to a committee to change the policy on Marijuana. I would like to see Marijuana change from a Schedule 1 drug to a Schedule 5.

Current Schedule List:
The drugs and the different Schedules:
- *Schedule 1: marijuana, heroin, LSD, ecstasy, and magic mushrooms*
- *Schedule 2: cocaine, meth, oxycodone, Adderall, Ritalin, and Vicodin*
- *Schedule 3: Tylenol with codeine, ketamine, anabolic steroids, and testosterone*
- *Schedule 4: Xanax, Soma, Darvocet, Valium, and Ambien*
- *Schedule 5: Robitussin AC, Lomotil, Motofen, Lyrica, and Parepectolin*

Marijuana fits more in line with Schedule 5. More states approving medical use results in more demand to reclassify marijuana. The only reason to deny changing the classification can only be from a political agenda.

Larry Bolinger
Candidate for Attorney General
Email: lb@larrybolinger.com
www.LarryBolinger.com
I am also looking for endorsements for my campaign to run for Attorney General in Nebraska.

Response from the FDA:

Dear Mr. Bolinger,

Thank you for writing to the Division of Drug Information in the FDA's Center for Drug Evaluation and Research (CDER).

The Controlled Substances Act (CSA) places all substances that were in some manner regulated under existing federal law into one of five schedules. This placement is based on the substance's medical use, the potential for abuse, and safety or dependence liability.

The Drug Enforcement Administration (DEA) is the entity that administers and enforces the CSA. You may review the CSA at DEA's website: https://www.dea.gov/drug-information/csa.

If you have further questions or concerns about the CSA, please contact the DEA directly: http://www.deadiversion.usdoj.gov/Inside.html#contact_us.

Best Regards,

TNC
Pharmacist
Division of Drug Information
Center for Drug Evaluation and Research
Tel: 855-543-DRUG (855-543-3784)
druginfo@fda.hhs.gov

Larry: "There was a guy that argued with me saying that the DEA created the law, passed the law, and was the only one that could change the law. I knew that the guy was full of crap. Legislatures are the ones who pass laws. I could take this argument to Congress or the state Legislature. It is both state and federal law so it would have to be argued at both levels. But if you can get an organization like the DEA or FDA to help argue the policy, that can help give a strong recommendation. The argument I tried to impose is that Schedule 1 has a medical use. Marijuana has several proven medical uses, so it does not qualify to be a Schedule 1."

<u>Response from the FDA:</u>

Dear Mr. Bolinger,

I am forwarding your inquiry to the FDA Center for Drug Evaluation and
Research (CDER) Division of Drug Information.

You may also contact the U.S. Drug Enforcement Administration (DEA)
regarding your concern with legalizing marijuana.

Their contact information is (202) 307-1000   info@dea.gov

Thank you for contacting the FDA Office of Regulatory Affairs.

ORAInfo
My response: Thank you. I have talked to the DEA. I know they can't change the law, but they
can make a recommendation.

<u>Letter from the CDER department of the FDA:</u>

Hello,

Information on the FDA's regulation of cannabis and cannabis-derived products, including cannabidiol
can be found at: https://www.fda.gov/news-events/public-health-focus/fda-regulation-cannabis-and-
cannabis-derived-products-including-cannabidiol-cbd.

The Drug Enforcement Administration (DEA) is the federal agency responsible for enforcing the
controlled substances laws and regulations of the United States and, as such, you may wish to contact
them directly. The link to DEA's website is https://www.dea.gov/.

Best Regards,

MM
Pharmacist
Division of Drug Information
Center for Drug Evaluation and Research
Tel: 855-543-DRUG (855-543-3784)
druginfo@fda.hhs.gov

My response: *"Thank you for the information. I do know the laws pertaining to cannabis. What I
am trying to accomplish is a recommendation to the Legislature. I am running for Attorney
General in Nebraska and I'm pushing for change on the Schedule but the Schedule needs to be
changed at both the State and Federal levels." (Larry)*

If you are failing to get your point across when addressing people in office, the next step could be going to the press. Sometimes the press can put pressure on elected officials to act or you may gain more support to put more pressure on elected officials to act.

This is the Article of Submission sent to more than 400 newspapers throughout the Nation.

<u>False Schedule Claim on Marijuana and how to fix the problem.</u>

Author
Larry Bolinger

Larry Bolinger has a Bachelor of Science degree from UNO and is a 2022 Nebraska Candidate for Attorney General.

Larry: My primary goal is to eliminate and/or decrease penalties pertaining to victimless crimes. There are some concerns about over-penalizing and false penalties concerning laws that target victimless crimes. Some of those policies are about drugs.

I would argue penalties for Marijuana possession as related to being falsely labeled as a Schedule 1 drug. Schedule 1 drug is defined as a drug that does not have a medical purpose. It is also looked at from its addictive nature. This has been knowingly labeled wrong for decades. Marijuana has been used for medical purposes for years. Marijuana was used to treat neuralgia, tetanus, typhus, tonsillitis, dysentery, insanity, excessive ministration, and uterine bleeding. It was used as a useful drug until the creation of the Marijuana Tax Act of 1937. How can something have medical use until the government creates a tax?

The Narcotic Control Act of 1951 created the drug classification and labeled Marijuana as a Schedule 1 drug. A Schedule 1 drug is said to have a high potential for abuse, no medical use, and is not safe even under medical supervision.

In 1997, the Institute of Medicine (IOM) conducted a study of marijuana's medical use. Their findings were that it is a safe effective medicine and patients should have access.

*In a political arena, one could argue that any drug offense pertaining to Marijuana could push for record expungement. The IOM proved that it does have medical value but the government refused its findings. That is putting politics over science. This could be argued **under The United States Code Title 18 10001 and the Federal Rules of Civil Procedure 9(b). Title 18, United States Code, Section 1001 makes it a crime to 1) knowingly and willfully; 2) make any materially false, fictitious, or fraudulent statement or representation; 3) in any matter within the jurisdiction of the executive, legislative, or judicial branch of the United States.***

In 1971 Marijuana was argued classified again as a Schedule I drug because they claimed there was no acceptable medical use and there was a high potential for abuse. But in the 1990's it was used to help treat chronic pain, glaucoma, Alzheimer's, Parkinson's, epilepsy, and other medical needs. As of 2022, 36 States allow medical marijuana. More than half of the States in the US agree that Marijuana has a medical purpose. I would like to see Marijuana change from a Schedule 1 drug to a Schedule 5.

Current Schedule List:
The drugs and the different Schedules:
- *Schedule 1: marijuana, heroin, LSD, ecstasy, and magic mushrooms*
- *Schedule 2: cocaine, meth, oxycodone, Adderall, Ritalin, and Vicodin*
- *Schedule 3: Tylenol with codeine, ketamine, anabolic steroids, and testosterone*
- *Schedule 4: Xanax, Soma, Darvocet, Valium, and Ambien*
- *Schedule 5: Robitussin AC, Lomotil, Motofen, Lyrica, and Parepectolin*

Marijuana fits more in line with Schedule 5. More states approving medical use results in more demand to reclassify marijuana. The only reason to deny changing the classification can only be from a political agenda.

What I would like to see is:
1. *Change the Schedule of marijuana to fit what is medically proven.*
2. *Since the Institute of Medicine proved that Marijuana has medical use in 1997, I would want to see all records of possession expunged from 1997 to date.*
3. *I would also want the government to pay back any fines or inconvenience.*
4. *I would want an investigation into pharmaceutical enrichment practices and any government official who received funds from pharmaceutical companies in violation of the Enrichment Act. This could require a regression research analysis that analyses the pharmaceutical companies that donate to elected officials and the elected official's fight to refuse the legalization of marijuana.*

   Imagine a pharmaceutical company endorsing a candidate to ignore what is medically proven to put more people in prison. Those prison systems are privately owned making those businesses 28k to 74k per person per year depending on what state you live in. To keep the money flowing the pharmaceutical and privately owned correction facilities continue to endorse elected officials to debunk Medical Marijuana at the expense of the people creating an overcrowding problem in our correctional facilities. Keeping people in prison makes someone a lot of money. Keeping people in prison from false labeling is criminal. Of course, this is all just "Theory."

The cost of repaying the false penalties for possession would be an extremely large sum of money. But hundreds of thousands of people were labeled criminals, many of whom were placed in prison because our government purposely mislabeled Marijuana. What price do we put on lives that were destroyed because of this mislabeling issue? How many jobs were lost, job refused, misdemeanor charges, felony charges, false incarcerations, and/or refusal of housing? The cost would be staggering.

Larry Bolinger
www.LarryBolinger.com

Resources:
Medical Marijuana Law, Richard Glen Boire, Kevin Feeney
http://www.safeaccessnow.org/section.php?id=175
https://nebraskalegislature.gov/laws/statutes.php?statute=29-3523
USlegal. "Medical use of Marijuana History."
https://medicalmarijuana.uslegal.com/medical-use-of-marijuana-history/

In 2006 24 members of Congress demanded that the FDA account for its disingenuous statement claiming that there was no sound scientific study that supports that there is a medical use for marijuana. Those Congressmen accused the FDA's decision was based on politics rather than on science. (entheology, 2006)

In January 2022, Senator Groene introduced a bill supporting Marijuana. The bill was a political stunt to try and get people to settle. It is a standard tactic for politicians to do in hopes that people will accept the bill because it is better than nothing. The policy proposal would only limit the medical use of Marijuana for 4 types of ailments and that to get marijuana prescribed, you would have to get approval from 3 different doctors.

Letter to the editor:

Concern about the proposed medical marijuana bill by Senator Groene:

I am writing to you because I have a concern about the medical marijuana bill proposed by Senator Groene and endorsed by Governor Rickets. The bill itself is far too restrictive. It looks like it was created to get people to settle on a bill. People will consider approving a bill because it is better than nothing. We should not settle on a poorly constructed bill. We need to do it right. In the bill, it will only allow people to be approved for the medication if approved by 3 doctors. It also states that it will only be allowed for 4 ailments. This is the only medication with those restricted guilds. All other medications are approved by one doctor. It should be the doctor's authority to give someone the prescription for whatever purpose he/she feels necessary just like all other prescriptions. Senators and Governors dictating a doctor's authority on how or what he can prescribe would be like a Senator or Governor giving their opinion on checking a prostate. They need to give the doctors the authority they earned.

Entheology. (2006). "FDA Makes False Claims About Marijuana
http://entheology.com/research/fda-makes-false-claims-about-marijuana-2/comment-page-1/?unapproved=355425&moderation-hash=f81880d92a3e4d3bbe2c6af89f39854c#comment-355425

https://www.brookings.edu/blog/fixgov/2015/02/13/how-to-reschedule-marijuana-and-why-its-unlikely-anytime-soon/

Associated Press. (22 January 2022). " Conservative Nebraska Sen. Groene Sponsors Medical Pot Bill." 1011 Now. https://www.1011now.com/2022/01/22/conservative-nebraska-sen-groene-sponsors-medical-pot-bill/?fbclid=IwAR3nWb3U-jPuWVNVsa7dKo5JT04UKnl-FIE-FkJwDNmoCAcnFFY7jwQn0f8

Associated Press. (22 January 2022). " Conservative Nebraska Sen. Groene Sponsors Medical Pot Bill." https://www.thestar.com/news/world/us/2022/01/20/conservative-nebraska-sen-groene-sponsors-medical-pot-bill.html

Chapter 5

Expunging Records:

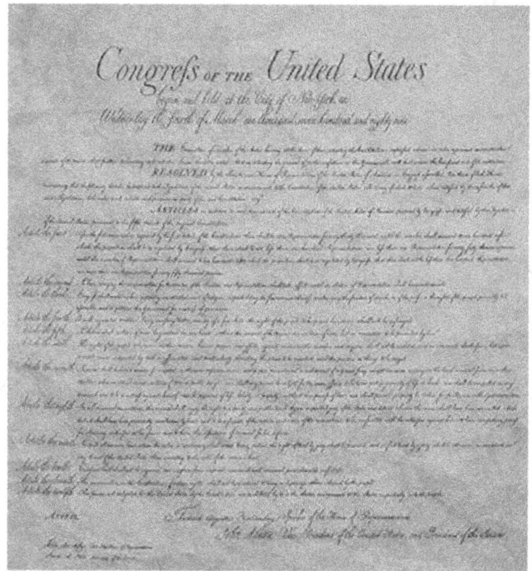

8TH AMENDMENT

The Eighth Amendment to the United States Constitution states: "Excessive bail shall not be required, nor excessive fines imposed, nor cruel and unusual punishments inflicted." This amendment prohibits the federal government from imposing unduly harsh penalties on criminal defendants, either as the price for obtaining pretrial release or as punishment for crime after conviction.

I. **Title**

Expunging Records

II. **State the purpose of the bill.**

To review over-penalization and correct errors that would conflict with the 8th Amendment.

III. **State who the bill will affect and how the bill will affect them.**

The bill to change yard code violations would affect the property managers or owners and would clear any legal records for petty crimes.

The bill for possession of marijuana would affect people who use marijuana. This would help them with obtaining better work, and gain support from Human Services, government support, and housing.

IV. **State what you want to accomplish**

a) Yard code violations: Most cities in Nebraska list yard violations as infractions, some increased the penalty to a misdemeanor and a fine. I want a law that says the highest penalty for a yard code violation is an infraction. I would want all penalties higher than an infraction to be expunged.

b) Marijuana possession: I would want to see all marijuana possession charges expunged unless other criminal acts were done along with possession. In 1951 the government falsely labeled marijuana a Schedule 1 drug when there was clear proof of medical use.

V.   State how you want to accomplish your goal

a) I would need the Attorney General to review the penalty violations and make his recommendation to change the penalties for yard code violations and expunge all exaggerated penalties in favor of the 8th Amendment.

b) I would need the approval of the commission on legalization to review expunging records for marijuana possession, conduct research analysis, and make their recommendation to the States Legislature.

VI.   Conclusion: This may be the area where you state the consequences of not acting and the benefits of acting to approve the bill.

Over-penalizing for petty crimes such as yard code violations does not stop larger crimes from happening. It does, however, make the local government look like bullies that are micromanaging people's yards by taking away individual property rights. Changing the penalties and expunging records helps restore individual property rights.

If we don't act to expunge records for marijuana, there is a possibility of a lawsuit that could affect every state that supports marijuana being given the false description as a Schedule 1 drug.

With the focus on law reform, we should also be looking at expunging records. Review laws that were changed from infractions to misdemeanors and have those reversed back to infractions. Look at victimless crimes and their severity and have a time frame that will automatically change in public availability. If new laws remove a penalty then records for that penalty will be expunged. Some policies allow a person to file to get records expunged if it is a case of child abuse or adult abuse if one can prove that the adult was vulnerable.

Larry: "I, myself have a misdemeanor charge for snow removal. A group of people and I shoveled snow in front of an old school building that I once owned. But the wind blew some snow on the sidewalk leaving less than ¼ inch of snow on the ground. I was charged with a misdemeanor charge and a $260 fine. The policy itself is petty. In most areas, something like this would have been considered an infraction rather than a misdemeanor. But a penalty such as this can keep a person from obtaining certain jobs."

Nebraska Expungement Law Review

"Expunging" a criminal record essentially means that the record will no longer be accessible to the public. Even an expunged record in Nebraska remains available to law enforcement, the courts, and certain government agencies in most cases. Many states allow an individual to expunge records of conviction for misdemeanors and even for certain lesser felonies. The State of Nebraska, however, *does not allow* **any** *convictions to be expunged.*

Section 29-3523 of the Nebraska Revised Statutes addresses the issue of Nebraska expungement. With regard to removing, or expunging, the record of an arrest, Section 29-3523(2) sets forth the time frames that a record of an **arrest** will remain on your criminal history, stating as follows:

- In the case of an arrest for which no charges are filed as a result of the determination of the prosecuting attorney, the arrest shall not be part of the public record after one year from the date of arrest;
- In the case of an arrest for which charges are not filed as a result of a completed diversion, the arrest shall not be part of the public record after two years from the date of arrest; and
- In the case of an arrest for which charges are filed, but dismissed by the court on motion of the prosecuting attorney or as a result of a hearing not the subject of a pending appeal, the arrest shall not be part of the public record after three years from the date of arrest.

Subsection (3) of that section also addresses expungement of an arrest due to an error of law enforcement, reading, in pertinent part:

"Any person arrested due to the error of a law enforcement agency may file a petition with the district court for an order to expunge the criminal history record information related to such error. The petition shall be filed in the district court of the county in which the petitioner was arrested.

The county attorney shall be named as the respondent and shall be served with a copy of the petition. The court may grant the petition and issue an order to expunge such information if the petitioner shows by clear and convincing evidence that the arrest was due to error by the arresting law enforcement agency."

(Nebraska Legislature)

28-381.

Amendment or expungement of records; good cause; notice.

At any time, the department may amend, expunge, or remove from the registry any record upon good cause. Upon request, written notice of any amendment, expunction, or removal of any record made pursuant to the Adult Protective Services Act shall be served upon the vulnerable adult who is the subject of the report or the person who allegedly abused the vulnerable adult. The department shall advise any other individuals or agencies who received a copy of the record pursuant to the Adult Protective Services Act to amend, expunge, or destroy such record. All information identifying the subjects of unsubstantiated reports shall be expunged from the registry.

Larry: "I would argue penalties for Marijuana possession as related to being falsely labeled as a Schedule 1 drug. Schedule 1 drug is defined as a drug that does not have a medical purpose. It is also looked at from its addictive nature. This has been knowingly labeled wrong for decades because Marijuana has been used for medical purposes for years."

Data

Marijuana was used to treat neuralgia, tetanus, typhus, tonsillitis, dysentery, insanity, excessive ministration, and uterine bleeding. It was used as a useful drug until the creation of the Marijuana Tax Act of 1937.

The Narcotic Control Act of 1951 created the drug classification and labeled Marijuana as a Schedule 1 drug. A Schedule 1 drug is said to have a high potential for abuse, no medical use, and is not safe even under medical supervision.

In 1997, the Institute of Medicine conducted a study of marijuana's medical use. Their findings were that it is a safe effective medicine and patients should have access.

In a political arena, one could argue that any drug offense pertaining to Marijuana could push for record expungement. The IOM proved that it does have medical value but the government refused its findings.

References:

Medical Marijuana Law, Richard Glen Boire, Kevin Feeney
http://www.safeaccessnow.org/section.php?id=175

https://nebraskalegislature.gov/laws/statutes.php?statute=29-3523

USlegal. "Medical use of Marijuana History."
https://medicalmarijuana.uslegal.com/medical-use-of-marijuana-history/

Chapter 6

Arguing Ideology

Introduction:

   Arguing ideology is arguing for or against a value of a party belief. Not necessarily a policy. It is more in line with promoting a social philosophy and utilizing that to create social changes. The argument of Critical Race Theory is argued on the "left" to express an awareness of racism in history and to continue to be aware of issues of racism and to act, while the "right" argues that supporting Critical Race Theory is creating racism in our social behaviors. Larry Bolinger argued Critical Ract Theory to try and educate both sides of the aisle on what CRT is because both were overreaching the ideals of CRT.

Critical Race Theory: (8/13/2021)

"Politicians use CRT as a political tool. The "go-to move" for politicians is to pick a topic, claim it's anti-American, or that it supports communism or Marxism. They make accusations that if you don't believe them that you are a Nazi. So in the argument of CRT, they claim all that, and the ones claiming it are the ones who are causing the hate, and misinformation and supporting the anti-American effort by taking away your First Amendment rights. During the Trump administration, the Democrats claimed Republicans were white supremacists supporting systematic racism if they backed Trump or the republican party. During the Biden administration, Republicans claimed the same thing against Biden. Anyone who supported CRT there was an opposition of misinformation, propaganda, and slander to create drama and incite people. Similar issues happened during the Obama administration. During Obama, if you supported law enforcement the far Left called you a fascist. The claim is if you don't think their way, then you are a communist, or nazi or you believe in fascism. Spewing hate all the time is a show of ignorance. Sometimes it is just best to be well-educated on a subject and ignore the propaganda in the media. The propaganda politicians create drama to gain support through hate and fear. I do support both parties, but I never supported extremist ideals.

Larry: "CRT was up to be voted on in the board of regency meeting on 8/13/2021 in Nebraska. I had messaged a couple of my sociology professors in support of how they taught CRT. I also sent a message to my district chairperson which reads":

"Hello

My name is Larry Bolinger.

I am writing to you to try and encourage you to support CRT.
I did attend UNO and took a couple of sociology courses. I graduated with a Bachelor of Science degree in 2021.
Those courses did cover CRT. How politicians describe CRT and how I was taught are two different things. CRT on the political screen is all smoke. It is just a biased political stunt to gain the support of one party over the other. The argument of CRT isn't about truth or education, it is only about political support.
I am running for the Nebraska States Attorney position in 2022. I'll do what I can to help support the University of Nebraska and support CRT or any other course they feel is necessary."

The false claim of CRT is that it creates hate towards America and that it teaches to segregate by race. At UNO, many of the studies were based on "critical thinking." Basically proving what is fact or opinions and how to go into depth in proving those facts. The CRT is a theory. If politicians want to get rid of it, then they should prove the theory to be wrong. But they can't because the theory is valid. In the past, there has been racism used to conduct government business. People eventually stood up against racism and fought for equal rights. People should be proud that we stood up against racism. It is not something that is to be browbeaten depending on what race you are. It is something that people should take pride in because we came a long way in equal rights whereas many countries are far behind in equal rights and human rights.

In a Sociology book by John Macionis called "Social Problems" examines the social-conflict approach. This theory sees society as divided by inequality and conflict. (Macionis, 2019) In any theory, you question and research to prove or disprove the theory. This theory can be easily proven by looking at our history and how people have fought for equal rights. There have been arguments to allow black people to vote, for women to vote, allowing women to work for equal pay, equal education opportunities, and fair treatment at work. There have been significant inequalities in our past. But people rose up, fought back, and were able to change our laws to support equality. That set the US above all others in advancing cultural changes because we have an established democracy and a government that is elected by the people. Many governments that don't have that are stagnant in their growth.

Some people argue that Marxism and CRT are the same things. Some things are similar, but they are two different theories. Karl Marx's theory has been studied for many years. Some of it is viable and some of it is overreaching. Marx's theories are based on analyzing and disputing capitalism. He states that capitalism will naturally have social problems as capitalism only focuses on the wealthy and does not help the poor. So in capitalism, the government does not serve the people. They pander to the elite business which results in a higher percentage of people in poverty because only a select few will be wealthy at the expense of the working class and poor. (Macionis, 2019) In theory, you can argue for and against this theory. It does have some truth to it because we have a system that allows banks and big business bailouts while small struggling businesses don't have those opportunities so they have a high failure rate. You can also argue the pay inequality. We have a system where the price of a product increases but the pay rates stay the same and at the same time cost of living increases. So people are not getting pay raises to keep up with inflation. The owners of the business are increasing the retail prices so the elite gets an increase in wages, but the working class stays the same with more of their money going to the cost of living.

You can also argue Marx's theory that capitalism spawns more social problems and poverty. Because any ideology has issues of poverty and eventually has to create programs to fix poverty issues. Most wealthy countries will have a mixed ideology. Usually, one ideology has a higher failure rate than a mixed ideology and most authoritarian ideologies have a high failure rate. The US is considered a capitalist society, but we are a mix of capitalism and socialism. People will argue or deny that we a partially socialist. We lean more toward capitalism but we have a mixed ideology. We have many government programs that are there to help people in need. Such as housing, people with disabilities, and food programs. Another example would be Germany. Today's Germany is primarily a socialist government. But they do dive into capitalism. Having that mix has made them the wealthiest state in Europe. Before WWII they were a strict socialist with an authoritarian ruler (Hitler) who hated communism and capitalism. Socialism can work but, if there is an authoritarian ruler it is bound to fail. Several European states had gone through bankruptcy after failing as a socialist society. There has to be a happy medium between socialism and capitalism to make it work right. It is a possibility that the US was leaning far too into capitalism which caused the depression and the 2008 recession. In the 2008 recession, Bush pushed his program to make banks unbreakable at the expense of the working class. This, in a way, does support Marx's theory. But the happy medium was to increase housing, improve the farming bill, support Snaps, put more into grants for college, federal loans for college, health care, and expanded health care.

Another failed government is Nigeria. They modeled the US government. But they have an authoritarian rule and the committees are made up of people that the ruler elects rather than elected by the people. They also put too much stock in just one commodity (Oil). They don't diversify so when oil prices drop, their economy collapses. The same thing happened to Venezuela. They are a socialist authoritarian rule that relied just on oil and now their money is worth little to nothing.

Conflict Theory looks at society as a competition for limited resources. **Critical Race Theory** looks at structural inequality based on white privilege and associated wealth, power, and prestige. Marxism which is also called class conflict theory is more based on the government system pandering to the wealthy where the different social classes compete for social, material, and political resources. (Rice University, 2017) 3 different theories but a far-right or far-left extremist will try and combine the three and assume it's the same ideology.

Larry: "I supported the teaching of CRT in college as it is a form for freedom of speech and it does teach a popular theory along with many others. We don't want kids to be closed-minded about ideologies because we don't improve by being biased or having a biased education. By supporting CRT, I was called a racist, a Nazi, a communist, a supporter of teaching kids to hate America, a supporter of segregation, and an anti-American. One clown told me that if I believed in CRT it was a crime against the state. It was a very stupid accusation as it is not a crime. The next thing you know, they will be banning "Dr. Seuss Books" (some of Dr. Seuss's books were forced off the shelf in 2020). An anti-American act would be to ban the teaching. The ones who were spreading the hate were the ones talking trash to me. Which in a sense proves the theory. I would hope that we would want to freely educate kids to help further their knowledge. To improve our future we have to know our pasts."

In critical thinking, we do an in-depth look into the theory and prove or des-prove the theory. All three theories can be argued as similar because they are arguments about inequality. Ultimately ignoring an issue doesn't make problems go away. In 2021 the far-Right extremist wants to deny that CRT ever existed and lay claim that it teaches racism rather than teaching that there have been decisions based on race or gender. It does not teach people how to be racist, but it identifies problems in our system. Identifying a problem and education will help us move forward.

Larry posted a write-up in a Facebook group called the Political Rumble. Which is made up of far-right extremists who are supported by a Republican Attorney General candidate Karen. They tried debating CRT by calling Larry every name in the book and then the discussion ended when one of them threatened his life. They thought threatening one's life was funny. Larry has always been a big supporter of anti-bullying programs. A threat on his life is something that he took seriously. Running for Attorney General and someone threatening his life is something he would have to act on. The threat gets reported to the IC3 which is a federal law enforcement agency that specializes in online threats.

Arguing with the far-left or far-right extremists is futile. There is no logical discussion. Larry had always been moderate so he never looked at CRT as being racist. He only looked at it as adding more education so that he could better understand and represent the people. Most of what was discussed in CRT was not new to him but it was put into perspective. Creates more awareness to help advance equal rights.

Politically the far-Right extremists and the far-Left extremists are fighting similar causes. The left is for CRT and freedom of expression. The far-right is against CRT which suppresses freedom of expression and speech. But, the far Left supports the WOKE movement and Cancel Coulter which limits or ends freedom of expression and freedom of speech. So both parties are fighting to limit freedom of expression and speech. Both utilize the fear factor to push each other's agenda.

An odd issue is that the far-Right fights against CRT but promotes supporting the Jewish community and Holocaust education to fight anti-Semitism which is educating in CRT.

An emailed question from Tom B.

Tom: Are you for or against CRT in schools?

Larry: It depends on how it is taught. When I studied CRT at UNO it wasn't presented in a way that was hate-mongering. Many policies and policy changes have been made because there was inequality based on race. The 1960s riots could be theorized by utilizing CRT because it was based on race inequality.

Some politicians are spreading rumors that teachers who teach CRT segregate students and that is not teaching theory. That is just segregation by a racist teacher. But you can argue that teachers could be utilizing an inequality of race and one can argue it as CRT. A teacher could lose their job if they segregate kids.

Grade school kids should not be put in a position to argue racism. But Teachers should be well versed in CRT as well as many other theories to help identify issues and to help them push for equality.

I do, to a certain extent support CRT as it is protected as a freedom of expression under the 1st Amendment. I do not support WOKE or Cancel Culture as those are programs that would violate 1st Amendment Rights and the freedom of expression.

Larry's argument with Karen who is a Republican candidate for Attorney General.

Karen: Your support for CRT would also not align you with the Republican Party.

Larry Bolinger: I support the 1st Amendment and responsible Legislation.

Larry Bolinger: Your statement makes no sense. CRT has never been part of what the Republican Party was in design. I would be very concerned about a person running for Attorney General who is backing speech and expression suppression. You are not backing what is Cons...

Larry Bolinger: you can take a political stance on CRT if you are running for positions such as Governor, Legislature, or School Board. But you can not as an Attorney General. You have to argue what is legal even if it's against your personal stance. Being an Attorney...

Karen: CRT promotes racism. I oppose racism.

Larry Bolinger: You promote a political lie. An Attorney General should not get caught up in spreading political lies. That is how you get petitioned out of office. You have to be legally correct. Taking this political stance would be in poor taste.

Karen: I will continue to be a strong opponent of CRT and CSE. The voters can decide what they want to support.

Larry *Bolinger: sounds good. I'll be a strong supporter of the Constitution.*

There are many complaints about CRT. There are complaints that the DOJ made threats to citizens that they better not show up at any school board meeting. There were even threats that the DoJ was going to have the FBI put them under investigation if they did show up at a school board meeting. Conservatives made the accusation that CRT is teaching black kids that white kids hate them. " (Bolinger, Politics Last Act of Defiance, Chapter 17, 2021)

There are some misconceptions of what Marxism is and what CRT is. Marxism is a theory of inequality of social status. But Karl Marx argued the inequality of social status and used Capitalism as a tool to argue his theory. He hated Capitalism and supported Communism. He blamed Capitalism for the inequality of treatment between social status. He went a little overboard in his theory. There are issues of inequality of social status that can be proven, but it is not based on ideology. There are proven issues of inequality of social status and in some cases, inequality by race but when adding ideology creates the issue of overreaching on a philosophy.

Chapter 7

Larry Bolinger 2024

Court Policy Reform

I.   Title

Court procedural change request

II.   State the purpose of the bill.

To ensure everyone is allowed a defense.

III.   State who the bill will affect and how the bill will affect them.

This will help secure people a proper defense, but may also be used to delay a hearing.

IV.   State what you want to accomplish

a)   After you are given papers in a suit, you have 10 days to send in your defense. After that date, the court will not allow any other papers to be sent in. If you miss the deadline, you will not have a defense. I would want to remove that procedure and allow a defense to be presented at any time. If there is a need to request a continuance to prepare an argument due to new evidence being presented, then you approve the continuance. Allowing the defense supports the 14th Amendment's due process.

b)   Coercion by a Judge: Stop judges threatening people from appealing to a higher court by using coercion. A judge should be educated about the process if a person is not satisfied with the judge's decision.

c)   Add more Drug Courts.

V.   State how you want to accomplish your goal

I would want this request to go to the States Attorney General for review and then make his recommendation.

VI.   Conclusion: This may be the area where you state the consequences of not acting and the benefits of acting to approve the bill.

By not acting we assure that many people will continue to be refused a defense and people will accept guilt or except penalties when they are innocent. Adding more drug courts will help with drug addiction and get people the needed rehab support. It will also help with reducing repeat offenders of drug-related criminal actions.

In some cases in politics, you may end up arguing procedures rather than a policy or statute. In this chapter, we argue a procedure rather than a State Statute. Many issues in our immigration policies are procedural issues rather than Federal or International law. In this case, we argue for defense and to stop coercion. To put pressure on change, we can argue it as an infraction of Constitutional Law. In politics being educated on the Constitution can help you argue issues of a government that is overreaching its legal authority. That is how you ensure accountability to the people and law.

Larry: "I am a firm believer in making sure everyone that has to go to court is allowed the due process of law. They are allowed a defense and allowed representation. The way our court system policy is run is that if you are summoned to court, you have 10 days after you receive your court date to present a defense. If you take longer than 10 days your defense will not be considered. I believe that needs to be changed. The change I would make is that you would be allowed to present a defense up to the date of the court date. If the people representing the prosecution and defense do not have a proper amount of time to argue the case, then they set another date to review materials to prepare the case."

Some people will take advantage of allowing a defense at any time to delay a hearing but we should not have a court that refuses a right to have a defense. Proper due process is protected by the Constitution in the 14th Amendment. But policymakers create more policies or procedures that take away or limit your Civil Rights.

Another issue in our court system is the issue of coercion that comes from the judge. Where he or she makes a decision and makes what would be considered a threat or coercion. There have been judges who made their decision on a penalty and then told the person being penalized that they should be thankful that they were only getting 3 years in the state penitentiary and then made a statement that they better not take the case to a higher court because nobody will overrule their decision. That, by definition, is coercion. A proper judge would make his decision and present policies that the defendant can pursue if they did not like the Judge's decision or proceedings. A judge, not following proper procedures should be penalized and should face an ethics board.

Chapter 8

Voting policy reform

I. **Title**

Voting Policy Reform

II. **State the purpose of the bill.**

To increase voter turnout.

III. **State who the bill will affect and how the bill will affect them.**

It will allow more flexibility on how to vote.

IV. **State what you want to accomplish**

a) Allow registration up to the day of the election.

b) Require poll stations to be opened from 8 am to midnight.

c) Change the policy on sign placement. Current policy says 200 feet from a polling station. The wording needs to be changed and read that campaign signs can not be within 150 feet of the front door of a polling station.

d) Registration for a political party: any person can change parties and run for office in that party up to the final day of registration

e) Improve internet capability and security to allow online voting, and voting through a phone app.

f) Early voting should be counted as they are registered. The Secretary of State's site should be updated daily to show early voting results.

g) Remove the policy that restricts prisoners and people with felony charges from voting.

h) Ballots will have all candidates listed based on your area not by political party. Candidates from all 4 parties will be listed on each ballot during the primary and regular elections.

i) Allow write-in votes in both the primary and general elections. Current policy states that if you are voting for a candidate in a different party and doing a write-in for the primary, your vote won't count.

j) State how you want to accomplish your goal.

I would need each bill drafted individually and presented to the Legislative Committee for review.

k) Conclusion: This may be the area where you state the consequences of not acting and the benefits of acting to approve the bill.

Our voter turnouts are usually less than 40% of the registered voters. There are a very large number of people who have not registered to vote and more than half who do register don't vote. Improving our voting process can help get more people involved and interested in our voting process and show more interest in how our government is doing.

During each election cycle, there are complaints of voter integrity, low voter turnouts, and accusations of voter fraud. Many states have changed to electronic counters to count votes and people argued that those are not accurate and that they should do away with them. But, before there were electronic counters, there were complaints of voter fraud. The process we have today is not infallible. When something is not infallible, there is room to improve. When creating new policies and procedures, you have to make sure you don't impede Constitutional Law. So each policy change needs to be reviewed and argued so that there is no infraction of the law if the policy is changed.

There are different areas people are arguing for voting reform. But the number one thing that should always be looked at is if there are policies that get in the way of people's right to vote. If there is a vote on voter ID, then there has to be a policy for people to obtain free IDs. You can't approve the first policy without the other intact.

Here is a list of suggested policy improvements:

1. Allow registration up to the day of the election.
2. Require poll stations to be opened from 8 am to midnight to allow people who work different hours of the day to vote.
3. Change the policy on sign placement. Current policy says 200 feet from a polling station. Change the wording that states that campaign signs can not be within 150 feet of the front door of a polling station. This policy is to deter people from putting up signs on the side of the street where the voting polls are on. It allows people who live across the street from a polling station to put campaign signs on their property. This allows those people their property rights and freedom of expression.
4. Registration for a political party. The policy states that you have to register by December for a party to be eligible to run for office in that part. A new party might not have enough time to file campaign slots due to a policy like that. The suggested change would be to say that "any person can change parties and run for office in that party up to the final day of registration."

5. Improve internet capability and security to allow online voting, and voting through a phone app.
6. Early voting should be counted as they are registered. The Secretary of State's site should be updated daily to show early voting results. If early voting starts 2 months before the regular election, there should be at the least, weakly updates on each candidate on the Secretary of State website.
7. Remove the policy that restricts prisoners and people with felony charges from voting. All people have the right to vote. Any type of voter restriction is against the law.
8. Ballots will have all candidates listed based on your area not by political party. Candidates from all 4 parties will be listed on each ballot.
9. Allow write-in votes in both the primary and general elections. Current policy states that if you are voting for a candidate in a different party and doing a write-in for the primary, your vote won't count.

Larry had written to several State Legislatures, requesting voting reform. Below is the response he received from Senator Erdman.

Arguments:

Steve Erdman:
 Message Body
 Larry, thank you for your email.
 Our current time of operation for the polling stations is adequate.
 I believe most people have some form of ID
 now.
 When you fly, cash a check, or about 50 other things you need a ID.
Another note from Erdman:
Take a look at this list where ID is required.
That comment about free IDs doesn't hold much water.
Oh there could be some (a few) that need a free ID. Very few!
We have more significant issues than how far signs are from a polling place.

My response to Erdmans message: I know there are more pressing issues, but the legislative job is never done. It is a multi-task position. You can't just focus on one policy. these are small issues that can easily be corrected.
I can see your argument about all the other things that need IDs, but none of them are for voting rights. If the policy is passed to force people to have an ID without a form of free ID's,
it will either get vetoed or it will get pushed to the Supreme Court for voter suppression violation. I am running for Attorney General and I for one would push it to the Supreme Court and have it overturned there. You have the chance to fix the issue before it fails.
On the issue of sign placement. the rewording is an easy fix. Not a big deal and should be easily passed. The big issue about sign placement is that in my own town, the County Clerk interfered in an election and refused people their right to place signs in their yards even though their yards were outside of that 200-foot mark. I live roughly 600 feet from the front of a polling station. I was not allowed to put up my campaign sign. I had to get some legal counsel to prove the clerk

violated state statutes. When she was proven wrong, my signs went back up. She misinterpreted the law and added her own personal policy to sign placement.
If these are such little issues, then they should be easy to pass.
Larry Bolinger
Attorney General Candidate 2022

Request sent to the Nebraska Secretary of State on 21 December 2021:

Data:
Election Policy Change Request:
32-1524. Electioneering; prohibited acts; penalty.

(1) No judge or clerk of election or precinct or district inspector shall do any electioneering while acting as an election official.

(2) No person shall do any electioneering, circulate petitions, or perform any action that involves solicitation within any polling place or any building designated for voters to cast ballots by the election commissioner or county clerk pursuant to the Election Act while the polling place or building is set up for voters to cast ballots or within two hundred feet of any such polling place or building. Any person violating this section shall be guilty of a Class V misdemeanor.
Source

Laws Policy Change Request:
Laws 1994, LB 76, § 423;

(2) No person shall do any electioneering, circulate petitions, or perform any action that involves solicitation within any polling place or any building designated for voters to cast ballots by the election commissioner or county clerk pursuant to the Election Act while the polling place or building is set up for voters to cast ballots or within two hundred feet of the front door of any such polling place or building. Any person violating this section shall be guilty of an infraction of the law.
The intent of the law: is to keep people from campaigning inside polling places, in front of the polling stations, and on the street on the side of the polling stations.
The reason for the change request: A couple of years back, I was running for Congress. The county clerk said that I could not put up my campaign sign. She said it was too close to a polling station. My family has lived at the property for more than 100 years and never had a problem. The Clerk said that during an election the County Court House and the Sheriff's Department are considered one building during election time. The county assessor's information shows two separate parcels of land. Voting is not being done at the Sheriff's Department. This would help

define this policy. Technically, the booth is the polling station, not the building. Most claim the entire building and that could be argued.

I also request changing this from a **misdemeanor to an infraction offense**. Many laws overreach penalties. Campaign signs are a form of freedom of speech and there should not be a serious penalty for being too close to a polling station.

2006, LB 940, § 2.

An issue in write-in voting during the primary election:

Larry: "I am in Box Butte County. I voted for myself and my wife voted for me. But in the Box Butte voting, it showed that I only received one vote. This is an error. I'm not sure if there are more errors, or if there were errors in all the times that I ran for public office. The missed vote would not do anything for my campaign. But it was an error and we both voted at a polling station. This error in the procedure needs to be fixed before the regular election."

The Nebraska Secretary of State Office: "Good afternoon Larry,

Thank you for reaching out. According to voter registration records, Marilyn Bolinger is registered as a member of the Republican Party. In primary elections, members of a party cannot choose to vote in another party's primary but instead are given the ballot for the party they're affiliated with. Voters can write in a candidate, but this vote does not count toward that individual unless they have submitted a write-in affidavit for that office (§32-615; §32-1005).

All voters are given the same ballot regardless of party affiliation during the general election; any registered voter, regardless of party, can certainly vote for you in the general election.

Hopefully, that information helps to clarify. If you have any other questions or concerns, feel free to let our office know."

All the best,

Ben Larsen
Elections Specialist I
Nebraska Secretary of State's Office
Phone: (402) 471-2555

The LMN party did not have a candidate for Governor, so everyone did a write-in. But according to state law, every write-in that the LMN party did, was not counted. If every vote was counted including the write-in vote, would that have made a difference in who passed the primary? In this election, 412,164 people voted. But in the governor's race, 370,071 votes were counted. What happened with the other 42,093 votes?

Crowdstrike argument:

Tim

"WHY IS CROWDSTRIKE SOFTWARE USED TO ENSURE OUR ELECTIONS IN NEBRASKA ARE SECURE?

The problems with our elections are so vast and so great that I can barely wrap my head around all of the different ways that they are subject to manipulation.

But anyone who knows anything at all about Crowdstrike will know that it is a tremendous conflict of interest for them to have anything at all to do with our election security. Their involvement alone should be enough to merit an audit in our very own state.

Am I the only one who thinks this is troubling?

If you share my concerns, please call on Secretary of State Evnen and all of our state senators to look into this."

Karen: So you agree with what I posted then? Kind of hard to tell if you even read it or not.

Larry Bolinger: I read it

Larry Bolinger: You propose a politically motivated audit, while I propose to fix the problems we already know exist.

Karen: You proposed nothing. And my post had nothing to do with voter ID. Nor is an audit politically motivated. An audit is necessary to ensure Nebraskans of any political party that election day isn't merely performed for the sake of theater....

Larry Bolinger: AN AUDIT IS NOT A FIX ALL. WE ALREADY KNOW THE PROBLEMS. THE BIGGEST PROBLEM TODAY IS PEOPLE THINKING WE NEED MORE AUDITS TO FIX PROBLEMS THAT WE ALREADY KNOW EXIST RATHER THAN FIXING THE PROBLEM!!...

Larry Bolinger: I understand that you get more attention by pushing the Audit rather than fixing the problems because you are politically motivated. You are not presenting solutions to the problem.

Larry Bolinger: On an audit, Nebraska has already had discrepancies and had already had a couple of audits. One of the audits had to be pushed through the Supreme Court. If you want a Nation Wide audit, you need an in-depth research analysis showing the discrepancies.

Karen: You are talking in circles and offering no solutions of your own. Keep keystroking yourself, Larry. Have a nice day.

Larry Bolinger: you are not listening. You are in your own world. We do not need people in the office who think they are above everyone else. I presented many solutions. You just want to push an item for political attention. You have not presented any solution.

Karen: I am the farthest thing in the world from being a self-promoter. I don't even post pictures of myself, much less give a damn about name recognition. My only concern is to secure the future of our state and our nation and without assurance.

Tim: You are off your rocker, Larry. You are a snowflake who reported a comment directed to you that was nothing more than the word, "RINO." Grow a spine. You do not have the mettle to be Nebraska's AG. Any more comments that you direct towards…

Larry Bolinger: my stance on CRT is that I support the 1st Amendment. You have the far-right trying to ban CRT, banning books from libraries, and banning books, then you have the far-left trying to ban books that the far-right approves of, and they have …

Larry Bolinger: Tim, you are just an extremist. The majority of Republicans are not extremists.

Karen: So—LIST the top 5 things you propose to do to fix the problem.

Larry Bolinger: with the issue of the Crowdstrike you have to filter out what is facts and what is political propaganda. It would be tough to win a case based on rumors. Presenting accusations without facts will be refused by the AG and it won't see its d…

Larry Bolinger: we need security but we have to be aware of suppression. If we create security programs that suppress the votes then there is room to argue to shut down the program.
Larry Bolinger: it is just an antivirus /anti-breech program to help stop hacks and viruses. Any government computer would have something similar. I would ask that if not that program, then what program should our government be using? There is also a question of intelligence. When part of their program is intelligence that means information gathering could mean privacy or security issues. The program has caught many hacks. Many countries do have government ran hack pods. Russia and China have several that are used against many countries. There needs to be a defense against that.

Karen: The provider of security software used to ensure that our elections are sound should not be businesses that have a history of covering for the DNC. Using Crowdstrike is a clear conflict of interest.

Larry Bolinger: what did they cover-up or attempt to cover-up? Cite a credible source.

Karen: My name is not Alexa, Larry. Look it up for yourself. I've already cited one source, and given that you are someone who thinks that CRT is a good thing, your idea of what constitutes a credible source is going to be vastly different from my own.

Larry Bolinger: if you can't cite your statement then I can only assume that you are just spreading false propaganda. You can't properly argue an issue without a credible source. Bringing up CRT again is stupid. It shows that you really don't have any i…

Larry Bolinger: with what was given with no credible source, you will lose your argument quickly.

Closing Statement:
Arguing for change in how votes are done should be just an argument of procedures. But it has become a political agenda. Politicians use it in a way to create propaganda and fear. If you create fear you gain media exposure. If people could look past party affiliation, positive changes would occur. Most support the propaganda spread by leaders in their party. That doesn't mean that you shouldn't try and create change. Utilize a basic form, and send in your request to change that policy. If there is a way to commit fraud in our voting system or some form of miscount, there is room to change and improve. When the issue is politically motivated, you may have to argue the policy several times so stay persistent and consistent and the policies will eventually improve.

Chapter 9

Meat Packing Policies

I. **Title**
   Ranching and Farming Policies
II. **State the purpose of the bill.**
   To help improve free enterprise in our Ranching community.
III. **State who the bill will affect and how the bill will affect them.**
   The policy changes would allow more flexibility in trade and the process of the product. This can result in more independent processing plants. That could bring the product into a fair market value and give the customer and lower price on products.
IV. **State what you want to accomplish**
   a) **Country of Origin Labeling for all Meats**: This must include imported cattle that are sent here to be slaughtered, so they can be stamped as a USA product. Products grown in another country, but packaged in the USA should not be allowed to be stamped with a "Made in the USA" stamp.
   b) **Milk Policies:** Alow raw milk to be sold without being processed. Allow a choice for customers to choose processed or non-processed milk. Some studies show raw milk and processed milk are good and bad for consumption. Let the people have the choice.
   c) **Meat Packing Inspectors:** There needs to be established 3 types of inspectors:

- State Meat Packing Inspector: To be qualified as a State Inspector the inspector has to be a veterinarian and follow state inspector guidelines.
- USDA Meat Packing Inspector: Follow federal guidelines for USDA Meat Packing Inspector.
- USDA Qualified State Meat Packing Inspector: Follow the USDA guidelines for a USDA Meat Packing Inspector.

    d) **Right to Repair:** This will allow people who buy a product to have ownership of that product. Congress passed the "Digital Millennium Copyright Act" in the 1990s which prohibits consumers from working or repairing computer programs. These programs are in such things as Apple cell phones, Tesla automobiles, and JohnDeer tractors. This is a copyright policy umbrella as a copyright. But, there is no copy and use. The Attorney General needs to argue that the "digital millennium copyright act" is a consumer rights violation. The state needs to pass the "Right to Repair" policy to allow consumer rights.

VI) **State how you want to accomplish your goal**

Each policy would need to be assigned to the proper state Legislative Committee and argued so that it can be added to the Legislative agenda.

VII) **Conclusion: This may be the area where you state the consequences of not acting and the benefits of acting to approve the bill.**

Our government has created a significant amount of red tape that business owners have to go through to conduct business. If we don't fix the problems our state will lose the business. If we make the change, you will add more jobs, give the consumer a better price on products, and improve our economy.

There is always a need to review policy and make proposals for change. In this case, they're a lot of red tape to conduct business. There is also a lack of policies that allow State Meat Processing inspectors that slow the process of meats, which stopped a lot of business. Larry saw a problem, then conducted research and questionnaires and found several other problems, and requested changes to help fix the problems.

One of the problems Larry found when he ran for Congress in 2018 and 2020 is that farmers and ranchers were settling with the elected official representatives they currently have so they don't risk their livelihood. So they did not want to speak out against current Congressmen. As a candidate, it was your responsibility to be the voice for the people so the people don't put themselves or their businesses at risk.

There has been a push for ranchers to put together their own coop packing plant. But there are still issues of federal policies that could cause a problem in selling their product between states and to other nations which is being overlooked. This creates a need to conduct more research and present your findings so that the ranching business isn't hindered.

Research Analysis by Larry Bolinger on the Meat Processing and Ranching Business:

Introduction:

"There are many policies that have been created to manage the farming and ranching industries. Federal policies started in the 1940s during the Roosevelt administration. Over the past few years that has become problematic. I theorize that several policies have been put in place that negatively affect the farming and ranching industries by forcing them to unnecessarily process meat through corporations. There are different arguments about the policies concerning the processing of meat. During the 2020 pandemic, there were problems in the processing of meat. From shutting down trade during tariff negotiations with China and businesses shutting down in the US, it bottlenecked the industry. Governor Ricketts (Nebraska Governor) has made his argument and refused to follow Wyoming's decision on meat sales under the Food Freedoms Act by claiming that we can only use USDA inspectors. During the 2020 pandemic, Wyoming was using both state inspectors and USDA inspectors to help ensure the processing of meat. Governor Rickets could simply make an executive order to allow ranchers to sell directly to consumers. He could have created policies to allow both state and federal inspectors. Why force using corporate processing? Why was the processing structure changed over the past decade that allowed putting a strain on the ranching business? What does the state or federal government have to gain or lose by forcing the policies or by showing flexibility on problem policies? Adding excessive red tape is not a free market or free enterprise.

Larry: "I do have some experience in the farming and ranching business that dates back many years ago. I had been a ranch hand for a couple of years back in the 1980s. In the 1990s, I helped out with many brandings and I worked at the Nebraska Boys Ranch. The NBR was a youth corrections facility with a working ranch. I also worked with a network marketing group that sold surfactants to farmers and ranchers. In 2018 and 2020 I ran for Congress in Nebraska Dist. 3 which is a very large farming and ranching district. There was a very big concern about policies in the agricultural industries. While on the campaign, I talked to several farmers and ranchers and listened to their concerns. I also reached out to a couple of farming interest groups who expressed their concern over some of the policies. The members of the interest group requested to remain anonymous so they would not endure any political backlash for any of their statements. I can certainly understand that because I have endured a fair amount of political backlash. Problems that were presented were policy changes in the Packers and Stockyard act and the Prime Act"

Larry conducted a questionnaire asking what the farmers and ranchers thought needed to be changed in our policies to help make the ranching and farming business easier to run. Tony S. stated that "the Prime Act, mandatory country of origin labeling, and stop importing all the foreign beef. Also, quit collecting the beef checkoff from cattle producers. All of these things can be done. It is a no–brainer. These are the things cattle producers need." (Tony) Mary V. stated that "she would want a country of origin labeling for all meats. This must include imported cattle that are sent here to be slaughtered, so they can be stamped as a USA product. Insist that there be a complete investigation of the 4 largest meatpacking plants in the US, with amounts of money being returned to the ranchers that have been ripped off for years. And let's put the Packers and Stockyard Act back in place as it was originally written. The government needs to support the smaller meat packers so they can sell directly to the consumer. Get more state inspectors educated. These are just a few thoughts from a rancher's daughter and the wife of a retired cattle buyer. The first thing we need to do is restore ownership of the American farmlands, oil rights, and companies to Americans. (Be sure to grandfather in purchases for the past 20 years)." (Mary) These are just a couple of the statements Larry received while talking in a ranching interest group on Facebook. There are many suggestions and areas of concern, but there will need to be some focus on the processing and how the system failed during the 2020 pandemic.

Sandy: We need something like the prime Act and some kind of legislation to protect the smaller packing plant. Our checked-off dollar should go to a Cooperative packing plant here in Nebraska. Feel free to contact me

Larry: I agree, there are several ranchers creating their own packing plant. But, policies need to be there to protect their business. I hope Senator Brewer got his policies approved. That would have been a step forward in protecting ranchers.

Sandy: Marketing is another issue hertzog's in Missouri marketing their beef in local grocery stores demand was high and they still got shut out. That sir is the kind of thing we are battling.

Larry: the way the law is right now, they would have to have a USDA inspector or a state inspector that is USDA certified to inspect the processing or the store would have to buy the cow to be able to get local beef. I'll look more into that and see if Senator Brewer got his Policy past. If he hasn't, it'll be a problem.

Sandy: Thank You.

In Larry's research, he reviewed Newspaper articles, scholarly research, and government websites to gain information on what has been argued and what is policy. He researched the effects of policies on the ranching business and how they created a bottleneck for the business.

Did the government overreach on the Packers and Stockyard act and the Wholesome Meal Act? Did those policies interfere with the ranching business's ability to operate profitably? There is value in researching this topic. To hold the government accountable for its actions or a failure to act, you have to be able to argue the policy to be able to better the ranching businesses. To ensure accountability you need to make sure the federal government did not overreach its authority by creating an unlawful or unethical policy. By creating research on the past business process over the past 10 years and reviewing the impacts of newer policies, you could argue the policy to the legislature and propose change. The 2020 pandemic created a bottleneck in the meat processing business where processing plants were slaughtering pigs and throwing them away and the dairy farmers were pouring out and destroying milk, while at the same time stores were running out of meat and milk. The bottleneck showed that there was a flaw in our system. It is a serious flaw that should not be ignored.

There was an article in the Times-Herald on 5 May 2020 written by Elise Balin in which Governor Pete Ricketts made a statement that Nebraska could not follow Wyoming in the revised "Food Freedom Act." The Food Freedom Act would allow meat producers to directly sell to consumers within the state by bypassing USDA meat inspections. According to the Governor, the Nebraska State statute says meat has to be inspected by the USDA. The Wyoming Department of Agriculture Public Information Officer said that they can conduct sales in the State without inspections but transferring out of State would need a USDA inspection. By federal law, the meat would need to be inspected by a USDA-approved inspector, not necessarily a USDA inspector. So you could have a state inspector that is USDA certified. The Wyoming and Nebraska governors both missed the boat on that one.

Governor Rickets made the excuse that Wyoming has state inspectors while Nebraska only uses the USDA. So Nebraska cannot get around utilizing other inspectors. However, he could have made an executive order to show leniency or add a policy to allow state inspectors. He also says that the meat lockers are already over capacity and that workers are working as hard as they can. He expressed the importance of the inspections as they should reduce the possibility of selling or processing contaminated meat.

 Governor Rickets could have allowed the use of the Food Freedom act by creating an executive order and then authorizing several state inspectors to do the work of the USDA inspectors. I'm not sure why Governor Rickets thinks we have to use the USDA. Would it be because of federal funds that are spent on inspections? It is a very big risk we face when the system is slowed down. During a time when Governor Rickets is refusing to bend on this issue, he puts people's jobs and homes at risk. If the main argument is of safety concerns, then what we would need is a guideline to follow. There should not be any difference between a federal inspector to a state inspector, except on who cuts their paychecks.

Three questions I would have are: Why is there a policy that restricts state and federal inspections that are controlled by the USDA? Does that interfere with the separation of federal and state governments? Was the policy created to enrich large corporations that are in the processing business?

Larry: "I remember about 20 years ago that people were skeptical about allowing corporate processing plants in our area. Now, I can see why allowing corporate processing may have been a bad idea. I do wonder which policies were the major factors in why beef sales were so badly managed during the 2020 pandemic. Stores were running low on meat, but ranchers were not allowed to sell directly to the stores and restaurants. During that time there were issues getting the meat processed."

When Larry talked to Senator Brewer about the issues of meat processing he said that "if the small town locker could be inspected, they can sell meat retail to the public. As it is, they are using the custom-exempt slaughtering rule and the ownership of the animal doesn't change hands. The Rancher has to find buyers and sell beef instead of selling cattle. If the locker could sell meat to the public we could ease the bottleneck and move a lot more heads through these local butchers and expand this market for ranchers, and bring back a little prosperity to these struggling little towns. " (Brewer) Brewer is also trying to gain support for his bill LR 380 which he says will help with trade across borders. But without the changes in the federal policy there could be difficulties in passing the policy, or if it is passed, would the USDA or federal government allow state-to-state sales? Larry had suggested that he needs to make a push on our congressmen to support the Prime Act to help ensure the success of his policy. Larry talked to Congressman Smith who is the Nebraska Congressman for District 3 about the policy issues. He had requested that he support Senator Brewer's bill and he also needed to support the prime act. Smith's stance is that everything is going fine. Stores were running out of meat, the retail price for meat increased from $25 a roll of hamburger to $80 a roll, ranchers were getting less for their product and the corporate slaughterhouses manipulated the prices to get a higher price, international trade was at a crawl, and the product was being destroyed because it was not allowed to the retail companies. But Smith says everything is going alright. That was his view in 2020. But in 2022 Larry brought up this issue of what needs to be done and told him he needed to support President Biden's proposal to support independent packers, his view had changed. 2 years too late that caused hundreds of Ranchers and Farmers to go bankrupt in Nebraska.

Literary Review

Hannah Cox wrote an article in the Washington Examiner in 2020 called "How to Stop the Coming Meat Shortage." She states that the problem with the policies has been an issue over the past couple of decades. Cox says that "these policies favor politicians rather than addressing health concerns. So in an emergency situation such as the pandemic, leaders had to temporarily repeal regulations." (Cox) I would question that if they had to temporarily repeal the regulation, then how important is that particular regulation? Cox said that "in 1967 the federal government blocked states from making their own decisions on how meat was processed and promptly handed the power to the Department of Agriculture / USDA".(Cox) By doing that limits how ranchers are able to get meat sold or processed. This forces the ranchers to sell to a USDA-approved slaughterhouse or slaughterhouses with USDA-certified inspectors.

The system we have today panders to Big Ag. Business. Big Ag. Businesses do get a bailout if they get into financial trouble, while the small farmers who are struggling are going bankrupt at an alarming rate. Cox states " that the Massie bill (also called the Prime Act) offers a free-market solution that could save the industry. She also says that the "Prime Act would repeal regulations and allow states to set their own standard on processing. " (Cox)

Larry: "One of my biggest concerns is that there are 50 congressmen that are co-sponsors of the Prime Act bill, but none of those congressmen are from Nebraska. It is disturbing that my own representatives chose not to support flexibility in the meat processing business."

Pete Kennedy wrote an article in the "RealMilk", in 2020 called "Prime Act Reintroduced in Congress." Kennedy states that "the Meat Exemption Act which is also called the Prime Act is a policy that would return power back to the states by allowing them to regulate the meat processing within their borders. This bill would allow the sale of meat directly to restaurants, hotels, grocery stores, and boarding houses. The current federal laws state that the individual would have to own the animal at the time of the slaughter. If the rancher wants to sell a portion of a cow, they would have to use an approved slaughterhouse with a federal inspector that is there throughout the processing." (Kennedy)

According to Kennedy, it was the Wholesome Meal Act of 1967 that gave the federal government power over meat processing. That took the number of slaughterhouses from 10,000 down to 2,766 slaughterhouses throughout the U.S. At 2,766 slaughterhouses, 4 companies control 80% of the beef processing, and 4 companies control 60% of the pork processing. That proves a couple of different things. One is that the issue of processing wasn't just over the past couple of decades. The problems started in 1967. It also shows that the business went from local slaughterhouses to a select few that do the majority of the processing creating a monopoly in the meat markets.

Pete explains that these large slaughterhouses that have USDA inspectors have had over 20,000,000 recalls while the small independents had few problems. Governor Rickets' concern was that if we did not use USDA inspectors, there would be safety concerns. The numbers show that independents who had processed less meat at a time ended up having fewer contaminants. A lot of contamination of meat can occur when you have mass slaughters on a daily basis and it can make things worse by mixing animals with other animals from several different suppliers. One group of contaminated meat can contaminate the whole lot.

According to the USDA website "under the Federal Meat Inspection Act and the Poultry Products Inspection Act, FSIS inspects all raw meat and poultry sold in interstate and foreign commerce, including imported products. The Agency monitors meat and poultry products after they leave federally inspected plants. In addition, FSIS monitors State inspection programs, which inspect meat and poultry products sold only within the State in which they were produced. The 1967 Wholesome Meat Act and the 1968 Wholesome Poultry Products Act require State inspection programs to be "at least equal to" the Federal inspection program. If States choose to end their inspection program or cannot maintain this standard, FSIS must assume responsibility for inspection within that State." (USDA) According to the USDA, to allow state inspectors the state would have to have a program equal to what is required by FSIS or USDA. So if Senator Brewer is able to pass his bill, he will also need to add a policy and procedure to that bill to ensure the inspectors are following the federal guidelines. So he would need to submit a resolution to the USDA inspection guidelines. On the USDA site, it does go through what they do as far as inspections. The site also assures that the Wholesome Poultry Products Act and Wholesome Meal act improved the meat processing business and that it is a safer way to process meat. That is contradictory to the actual numbers given earlier quoting more than 20,000,000 recalls.

Gavin Wax wrote an article in the "Human Events" in 2020 called "Pass Thomas Massie's Prime Act." Wax wrote about Thomas Massie who is a Republican representative out of Kentucky who has raised cattle, has a master's degree in mechanical engineering from MIT, and has been lobbying for the prime act for several years. According to Massie, the current regulations have put restrictions on over 1,000 mom-and-pop meat processing plants and it pushes to funnel their business through big businesses. Through strict policies, we have seen a bottleneck in processing during the 2020 pandemic. This has limited how people can get their food and how growers and ranchers can sell their products. The limits have forced the producer to shut down. The pandemic shut down restaurants all over. Stores were running out of meat and milk while the big business was over their limit so they had to destroy supplies rather than distribute them. This also created an issue of the consumer paying significantly more for meat while at the same time, the ranchers are getting a bottom dollar for their cattle. (Massie) Imagine that. The large corporations get a bailout, farmers and ranchers get the bottom dollar on sales, and the consumer gets to pay a significantly higher price. Corporate slaughterhouses were allowed to price gouge during the 2020 pandemic.

Catherine Paul researched the meat market business and trends. Her research article was called the "Production Structure and Trends in the U.S. Meat and Poultry Products Industries," which was published in the Journal of Agricultural and Resources Economics in 1999. Paul states that there is concern about the effects of the policies on the flow of a business. Distorting the flow can create a monopoly by marking up output product over production cost while creating an artificially low price. She weighed the results of the cost, the cost impact, and trade changes as well as the markups and downs. She weighed this against the input and output markets by utilizing an algebraic formula and a generalized method of moment procedures. This proves the monopoly prevailed across most specifications. By proving the monopoly and ability to force cost helps prove that by utilizing the USDA inspections through corporations creates a bottleneck in the meat industry while forcing specific prices and manipulating the prices.

Data:

Larry: "After reviewing the policies and what the legislature is proposing I have found some issues that could be flawed. Passing the policy to allow State Inspectors is a good idea, but the policy itself would limit the ranching business. What we want to eventually achieve is decreasing limitations when it comes to both inter-state and out-of-state sales. What is proposed could limit sales to just interstate sales. There would also be a need for a cooperative interstate shipment program to do business across state lines. When you see flaws in a policy, you hold the Legislature accountable to make the necessary changes."

LR 380 is the request to do a study to allow a state meat inspector and LB235 is the bill that was introduced on 11 January 2021 to officially add state meat inspectors. The qualification is that an inspector has to be a veterinarian.

What needs to be done is a policy to address and allow 3 different types of inspectors under the State Packing Inspector policy.

1. State inspector
2. USDA inspector
3. State Inspector who is USDA-certified

The USDA Food Safety and Inspection Service requirement:

- The state has to enforce requirements to be at least equal to those imposed under the Federal Meat and Poultry Products Inspection Act and the Humane Methods of Slaughter Act of 1978.
- need a cooperative interstate shipment program to do business across state lines.

Must have policies to meet:

- Federal Meat Inspection Act
- Poultry Products Inspection Act
- Humane Methods of Slaughter Act of 1978

FSIS provides up to 50% of the State's operating funds, as well as training and other assistance. FSIS provides guidance to state MPI programs under these agreements. FISA evaluates state inspection programs by looking at:

1. Statutory Authority and Food Safety Regulations
2. Inspection
3. Product Sampling Programs
4. Staffing, Training, and Supervision
5. Humane Handling
6. Compliance
7. Laboratory Methods and Quality Assurance Program
8. Civil Rights
9. Financial Accountability

Must meet the State Meat and Poultry Inspection Program Laboratory Quality Management System Checklist

Must meet the compliance guidelines for state meat and poultry inspection programs for residue testing.

Would need to add a "Cooperative Interstate Shipping Program" to be allowed to sell to other states or countries.

https://nebraskalegislature.gov/FloorDocs/107/PDF/AM/AM799.pdf

LR 380 is the request to do a study to allow a state meat inspector and LB235 is the bill that was introduced on 11 January 2021 to officially add state meat inspectors. The qualification is that an inspector has to be a veterinarian.

https://www.fsis.usda.gov/inspection/apply-grant-inspection/state-inspection-programs
the USDA Food Safety and Inspection Services:
• The state has to enforce requirements to be at least equal to those imposed under the Federal Meat and Poultry Products Inspection Act and the Humane Methods of Slaughter Act of 1978.
• State inspections could limit intrastate commerce

https://www.fsis.usda.gov/sites/default/files/media_file/2021-02/State-MPI-Legislation-Letter-041817.pdf

Must meet the State Meat and Poultry Inspection Program Laboratory Quality Management System Checklist
Must meet the compliance guidelines for state meat and poultry inspection programs for residue testing.
Would need to add a "Cooperative Interstate Shipping Program" to be allowed to sell to other states or countries.

Conclusion

Larry: "With the research, I have done, I have concluded that at least in part my theory is true. My theory was to prove that several policies were put in place and that they had negative effects on the farming and ranching industries by forcing them to unnecessarily process meat through corporations. In a sense, the USDA regulations have created a monopoly on meat processing."

The meat inspection policies started back in the 1940s under Franklin Roosevelt. Then there was the implementation of the Wholesome Meals Act of 1967. The WMA restricts local ranchers from direct sales. By doing that, it forces them to have to utilize corporate processing plants that have a USDA inspector to inspect the entire process. However, the USDA website does state that a state can have its own inspector if it follows USDA guidelines. The USDA does create a monopoly by forcing ranchers to utilize corporations to get meat processed and inspected. Out of the 2766 slaughterhouses, 4 corporate slaughterhouses have 60% to 80% of the business. The states could have their own inspector by creating a resolution and adopting the USDA inspection guidelines into their own state inspection guidelines. That could create flexibility to pander to the independent ranchers rather than the corporate processing plants and it would help break up the monopoly. " (Bolinger, 2021)

References

Bolinger, Larry. (2021). "Politics: Last Act of Defiance." Chapter 21.

Cox, Hannah. "How to Stop the Coming Meat Shortage." *Washington Examiner* https://www.washingtonexaminer.com/opinion/thomas-massies-prime-act-can-stop-the-coming-meat-shortage . May 2020

Kennedy, Pete. "Prime Act Reintroduced in Congress." *West A. Price Foundations. Real Milk.* https://www.realmilk.com/prime-act-reintroduced-in-congress/ . 2020

Congress.gov. https://www.congress.gov/bill/116th-congress/house-bill/2859/text . 2019

Senator Brewer, Tom. "There is a lot of government "virus Money" out there right now."
https://www.facebook.com/permalink.php?story_fbid=2751256741775137&id=1895775163989
970&comment_id=2751273485106796¬if_id=1595618027019030¬if_t=feedback_reacti
on_generic July 2020

USDA. "Inspection & Grading of Meat and Poultry: What Are the Differences?"
https://www.fsis.usda.gov/wps/wcm/connect/5d43763f-a9aa-459b-94e0-
cdf9e3543923/Inspection_and_Grading_What_Are_the_Differences.pdf?MOD=AJPERES
Revised April 2012

Wax, Gavin. Massie, Thomas. "Pass Thomas Massie's Prime Act," *U.S. Politics. Human Events.*
Parallel Media L.L.C. https://humanevents.com/2020/05/06/pass-thomas-massies-prime-act/
May 2020

gov.track. *H.R. 2859: PRIME Act*
https://www.govtrack.us/congress/bills/116/hr2859/summary revised 1 June 2020
Bullard, Bill. *Ranch Group Grateful for Swift Senate Action to Fix Broken Cattle Markets.* R-
Calf USA
https://www.r-calfusa.com/ranch-group-grateful-for-swift-senate-action-to-fix-broken-cattle-
markets/?fbclid=IwAR3U9jhiUKg5pXRu3og7r5ygZWTosCzs8xZEpQdJdlZ54g1TmQsufvQW
Lbw 12 May 2020

Balin, Elise. Star-Herald," Ricketts: Meat Processing Approach similar to Wyoming's unrealistic
for Nebraska https://www.starherald.com/news/local_news/pete-ricketts-nebraska-needs-state-
meat-inspection-for-direct-to-consumer-sales/article_4d9cbe97-2641-543b-a76f-
59142f245574.amp.html?fbclid=IwAR3IA-aBvB8G-
JTKc85nHtCvsgjOED4hiAHcLupLIZRrYBHiz6EbcZPlH-A (5 May 2020)

Grossman, Margaret Rosso. "United States: Preemption under the Federal Meat Inspection
Act." *European Food and Feed Law Review*, vol. 7, no. 2, 2012, pp. 101–105. *JSTOR*,
www.jstor.org/stable/24325497. Accessed 26 July 2020.

Paul, Catherine J. Morrison. "Production Structure and Trends in the U.S. Meat and Poultry
Products Industries." *Journal of Agricultural and Resource Economics*, vol. 24, no. 2, 1999, pp.
281–298. *JSTOR*, www.jstor.org/stable/40987023. Accessed 26 July 2020.
https://nebraskalegislature.gov/FloorDocs/107/PDF/AM/AM799.pdf

The letter that was sent to the Nebraska Legislature on 11/28/2021:

Hello
This is Larry Bolinger. I am a candidate for Attorney General.

I saw in the Missouri Farm Burau that they had created a directory for meat producers to sell beef, pork, lamb, and poultry directly to consumers. they also have a directory for agriculture to help connect farmers and consumers. Is that something that we can get done to help connect farmers and ranchers directly to the customers?

Also. I saw that the legislature was trying to pass a policy to allow state meat inspectors. I am in support of that, but how it is
written limits sales. Were there going to be additional policies added to that so that ranchers can sell to other states and on the international markets?

When the State Legislature failed to act, Larry decided to write a letter to the editor. If our representatives fail to act, then a good go-to move is to hold them accountable for posting the failures and what needs to be done in the newspaper and other media outlets.

Letter to the editor

1/4/2022

Problems in Our Meat Processing Policies

I do have a concern about price gouging in the meat industry. But we need to blame the ones who took control of the prices. This is in response to President Biden's write-up to attempt to reduce food prices.

The price gouging was done because the processing companies jacked up the prices, then decreased the payout to the Ranchers and Farmers. Utilizing the Packers and Stockyard act and the Wholesome Meal Act created a monopoly that allowed the manipulation of prices. I conducted research analyses and tried to get our Federal and State representatives to fix the problems. They said they liked things the way it is. There could have been a simple Governor executive order that could have fixed the issue. But they wanted to wait and do their own thing so they could have more control. Senator Brewer did present a bill to allow State Inspectors. But it lacks policies. It does not allow state-to-state sales or international sales. So you will continue to have 4 corporate packing plants controlling 80% of the packing business in the US. I joined the LMN Party to try and fix this failed system. Each State Legislature knows what needs to be done because I told them what needs to be done, but they have failed to act.

Larry Bolinger

<u>Resources:</u>

https://nebraskalegislature.gov/FloorDocs/107/PDF/AM/AM799.pdf

https://www.fsis.usda.gov/inspection/apply-grant-inspection/state-inspection-programs

https://www.fsis.usda.gov/sites/default/files/media_file/2021-02/State-MPI-Legislation-Letter-041817.pdf

https://panhandlepost.com/posts/b17bf515-8b42-4d0c-9735-e1e8aa0247e3?utm_source=dlvr.it&utm_medium=facebook

Chapter 10
Helping the Housing Market

I.   **Title**

Housing policy reform

II.   **State the purpose of the bill.**

To help secure people's right to property ownership

III.   **State who the bill will affect and how the bill will affect them.**

The bills will help property owners by addressing options that can stop and fix the loss of a home. This may change the process of how banks address foreclosures. This will also ensure that banks pay contractors for the work they do.

IV.   **State what you want to accomplish**

a) Buying past due land tax: 3rd party can no longer buy past land taxes unless taxes are 4 years past due. After 4 years, the land owner has one year to pay the past taxes before the property could be foreclosed.

b) Broker agreements: When a property is at risk of foreclosing, the land owner is able to contract with a Broker to sell the property. This contract stops the foreclosing process.

c) During the foreclosure process: During the foreclosure process, the banks would not be allowed to publicly announce the state of the property or promote any sales intent of the property. This can only happen after a Bank fully acquires a property and will be considered fraud if they announce a property under a tax lien, bankruptcy, or foreclosure and have not taken full ownership. Failure to comply will penalize the bank the market value of the property.

d) Mechanical Lien: when a contractor puts a mechanical lien on a property it should be able to last for 10 years before the consideration of dropping the lien.

e) Mechanical Lien Waiver: Create a policy to make it illegal for companies to force contractors to sign a mechanical lien waiver.

f) Mechanical lien payback: When a bank sells a property that has a mechanical lien on it, the bank is liable to pay the mechanical lien.

V.   **State how you want to accomplish your goal**

Each of these policies would need to go before a Legislative committee and be argued at the state level. The mechanical lien policies would need to be argued at the state level and federal levels.

VI.   **Conclusion: This may be the area where you state the consequences of not acting and the benefits of acting to approve the bill.**

By not changing we will continue with a high rate of foreclosures. By creating these changes it assures people's property rights and a way to sell a property that is agreeable to the bank and land owner. The mechanical lien policies will help ensure contractors are being paid. The state of contractors working with banks has created a significant loss of income over the past decade.

Over the past couple of decades, policies have changed in the housing section. They were more focused on creating penalties on property owners to help make more money for the banks and the County's tax collection efforts. That created a business to take over people's property from their misfortunes. Years ago, people might pay off taxes on a property to take it over when a property was abandoned for several years and then sold at a public auction. Today, 3rd party investors pray on the less fortunate to pounce when a land owner is just a day late on their taxes to add hefty penalties. When people are down on their luck, lawmakers created a system to keep them down.

Crunching the numbers of the housing market in 2018 and comparing that of the time frame just before the 2008 recession, the numbers are very close to the same. We have had several issues that have worsened the housing markets and economies such as the 2016 presidential order on EPA regulations, the 2019 floods, the 2020 Tariff negotiations, and the 2020 Pandemic. Outside of that, bringing down the housing market, there are unethical policies that were created to make it easier for the government or 3rd party investors to buy out your property. Making this easier to landgrab. This change started back during the Bush administration, in his build-up of the banking system to make it unbreakable. The government and 3rd party investors have held the reigns long enough, now it is time to flip that switch and get back to helping people in need. Proposed changes.

Improvement in policies:

- We change how a tax lien company can buy people's taxes. At the moment a homeowner could be one day late and someone can buy the taxes and tack on a large fee. The change I would recommend is to set the time frame at 4 years before a company can buy someone's taxes.
- After the 4 years have passed the landowner would have 1 year to pay off the lien or it could go into foreclosure for the lien.
- To stop a property from going to foreclosure a landowner could contract with a Broker to sell the property and upon the sale, the lien and interest not exceeding 14% are paid to the investment company, and the landowner gets paid if the property is sold for more than what he or she owes, and the broker gets his/her commission. As long as the landowner is contracted with a broker, the property can't be finalized and go into post-foreclosure. If the property is not occupied, then the Broker will have to make sure the property is up to FHA code and being maintained. The Broker would have a choice to hire a Property Preservation specialist to bring the building up to FHA code and do

reoccurring services or have the property preservation specialist do an inspection and fill out a form to show what needs to be done to bring a property up to FHA code and the landowner would have to do the work. Inspections on the property would be paid out within 6 weeks, and payouts on Property Preservation service would be upon sale of the property.

- Extending the Mechanical Lien times to 10 years. A tax lien is 10 years, might as well expand a mechanical lien to 10 years and keep it the same. Only having it for 2 years, makes it easy for people to not pay contractors.
- When a bank forecloses on a property, it should have to pay off any Liens just like anyone else who buys a property. If someone's sales property, and has a Lien and the lien isn't settled at the time of the sale, it could be considered fraud. But a bank is given a free pass on this fraud.
- During a foreclosure: it should be unlawful for a bank to publicly announce the foreclosure and time of the public auction. If the bank is taking a property, they should have to assume the loan. If the property is for sale by the mortgagor, and the bank has it in pre-foreclosure and the bank is putting up ads in the paper for the public auction, that undermines the mortgagor's sales. Interested investors have turned away because of that so that they can try and pick up the property cheaply at the public auction.

Resources:
Bolinger, Scott. (2021). "Politics: Last Act of Defiance Volume I." Chapters 16, 19, 21, 24

Larry Bolinger had been in the property management and contracting business for over 20 years, so he knew the trends and the changes in laws concerning realty. Below is one of the arguments he had on a policy that would have created another policy that would stop a business from running and created another way to conduct government ran landgrabs.

LB695

Prohibit conditional use permits and zoning exceptions for delinquent property taxpayers

Larry did make a post on the Legislature website on LB695 BloodProhibit conditional use permits and zoning exceptions for delinquent property taxpayers in opposition to the bill. This creates an issue that if you are trying to create a business or run an existing business it could be stopped because you owe land tax. Stopping one's ability to make a living to be able to pay those back taxes.

Senator Blood's (who was running for governor at that time) office did contact me to try and change my mind on that. However the reasoning behind the bill was due to the alcohol plant in Mead that took advantage of the system and failed to follow county, state, federal, and EPA policies. That is something that should be considered a completely different ordeal. You can't hold the entire state accountable for one company. But we need to get that environmental disaster cleaned up.

Respons by Senator Bloods' office:

Good afternoon Larry

From Senator Bloods' office: We spoke on the phone last week about your opposition to LB695. I've attached the amendment to the bill that should address your concerns by offering some wiggle room to businesses looking to apply for CUPs and TIF. If you are satisfied with the amendment, I would ask that you rescind your opposition by emailing Trevor Fitzgerald, the legal counsel for the Urban Affairs Committee, at tfitzgerald@leg.ne.gov.

My response: I believe the proper course of action is if someone owes state back taxes and is more than 180 days past due, may not receive additional state funds until those back taxes are paid. That would focus on the real problem of paying taxes by a penalty of not getting more funds, rather than shutting down a business completely so there is no way for them to make money to pay those taxes. If you change it, I'll support it.

From senator Blood's office: *That is exactly what the bill does - it makes it so businesses may not receive city, county, or state funds. It does not shut down businesses just because they owe taxes.*

My response: What I'm reading is that it is refusing to allow people a conditional use permit for people who owe back land taxes. That is not a loan, that is just a conditional use permit so someone could run a business.

It looks like there are some questionable areas such as: in section Sec. 3. Section 18-2119, (b) gives redeveloper authority to take over one's property at 180 days of delinquent land tax. Usually, it's 3 years. At the 3-year mark, the landowner is given 1 year to pay up the back tax or may face a tax lien foreclosure. I would rather see a policy of no third-party interest at 4 years and no finalizing of a tax lien a year after the initial filing from the 4-year mark.

From Senator Blood's Office: *Denial of a CUP in itself will not make a business fail. A CUP is a tool that responsible business owners can use to expand their business in some way. A business should not be expanded by way of state funds or special permits if they can not pay their property taxes.*

My response: If you owned a business and had a business loan with a bank and defaulted on that loan payment, the bank would decline any more loans until the payments were caught up. They would not take your business away because you're late on a payment. I expect our government to work in the same way. You decline more loans until the back payments are paid up. You don't take their business away. That is not a fitting penalty. You propose to stop the business from running and then conduct a government land grab. The refusal of the special use permit and the property land grab do not fit within the policy of the tax lien statute. The policy is overreaching and does not fit a proper penalty for late payments.

Chapter 11

Unethical Billing Practices

I. **Title**

Review of billing practices

II. **State the purpose of the bill.**

Review complaints about IRS billing practices.

III. **State who the bill will affect and how the bill will affect them.**

This will affect the taxpayer. Tax audits and appeals should be easy to request. If unethical billing practices are found, this could mean changing IRS procedures.

IV. **State what you want to accomplish**

a) The billing practices at the IRS have several issues of misrepresentation. Charges on paperwork and online may not show or reflect the same payments or invoices. This is sloppy bookkeeping that one could manipulate. Sloppy bookkeeping can lead to others making mistakes.

b) They have the policy to increase interest rates instead of staying with the agreed interest. When you enter an agreement you have a specifically agreed payment per month that would include a monthly interest rate. But the IRS will increase the interest rates because it is their policy to do so. It creates an issue of a violation of contract law.

c) There is an issue with when they apply returns to taxes owed. Instead of applying the returns in January, they wait until august to apply those returns. By doing so they are able to collect 8 months of interest, late fees, and other fees on an amount that is no longer there. This could be argued as unbundling as they are trying to get ahead or receive higher reimbursements.

d) There are late penalties when payments are made on time.

e) There is roughly a $250 charge to enter a payment plan. We the taxpayers, pay for the people at the IRS to do a job. But they charge people extra for doing their job. They are already being paid. So this is a double payment issue.

f) There are penalties called "Other." It is a penalty created to be able to add another penalty to a payment plan that is not past due. This can be argued as phantom billing as there is little to no description. The lack of description on the bill is a red flag.

V.   **State how you want to accomplish your goal**
Reviewing IRS procedures would need to be a request of Congress or an investigation that is started by the State's Attorney General. I would first request the Attorney General to review the billing procedure, order an audit of those procedures, and then file a lawsuit.

VI.   **Conclusion: This may be the area where you state the consequences of not acting and the benefits of acting to approve the bill.**
If we act now, we set a billing trend that could hold the IRS and other businesses accountable for their billing practices. This would encourage a straight billing practice and discourage adding overwhelming added penalties which could lead to an infraction of enrichment practices.

Unethical billing practices in our banking industry, medical industry, legal industry, and the IRS:

Introduction:

Bolinger: "Over the past several years there has been a trend of unethical billing practices in our banking industry, medical industry, legal industry, and the IRS. In the medical field, there are issues of creating multiple charges from several entities for seeing one doctor, which includes phantom billing practices. The banking industry has created some odd or unethical practices when they are preparing a house to be foreclosed. There is a procedure that strings along the homeowner with promises of refinances until the 9-month period where they can finalize foreclosure and that is when they deny your application. The IRS billing practices aren't much better when you look at their phantom billing system and overcharging late fees. Some say they do that to force you to get a loan and pay them off. I say they do it, just to enrich the banking system. I have dealt with unethical banking or billing practices in the banking, medical, and IRS. There was enough that I had dealt with that warranted more investigation to see at what scale this was happening. If there is a large enough issue, it could create a need to address the issue with the Legislature or Attorney General to order an investigation or to review policy and procedures.

Many people won't argue against those industries because they are very wealthy industries that can afford expensive lawyers. I've talked to politicians about fighting against the banking system and they won't because the banks are too powerful. Politicians won't fight the IRS for fear of being audited. If they fear being audited, then they probably need to be audited. Many of these industries have a system that if you don't pay them, they will take everything you got and they will make it as difficult as they can for you to pay them. Creating a wall of penalties so you can not afford to pay them is unethical. I have reviewed many of these practices and feel that there is cause to argue these procedures further."

I conducted a research analysis on the Banking industry that is documented in the first series of "Politics: Last Act of Defiances" in Volume I, Chapter 15. From what I reviewed there were issues of the banks not paying contractors for the work they did on a bank-owned property. In some cases, the companies they contracted would penalize contractors, create charges, and decrease prices after the job was completed to satisfactory as per the approved work bid. The unethical property preservation business run by the banking industry has cost contractors hundreds of thousands of dollars. If you count the entire nation, the banks did not pay millions of dollars in contractor work. That warranted an investigation. So I conducted a research analysis and sent that information to the Legislature. Very little was done. When nothing is done on such an important issue, you run for office and fix the problem when you get voted in. My experience as a contractor for over 20 years in the Property Preservation field. So I got to know all the things that the banks and their contracting companies do to contractors and sub-contractors and through my research, they are doing that nation wide to thousands of contractors.

When a person is facing forecloser on their property, they are usually given several options to choose from. A bank can not officially foreclose on a property until 9 months of missed payments and can not finalize until a contractor secures the property. What seems to be the norm of banking practices is when a homeowner falls behind on their house payment and they send in their refinance papers, the bank will contact them every 3 weeks or so asking for more information or request that they resend the information because it's blurry. At the 9 months, they will say it has gone too long for that application to be approved and have you resend all of the paperwork all over again. From the day you send in the second set of paper work, you have roughly 30 days before they deny your refinance request and they put your property into pre-forecloser until the bank finalizes the sale. It is a terrible process, but it is a banking procedure that is the norm of the banking function. The IRS acts similarly. They will do everything they can to squeeze as much money out of you as they can get away with.

The IRS is just another banking system. It is just focused on tax collection. One of the things you always have to keep up with is paying your taxes. If you don't the IRS will go after you. They will get access to your bank account and wipe out all your money or try and take your house. If you enter into a payment agreement, you have to pay some of the money for them to do the paperwork. They are government workers who get paid with your tax dollars but charge you extra for doing a job that they are already paid to do. After you get your contract done and a payment plan all set up to make monthly payments, you will be charged an interest fee. Intrest fees are part of any loan so that's not a big deal. But they tack on late fees. You are charged late fees even if your payments are on time. Then they charge a thing called "Other." "Other" is just a charge just to charge. If you find fault in their bill system you have an allotted time to file for a "tax appeal." From my experience in running my own business, managing properties, and working in the property preservation business, I would theorize that the legal issues in phantom billing have increased over the years. 10 years ago, there were significantly lower issues of contractors being paid by the banks. Today, you have to fight every work order to get paid. Before 2008, you could file bankruptcy or chapter 13 and wipe your bills clean and keep your house. During the 2008 recession, lawmakers focused more on making banks unbreakable. By focusing on making banks unbreakable, I would theorize that some of their procedures were changed and have become unethical. Unethical billing practices or unethical banking practices should have an increase in legal actions to argue those processes. I would have to argue that the "tax appeals" have increased over the years for unethical practices.

Article Review:

Lee Kongoh conducted research in 2015, called "Timing of Penalty, Tax Rates, and Evasion" that reviewed the relationships between tax rates and tax evasions and how they relate to the risk and penalty rate. Lee's research showed that an increase in penalties on evaded tax had decreased tax evasion. Further review of the different analysis showed conflicting arguments. If tax penalties increase, some research showed an increase and some showed a decrease in tax evasion. Some people try to evade paying taxes to save. Some people are scared to file because of what they might owe. Some are scared to pay late taxes because of the penalties. The relationship between tax rates and evasion depends on the penalty structure, the magnitude of the fine, and the magnitude of the income. (Kongoh, 2015) You can conclude the argument that creating stiffer penalties is created to force people to pay their taxes, but also creates an issue of evasion because of over-penalizing. The government over-penalizes to force compliance.

Del Write Jr. conducted a research analysis in 2015 called "Improperly Burdened: The Uncertain and Sometimes Unfair Applications of Tax Penalties." He researched issues of unfair penalty practices and issues of taxpayers having little support and not having legal representation. Penalties were used to negotiate positions with taxpayers. Congress did pass the "IRS Reform Act" to decrease abusive penalty behaviors. The IRS Reform Act added three provisions:

- The IRS must include detailed information about the bases for penalties.
- IRS supervisors to approve, in writing, all discretionary penalties.
- The IRS is to bear the burden of production with respect to tax penalties in court proceedings.

Wright states that the IRS has for the most part complied with the first provisions but routinely evades the other two. In 2014 30,000 cases were filed in tax court. 18,000 of those cases were Pro Se or cases where the taxpayer did not have any legal representation. Underrepresented taxpayers have a high rate of losing their case in court even after the IRS and the courts acknowledge that the penalties should have been assessed in the first place. (Wright, 2015)

Data:

IRS Penalties:

- **5% for not filing, imposed every month**
- **If 60 or more days late, there is a minimum penalty of $435**
- **If you are underpaid it is 4% per year, compounded daily**
- **If you pay less than 90% of your taxes, you pay a penalty of 4% and a half percent penalty accrued each month.**

- **If you file an extension there is a 5% penalty plus 4% interest compounded daily.**
- **If you wait too long to file, you may lose your return.**

(Ivanova. 2022)

Conclusion:

Over the past several years there have been many issues of unethical billing practices that were created to enrich those industries through unethical means. Kongoh's research shows that the government may over-penalize taxes to force compliance. But does over-penalizing create an ethics problem or possibly a constitutional problem? The 8th Amendment argues over penalizing. In this case, the government is in control forcing compliance by any means, and is not being held accountable for not following standard banking procedures. You can argue whether the IRS is a bank or not, but they are a banking institute for the Federal Reserve and should have standard banking procedures. Any phantom billing is against the IRS Reform Act.

We want people to pay their taxes. We don't need the IRS creating phantom billing practices to make it harder for people to pay off those taxes. The IRS examples are being done in other industries as well and it needs a legal review.

The next step should be to appeal to Congress and review the IRS Reform Act and come up with a better plan to hold the IRS accountable for following federal policies.

Resources:

https://www.lawsuitlegal.com/phantom-billing.php

https://www.irs.gov/payments/interest-on-underpayments-and-overpayments

SESSIONS, W. S. (1990). WASHINGTON: The FBI's War on Bank Fraud: Facts and Figures. *Challenge*, *33*(4), 57–59. http://www.jstor.org/stable/40721179

Ivanova, Irina. (2022). "What are the penalties and interest for filing taxes late?" https://www.cbsnews.com/news/tax-late-filing-penalty-interest-irs-extension/

Lee, K. (2015). Timing of Penalties, Tax Rates, and Tax Evasion. *FinanzArchiv / Public Finance Analysis*, *71*(1), 37–52. http://www.jstor.org/stable/24807711

Wright, D. (2015). IMPROPERLY BURDENED: THE UNCERTAIN AND SOMETIMES UNFAIR APPLICATION OF TAX PENALTIES. *Proceedings. Annual Conference on Taxation and Minutes of the Annual Meeting of the National Tax Association*, *108*, 1–68. https://www.jstor.org/stable/90023178

Chapter 12

Addressing The Local County Commissioners

One of the County Commissioners put in her resignation to leaving office and they need someone to finish out her term. Larry decided to hand in his Resume for the County Commissioners position in Box Butte County on 30 December 2021. Larry put his name in the hat for that position but would continue his campaign for Attorney General. Some of the policies on law reform can be started at the County level. As new policing policies are introduced to the city, many of those policies and procedures can be implemented at the county level to help improve our Sheriff's department and court system. Making the changes locally could help set an example for the rest of the State to follow.

Larry: "The interview was a bit odd. Seemed like the County Clerk and the County Attorney still have personal issues. One of the questions was "do you have any resentment toward the county because of the past." I might not have any, but it tells me that they still have some issues with me. Those two errored and I pointed it out. They shouldn't hold a grudge about that. If they make an error, they should learn from the error and correct the mistake.

However, If a government targets you for several years and causes you significant harm, of course, there will be personal issues. Anytime a government targets a citizen to bully them around would always be considered personal. Any government official thinking they can attack a civilian and don't think it is personal is an ignorant fool. As an elected official, you should always take into consideration that your actions do affect people.

The issue with the County Clerk was when she interfered with my campaign when I ran for Congress in 2018. I discussed that in my book called "Politics: Last Act of Defiance" Volume I. She created the idea that during election time that the Court House and the Sheriff's Department are were considered the same building. She said that since they are one building during election time, my campaign signs were too close to a polling station, and she forced me to take them down. I argued against it and proved her wrong. Both properties are on two separate parcels of land. She, at one time, referred me to the Count Attorney. The County Attorney said that the ruling on, "if I was placing my sign correctly or not is whatever the County Clerk said." I expected the Attorney to quote the law or state statute. But she did not. But, in the end, I was right, and she was proven wrong. The issue that the County Attorney had with me was when there was a Sheriff Deputy who refused to follow state statutes and judicial procedures and I had addressed those issues to him and several other entities. The Deputy was told more than a dozen times what specific laws and procedures he had to follow, and he refused. The prosecuting attorney refused to penalize the unlawful act and said that law enforcement is allowed to error and that they are allowed immunity. I had studied law and I knew his statement was false. Law enforcement does have some protections if they unknowingly do not follow procedures. You can't expect law enforcement to know every single law or procedure so there needs to be some flexibility. But in this case, that wasn't what was done. The Deputy knew the law and procedure and he refused to follow the law. I expect when a law enforcement officer errors that they receive an education, so it doesn't happen again. In this case, they refused to acknowledge or correct the error, so I filed a complaint with the state. In both cases, they were given the chance to correct the error themselves. In both cases, they refused to fix the error, so I filed official complaints. The bad thing about today's politics is if government officials make an obvious error, they refuse to fix the error because they have far too big of a chip on their shoulder, or do they think it is a liability to accept fault and then fix it? It is hard to understand because if I make a mistake, I try and correct the mistake.

Another issue that was a bit odd about the interview was that we were still talking, and all of a sudden one person said thank you, then the other two said thank you. Just out of the blue as a way of saying we're done, you're dismissed, you can get the hell out of here now. I don't think I did my best interview, but I think they should have been respectable.

We do need things changed in our county procedures. I went to bat to help change our local government and we are doing far better today than we were 5 years ago. So, I will do a few write-ups, get on the county agenda, and present what needs to be done. I would like the Sheriff's Department to get the education needed and bring it into the 21st century. I would like our prosecuting attorney and judges to get on the same page as our police chief. We have a new police chief that is well-educated on 21st-century policing. Many other law enforcement agencies are still stuck in the '80s. We need to end Truancy as a status offense. Start utilizing what we have in a community to help these kids rather than putting them through a juvenile court system. We need to have a drug court system and we need to start utilizing rehab, counseling, intense supervision, and community services instead of jail time for drug-related offenses.

Since I did not get selected for the county position, I will send them a recommendation on what they should work on. (Bolinger, 2022)

To the Box Butte County Commissioners.

Bolinger: Since I was not selected to be A commissioner here is my list of areas that need improvement. For in-depth analysis, I would have to make my books on politics available to you. Volume one was completed last month. Volume two won't be completed until next year. This is the short version. My suggestions are from my many years in politics and the education I received at UNO obtaining a Bachelor of Science degree, majoring in Political Science, minoring in Criminology, with a concentration in Government Affairs and Civic Engagement.

- With the snafu of the Central School building, there was a flaw in the procedure. There was a tax lien foreclosure completed on the property that failed to be listed on the county treasurer's computer or with the county clerk. The paperwork was in the Clerk of the District Court's office. After 8 months it was still not on the county computer. So I got a clean bill of health when I bought the building to find out several months later that there were significant liens on the property. This may need a procedural improvement.
- There have been procedural violations conducted by the Sheriff and Sheriff's department. What I would like to see is, if there is an error in a procedure that they receive the proper education. What has been done in the past is, that the government backs the government rather than gaining education and improving. Let us educate, not ignore. Failing procedure is a burden on the people.
- I would like to see our law enforcement receive more education on 21st-century community policing. They are still utilizing the 1980s-1990s era community policing. Which may stand to reason why they have failed in procedures. I have studied both law enforcement procedures and judicial procedures.
- More focus on mediation, drug courts, rehab programs, and counseling.
- End truancy as a status offense. Utilize mediation and counseling rather than Juvenile courts. The juvenile court system has been shown to do more harm than good. While mediation and counseling have reduced recidivism by 40%. I have done extensive research on this issue. The Alliance Police Chief is trying to utilize more mediation/counseling options for kids and I'd like to see our county/prosecuting attorney and judge on the same page as the Police Chief.
- Drug Courts: there are state grants to start up a drug court system. Utilizing drug courts, mediation, community services, intensive parol/supervision, and rehab has been shown to decrease recidivism by as much as 60%. With the overgrown population in our correctional facilities, we need to look at this option.
- Drop Marijuana as a Schedule 1 offense. In 1971 Marijuana was classified as a Schedule I drug because they claimed there was no acceptable medical use and there was a high potential for abuse. But in the 1990's it was used to help treat chronic pain, glaucoma, Alzheimer's, Parkinson's, epilepsy, and other medical needs. In 1997 the Institute of Medicine proved medical use so Marijuana does not legally fit a Schedule 1 description.
- Any county or city vehicle that is 4-wheel drive should be outfitted with a snow blade to help with snow removal.
- Improve our disaster readiness. There were issues with water pressure at the airport. Fueling the water tanks for the airplanes was very slow. The option that was presented was to tie in all the wells around that area to the airport. Doing that

would cost significantly because of the cost to test each well. It may cost less to send a County worker to college to get an education so the County can test the water rather than hire an outside source. The other option would be to run the airport water off the city main to gain enough water pressure which would cost roughly $800,000. We are centrally located, so we should have a better disaster program. I would suggest putting together a think tank on this to improve this.

I would also express concern about equal employment. Such as when I had the interview for the county commissioner's position. It seemed like the county clerk and county attorney continued to have personal issues with me. They made mistakes and made me pay for them. That should not happen. When there are mistakes, those mistakes should be corrected. They should not try and make an innocent person feel guilty. The clerk interfered in an election, the county attorney failed to support state statutes and judicial procedures. They refused to correct themselves, so I used the chain of command and filed a report. I could have filed a lawsuit, but I chose to just file a report to give them another chance for redemption. Maybe we need mediation to resolve this issue. If I'm applying for a government job, their personal issues should not be the reason I don't get the job. If it is, they should not be allowed to be in those positions.

I am running for Attorney General and these areas are of concern to me. I'd like to see some focus in those areas. The book I wrote is 274 pages with in-depth research analyses. I can make that available to the County Commissioners upon request. I fixed a corrupt system in my town, and I should not be treated poorly because of it. The book covers in detail what happened. It also covers several research analyses that can help our local and state policies. (Bolinger, 2022)

Chapter 13
Consumer Rights

I.	**Title**

Addressing Consumer Rights Violation concerning "The Digital Millennium Copy Right Act"

II.   State the purpose of the bill.

The purpose of this bill is to impose a "Right to Repair" policy to assure consumer rights.

III.   State who the bill will affect and how the bill will affect them.

This bill helps support the consumers who buy electronics or items that have electronics in them such as a cell phone, computer, Tesla vehicle, John Deer tractor… etc. The Digitial Millennium Copyright Act makes it a federal crime for people to work on computer items. The Right to Repair Act overrides that policy and allows people's consumer rights.

IV.   State what you want to accomplish

There are two things that I want to accomplish:

- Pass the Right to Repair bill to allow consumers the right to repair products they buy and let them hire whoever they want to work on the product they bought.
- I would want our Attorney General to file a lawsuit against the Federal Government for approving the Digital Millennium Copy Right Act as it is a violation of consumer rights laws.

V.   State how you want to accomplish your goal.

Both the Legislature and Attorney General will need to review this in committee. This will need to be addressed at both the State and Federal levels.

VI.   Conclusion: This may be the area where you state the consequences of not acting and the benefits of acting to approve the bill.

There will be issues where the hometown mechanic will lose business because federal policies will not allow them to fix a car or tractor. This policy takes away business for each city. This policy creates more downtime for machinery brake-downs because you have to use an approved vendor mechanic. By not fixing this consumer rights violation, you decrease jobs in each town and you decrease productivity.

Approving "Right to Repair" policies would help improve secondary raw material markets, it will help get equipment fixed quicker, decrease equipment downtime, and reduce electronic waste.

Right to Repair

Introduction:

There are many areas where the Right to Repair policy is being argued. The primary issues are with companies such as Tesla, Apple, and John Deer. They refused to allow a consumer who bought equipment from them to work on their own equipment and can utilize the " Digital Millennium Copyright Act" (DMCA) to justify not allowing owners and independent contractors to work on those products. Some companies go to the extent of making programs that will make your equipment shut down or fail if you try and repair it. One of those such programs is the "Error 53" program that Apple used on their phone. "Error 53" caused the phone to shut off if someone tried working on the phone or it would shut down if you tried installing third-party components. Apple was fined $9 million for violations of Australian Consumer Laws. Similar Error 53 programs are installed in John Deer and Tesla. However. John Deere requires the purchaser to sign an end-user license agreement to limit the user's right to the software and forbids any repairs to the equipment.

After the DMCA was implemented in 1998, the EU adopted the Electronic Commerce Directive that provides certainty for businesses and consumers. Establishes requirements for information requirements for online services provider's commercial communication and electronic contracts and limitation of liability of intermediary service providers. (European Commission). Under the 2001 Information Society Directive Article 5 (3), allows the demonstration or repair of equipment. The European Parliament is trying to pass policies for the right to repair. They are promoting reuse and repair arguing against the practice that shortens the lifespan of a product. They want clear labeling that would have an estimate of the lifespan of a product. They are working on decreasing electronic waste. This would include rules for waste management and the removal of legal obstacles that prevent repairs, resale, and reuse. Which will benefit the secondary raw material market.

The Right to Repair policy will give the option to go to someplace other than the dealer or manufacturer to get repairs done. This should also give people the right to the information to be able to fix the items. Manufacturers need to provide spare parts to sell so that consumers can buy them. Parts should be readily available.

Right to Repair laws have been passed in the UK and Europe.

Nobody signed a warranty so they are not bound by warranty policies. It could be argued as not boundable under contract law.

Many farmers and ranchers do most of their own maintenance. In many areas, there are traveling mechanics that would cover a region. Mechanics would go out to the farms or ranch or do the maintenance in the field. Loading up a tractor would be a big undertaking. Taking a tractor to the manufacturer could result in considerable losses due to extended mechanical downtime.

Pros:

- Items get fixed quicker
- Improve secondary raw material markets
- Reduced equipment downtime will increase productivity
- Reduce electronic waste

Cons:

- improper installation
- repairing could cause harm to the property
- company may have to provide blueprints to the public.

Article Review:

An article was written by Elizabeth Moore in 2016 in the Newser titled "Farmers Fight for Right to Repair Own Tractors." Moore stated that according to the "Modern Farmer" if a farmer opens the compartment to check the computers they could be in violation of federal law under the 1998 Digital Millennium Copyrights Act. (Moore, 2016)

In a 2015 letter to the United States Copyright Office, John Deere, the world's largest tractor maker, said that the folks who buy tractors don't own them, not in the way the general public believes "ownership" works. Instead, John Deere said that those who buy tractors are actually purchasing an "implied license for the life of the vehicle to operate the vehicle."

Dan Nosowilz wrote an article in the Modern Farmer titled "Farmers Demand Right to Fix Their Own Dang Tractors." In that article, Dan states that "in a 2015 letter to the United States Copyright Office, John Deere, the world's largest tractor maker, said that the folks who buy tractors don't own them, not in the way the general public believes "ownership" works. Instead, John Deere said that those who buy tractors are actually purchasing an "implied license for the life of the vehicle to operate the vehicle." (Nosowilz, 2016) That could only be true if you are on a lease agreement. The owner of the property is not under any contractual law unless he actually signs an agreement that there is an agreement for the owner to not do work on the equipment. I would say that if you bought the equipment it is yours. Creating policies that say that you cannot work on your own equipment is denying one's right to their own property and is a violation of the 14th Amendment. Refusing to allow one to work on their own property is like buying a book and only being allowed to look at the cover.

An article was written by David Cormand in the News European Parliament in 2020 titled "Parliament wants to grant EU consumers a right to repair." The article talks about the policies that the European Parliament is trying to pass to advance the right to repair. They are promoting reuse and repair and arguing against the practices that shorten the lifespan of a product. They want clear labeling on the estimated lifespan of a product. They are working on decreasing electronic waste. This would include rules for waste management and the removal of legal obstacles that prevent repair, resale, and reuse. Which will benefit the secondary raw material markets. (Cormand, 2020)

President Obama signed the "Unlocking Consumers Choice and Wireless Competition Act," to unlock cell phones to be able to use with other services. Many wireless operators have software locks on them to prevent the phones from being used on other networks. This has been argued as a circumventing technology, but there is no hacking, no code manipulation, or anything being done as per the definition of circumventing technology. (Marquerite, 2014)

DATA:

"The **Digital Millennium Copyright Act (DMCA)** is a 1998 United States copyright law that implements two 1996 treaties of the World Intellectual Property Organization (WIPO). It criminalizes the production and dissemination of technology, devices, or services intended to circumvent measures that control access to copyrighted works (commonly known as digital rights management or DRM). It also criminalizes the act of circumventing an access control, whether or not there is actual infringement of copyright itself." (Wikipedia) (copyright.gov) DMCA § 1201(a)(2) and (b)(1), and tortious interference with contract."

- In order to violate § 1201(a)(2) an individual must "(1) traffic[] in (2) a technology or part thereof (3) that is primarily designed, produced, or marketed for, or has limited commercially significant use other than (4) circumventing a technological measure (5) that effectively controls access (6) to a copyrighted work. Corporations claim that through the use of EULAs (end-user license agreements), prosecute those who are attempting to facilitate repairs by developing and distributing software to circumvent TPMs during the repair process. (UIOWA. Edu)

  When an electrician or mechanic repairs an item, they are not circumventing technology under this definition. They are repairing or replacing a part. If the computer needs to be reformatted and reprogrammed it is reformatted to specified specs. No technology is taken to install in other products. That is pretty standard for any computer.

- The EU adopted the Electronic Commerce Directive in 2000 which provides certainty for businesses and consumers. Establishes requirements for information requirements for online service providers, commercial communication, and electronic contracts and limitation of liability of intermediary service providers. (European Commission) Under the 2001 Information Society Directive Article 5 (3) allows the demonstration or repair of equipment.

- **Circumvention of Technological Measures** When we say circumvention of technological measures, we're referring to **tools that allow users to evade a software's licensing protocol**. This can mean serial numbers, keygens, passwords, and other methods to hack software or games or to hack to manipulate codes.

  In conducting repairs, there would be replacement of parts, reboot software, reformat programs if the computer system goes bad, and software diagnostic equipment to show errors in the product. The policy the US has is to stop the circumvention of technology but does not use the definition of circumvention of technology. They assume general maintenance as part of that definition which may be an infraction of Title 18, United States Code, Section 1001. 1) knowingly and willfully; 2) make any materially false, fictitious, or fraudulent statement or representation; 3) in any matter within the jurisdiction of the executive, legislative, or judicial branch of the United States.

- Antitrust laws are statutes developed by governments to protect consumers from predatory business practices and ensure fair competition. Antitrust laws are applied to a wide range of questionable business activities, including market allocation, bid-rigging, price-fixing, and monopolies. Core U.S. antitrust law was created by three pieces of legislation: the Sherman Anti-Trust Act of 1890,[1] the Federal Trade Commission Act, and the Clayton Antitrust Act.[3]

Methods

- Expand the "Unlocking Consumers Choice and Wireless Competition Act" to support all computers. This act allows independents to work on cell phones.
- Could be argued under the "Antitrust Law' or "Sherman Act. Corporate giants are taking advantage of the people. The Digital Millennium Act creates a monopoly on who can work on equipment and takes away free competition.
- Could be argued under consumer rights.
- Title 18, United States Code, Section 1001. 1) knowingly and willfully; 2) make any materially false, fictitious, or fraudulent statement or representation; 3) in any matter within the jurisdiction of the executive, legislative, or judicial branch of the United States.

Conclusion:

We would need to pass the policy for the right to repair. Right-to-repair is a consumer right. The Digital Millenium copyright infringes on Consumer Rights and therefore should be dissolved.

Where there were issues with companies creating items that last for a short time so as to have more maintenance, there should be a policy that there should be labeling on the estimated amount of time the item should last. If we cannot get the right-to-repair policy to pass there may be a need to pass policies that prevent the sale of the device in the state that are not easily repaired by independent repair providers. Owners and maintenance persons should be allowed to buy diagnostic equipment.

Resources:

Moore, Elizabeth. (2016). *"Farmers Fight for Right to Repair Own Tractors."* Newser. https://www.newser.com/story/228367/farmers-fight-for-right-to-repair-own-tractors.html#:~:text=%28Newser%29%20%E2%80%93%20Farmers%20in%20Nebraska%2C%20Minnesota%2C%20Massachusetts%2C%20and,tractors%20or%20get%20an%20independent%20mechanic%20to%20help.

Nosowilz, Dan. (2016). "Farmers Demand Right to Fix Their Own Dang Tractor." Modern Farmer. https://modernfarmer.com/2016/07/right-to-repair/

European Commission. https://digital-strategy.ec.europa.eu/en/policies/e-commerce-directive

https://www.copyright.gov/legislation/dmca.pdf

Cormand, David. (2020). "Parliament Wants to Grant EU Consumers a Right to Repair." News European Parliament. https://www.europarl.europa.eu/news/en/press-room/20201120IPR92118/parliament-wants-to-grant-eu-consumers-a-right-to-repair

Reardon, Morquerite. (2014). *"President signs cell phone unlocking bill into law"* https://www.cnet.com/tech/mobile/president-signs-cell-phone-unlocking-bill-into-law/

UIOWA. Edu . https://ilr.law.uiowa.edu/print/volume-105-issue-5/defending-the-right-to-repair-an-argument-for-federal-legislation-guaranteeing-the-right-to-repair/

Speech

Right to Repair

Topic: Right to Repair

Specific Purpose: To allow farmers and ranchers the right to work on property they bought.

Central Idea: To argue and protect consumer rights to property they have bought.

Introduction:

1) **Attention:** Hello: my name is Larry Bolinger. I'm a candidate for Attorney General in Nebraska. Today I am going to talk about a policy for the "Right to Repair." Right to Repair is being argued to allow the consumer, maintenance people, computer experts, and mechanics the right to repair products.

2) **Importance:** The importance of this policy is to support consumer rights. To allow them the right to work on their property or give them the right to allow a qualified person to do the work.

3) **Credibility:** I have a Bachelor of Science degree from UNO and I have studied policy and procedures. I also worked for several years as a contractor and as a ranch hand.

4) **Preview:** I will go through some of the issues of the "Digital Millennium Copyright Act" and its impact and talk about how some corporations have overreached their authority in violation of consumer law. I'll review some of the issues of the Error 53 programs, John Deers' "End User License Agreement," and the circumvention of technology.

I) John Deere created a policy called the End User License Agreement to limit what the owner can do to a tractor.

    A) Back about 40 years ago when I was a ranch hand, when a tractor broke down out in the field, you fix it in the field. There was also a roving mechanic who would go from farm to farm to work on equipment. This helped get equipment up and running at the quickest possible time.

    B) The passing of the "Digital Millennium Copyright Act" created a system where companies such as John Deere can tell you that you can no longer work on John Deere tractors. With the newer tractors that are computerized, they claim copyright violations if someone works on the tractors. That includes owners of the tractor and any mechanic who is not directly employed by John Deere.

C) John Deere claims that when you buy tractors, the consumer is actually purchasing an implied license for the life of the vehicle to operate the vehicle rather than traditional ownership. To satisfy contract law, they have every new owner sign an "End User License Agreement" which puts a limit on the user's right to software and forbids any repairs to the equipment. It restricts the owner's ability to perform maintenance or hire a mechanic to perform maintenance.

Transition: *Outside of the EULA, some programs will create an automatic fail or shutdown of the computer system. Such as what was happening with the use of the Error 53 program.*

II)   Error 53 Program was used by Apple on their cell phones.
A) The program shut down the phone if someone tried working on the phone or tried installing a third-party component. Apple was fined 9 million dollars for a violation of Australian Consumer Laws.
B) Error 53 programs were installed in Apple, John Deere, and Tesla.
C) Programs that are created to make your property fail or have a limited life can be argued as Consumer Rights violations. Items break and that is understandable, but making items last a limited amount of time is not ethical.

Transition: *The policy that allowed approval of Error 53 was the Digital Millennium Copyright Act.*

III)   The Digital Millennium Copyright Act was passed in 1998.
A) It criminalizes the production and dissemination of technology, devices, or services intended to circumvent measures that control access to copyrighted works. It also criminalizes the act of circumventing an access control, whether or not there is actual infringement of copyright itself." If a person works on their Apple phone, tractor, or Tesla automobile could be in violation of Federal Law. Under this law, if you even open the compartment to the computer could be a violation of this federal law.
B) The DMCA policy is under the Copyright Law, but people are not copying the program for use for another program or creating their own product. You have to prove a "copy and use," to be proven as a copyright infraction. The policy itself does not fit within the intent of Copyright Law.

Transitions: There is another claim that allowing people to work on computer systems for phones, vehicles, and tractors could be an issue of circumvention of technology.

IV)   Circumvention of technology refers to **tools that allow users to evade a software's licensing protocol**. This can mean serial numbers, keygens, passwords, and other methods to hack software or games or to hack and manipulate codes.

A) When conducting repairs, there would be replacement of parts, reboot software, reformat programs if the computer system goes bad, and there would be software diagnostic equipment that would show errors in the product. The policy the US has is to stop the circumvention of technology but the actual maintenance that is being performed is not by definition, "circumvention of technology." They assume general maintenance as part of that definition which may be an infraction of Title 18, United States Code, Section 1001. 1) knowingly and willfully; 2) make any materially false, fictitious, or fraudulent statement or representation; 3) in any matter within the jurisdiction of the executive, legislative, or judicial branch of the United States.

Conclusion:

There are many ways to fix this problem. There needs to be policy approval to allow owners of property to be able to work on that property. We need to hold the government and businesses accountable when they violate laws. Many of the law violations can be argued under consumer laws, Antitrust laws, infractions of the Federal Trade Commission Act, Infractions of the Clayton Antitrust Act., Sherman Act violations, or violations of the Title 18 policy.

Approving "Right to Repair" policies would help improve secondary raw material markets, it will help get equipment fixed quicker, decrease equipment downtime, and reduce electronic waste.

The next course of action would be to contact our state and federal legislatures and change these policies. If they refuse to change the policy, we start filing charges.

<u>Press Release</u>

Attorney General Candidate Larry Bolinger argues in support of the "Right to Repair " policy.

Author: Larry Bolinger
Alliance, Nebraska

The Right to Repair policy would allow consumers, maintenance people, computer experts, and mechanics the right to repair equipment. The importance of this policy is to reestablish support for consumer rights. To allow consumers the right to work on their property or give them the right to allow a qualified person to do the work. Several policies were put in place to safeguard Consumer rights and some policies were created to undermine consumer rights such as the "Digital Millennium Copyright Act" which allows corporations to overreach their authority in violation of consumer law. There have been problems with companies utilizing Error 53 programs, John Deeres' "End User License Agreement," and circumvention of technology.

John Deere created a policy called the "End User License Agreement" to limit what the owner can do to a tractor. Back about 40 years ago when I was a ranch hand when a tractor broke down out in the field, you fix it in the field. There was also a roving mechanic who would go from farm to farm or ranch to ranch to work on equipment. This helped get equipment up and running at the quickest possible time. The passing of the "Digital Millennium Copyright Act" created a system where companies such as John Deere can tell you that you can no longer work on John Deere tractors. The newer tractors are computerized so they claim copyright violations if someone works on the tractors. That includes owners of the tractor and any mechanic who is not directly employed by John Deere. John Deere claims that when you buy tractors, the consumer is actually purchasing an implied license for the life of the vehicle to operate the vehicle rather than traditional ownership. To satisfy contract law, they have every new owner sign an "End User License Agreement" which puts a limit on a user's rights to the software and forbids any repairs to the equipment. It restricts the owner's ability to perform maintenance or hire a mechanic to perform maintenance. That seems like a very clear consumer rights violation and it takes away your right to property ownership of something you bought.

Outside of the EULA, some programs will create an automatic fail or it will shut down the computer system. One of those programs is called the "Error 53" program. Error 53 Program was used by Apple on their cell phones. The programs were also used in John Deere trackers and Tesla automobiles. The program shuts down the phone if someone tries working on the phone or tries installing a third-party component. Apple was fined 9 million dollars for a violation of Australian Consumer Laws. Programs that are created to make your property fail or have a limited life can be argued as Consumer Rights violations. Items break and that is understandable, but making items last a limited amount, or creating a program to start failing at a one-year or two-year mark is not ethical. Have you ever noticed that by the time your phone is paid off, your phone starts to fail, so you have to upgrade every two years? Another example is when it is near the time to renew your virus protection for your computer at the same time your computer starts to fail.

The policy that allowed approval of Error 53 was the Digital Millennium Copyright Act of 1998. It criminalizes the production and dissemination of technology, devices, or services intended to circumvent measures that control access to copyrighted works. It also criminalizes the act of circumventing an access control, whether or not there is actual infringement of copyright itself." If a person works on their Apple phone, tractor, or Tesla automobile could be in violation of Federal Law. Under this law, if you even open the compartment to the computer could be a violation of this federal law. The DMCA Policy is umbrella under the Copyright Law, but people are not copying the program for use for another program or creating their own product. You have to prove a "copy and use," to be proven as a copyright infraction. The policy itself does not fit within the intent of Copyright Law.

Another claim states that allowing people to work on computer systems in phones, vehicles, and tractors could be an issue of circumvention of technology. Circumvention of technology refers to **tools that allow users to evade a software's licensing protocol**. This can mean serial numbers, keygens, passwords, and other methods to hack software or games or to hack to manipulate codes. When conducting repairs, there would be replacement of parts, reboot software, reformat programs if the computer system goes bad, and software diagnostic equipment that would show errors in the product. The policy the US has is to stop the circumvention of technology but the actual maintenance that is being performed is not by definition, "circumvention of technology." They assume general maintenance as part of that definition which may be an infraction of Title 18, United States Code, Section 1001. 1) knowingly and willfully; 2) make any materially false, fictitious, or fraudulent statement or representation; 3) in any matter within the jurisdiction of the executive, legislative, or judicial branch of the United States.

There are many ways to fix this problem. There needs to be policy approval to allow owners of property to be able to work on that property. We need to hold the government and businesses accountable when they violate laws. Many of the law violations can be argued under consumer laws, Antitrust laws, infractions of the Federal Trade Commission Act, Infractions of the Clayton Antitrust Act., Sherman Act violations, or violations of the Title 18 policy. Approving "Right to Repair" policies would help improve secondary raw material markets, it will help get equipment fixed quicker, decrease equipment downtime, and reduce electronic waste. The next course of action would be to contact your state and federal legislatures and change these policies. If they refuse to change the policy, we start filing charges. There are two courses of action. We can fight to Instow a Right to Repair policy or we fight to repeal the Digitial Millennium Copyright law as it is a consumer rights violation.

Resources:

Moore, Elizabeth. (2016). *"Farmers Fight for Right to Repair Own Tractors."* Newser. https://www.newser.com/story/228367/farmers-fight-for-right-to-repair-own-tractors.html#:~:text=%28Newser%29%20%E2%80%93%20Farmers%20in%20Nebraska%2C%20Minnesota%2C%20Massachusetts%2C%20and,tractors%20or%20get%20an%20independent%20mechanic%20to%20help.

Nosowilz, Dan. (2016). "Farmers Demand Right to Fix Their Own Dang Tractor." Modern Farmer. https://modernfarmer.com/2016/07/right-to-repair/

European Commission. https://digital-strategy.ec.europa.eu/en/policies/e-commerce-directive

https://www.copyright.gov/legislation/dmca.pdf

Cormand, David. (2020). "Parliament Wants to Grant EU Consumers a Right to Repair." News European Parliament. https://www.europarl.europa.eu/news/en/press-room/20201120IPR92118/parliament-wants-to-grant-eu-consumers-a-right-to-repair

Reardon, Morquerite. (2014). *"President signs cell phone unlocking bill into law"* https://www.cnet.com/tech/mobile/president-signs-cell-phone-unlocking-bill-into-law/

UIOWA. Edu. https://ilr.law.uiowa.edu/print/volume-105-issue-5/defending-the-right-to-repair-an-argument-for-federal-legislation-guaranteeing-the-right-to-repair/

Note: My standard practice when trying to push a policy is to do an in-depth research analysis. The format is for a speech. While running for office and could do a Town Hall meeting and use that in my speech. I also do a recording of my speech and put it on my website and in any instant messenger group. Then I reformat it for a press release or article of submission. If it is just a state issue, I send it out to state media outlets and the state legislature. If it is a national policy, I do the same thing but also send it out to media outlets in every state.

Bolinger Quote in 2024 campaign for Nebraska State Legislature 2024:
   A politician that is motivated by donations is not honest representation.
I have been in politics for 20 years. If you need help with a policy, feel free to contact me. I've always had an open-door policy.
   Many of these big tech companies have been hiding behind the "Digitial Millennial Copy Right Act." That federal policy makes it illegal for Consumers to work on or fix certain products that have a computer in them such as cell phones, computers, electric vehicles, and John Deere tractors. That is why in my 2020 campaign for Attorney General I endorsed the fight for "Right to Repair." But, I also fought to claim the "Digital Millennial Copy Right Act" as a Consumer Right violation.

I do not bend to corporate greed. My only concern is for my community.

Chapter 14

The ever-expanding fight for Equal Rights

I. **Title**

Implement a Statewide "Fairness Ordinance."

II. **Purpose of the bill.**

To secure equal protection under the law that the 14th Amendment to the Constitution demands. This will ensure that people will not be discriminated against because of their gender or sexual orientation.

III. **State who the bill will affect and how the bill will affect them.**

This will affect the LGTBQ community. This will ensure that they will be treated with equal rights when obtaining a job, treated fairly at the job site, and have equal and fair treatment in regards to housing.

IV. **What I expect to accomplish with this bill.**

Lincoln Nebraska has been trying to secure and pass the Fairness Ordinance. What I want to accomplish is to make this a statewide program by approving it through the State Legislature.

V. **State how you want to accomplish your goal**

I would want the Committee to review my request and create the policy to make it a state statute.

VI. **Conclusion: The consequences of not acting and the benefits of acting to approve the bill.**

By approving the policy you are ensuring equal protection under the law. Not approving such a policy will end up just like any other discrimination case. It will be costly. Over the years, many cases of discrimination have been fought. Discrimination will eventually lose and it will cost the state significantly if the state refuses to act in accordance of the law.

The fight for equal rights for the gay and LGTBQ community over the past several years has brought some very odd arguments. Some arguments created more division between parties. Many issues that showed that racism was fought with racism or discrimination are fought with racism. Which created more division rather than acceptance. The change in how one identifies themself or how they identify their gender has created a stir. The left argues for gender identity, the right argues they don't want men in the women's bathroom. By arguing it in this fashion when LGBTQ argue for equal rights, the arguments from the right result in focusing on men in women's bathrooms. This led to the creation of WOKE and Cancel Culture on the Left and the fight for and against Critical Race Theory that is argued on the Left and Right. In many cases, Critical Race Theory was argued that it was created to shame white people for events in history and to focus on making sure other than a white man advances. President Trump and President Biden put some focus on hiring people in office based on the sex and color of a person. Such as hiring representatives to the Supreme Court based on sex and/or color, or electing a vice president based on sex and color. That set an example to follow.

Bolinger: "I spent two weeks in Lincoln Nebraska campaigning for Attorney General and I pushed to help fight against discrimination and was told not to help the LGBTQ by a member of the LGBTQ community because I was white and straight. When such things happen and people are not treated equally, it always ends up with some form of backlash."

To Shame or Not to Shame
20 March 2022 debate review

Bolinger: Going to a debate for Attorney General as a moderate in a 90% extremist far-Right group is just asking for trouble. Assume and prepare for the worst. Extremist groups only have one thought pattern, are very narrow-minded, and are not going to change anything. Listening to reason is thrown out the door. This was the setup at the debate in York that was conducted on the 20th of March. It was comparable to the Snake-Pit in basic training.

The debate did not go as well as I would hope. I did get a chance to talk with some pretty good people but was met with opposition and hecklers when I supported a child's Rights. One of the questions that was asked was "what would I do in a case in Texas where a teacher sexualized a child." I chose to defend the child as they are protected under the 14th Amendment equal protection under the law. Several people were in an uproar that I would be against a teacher who would shame a kid over their sexuality. It was a disgusting display of discrimination. This was a 90% conservative group. It is troubling when a political group supports shaming children. One lady claimed that she was a Christian. It is troubling that people use being Christian to gain the acceptability to discriminate against others. Many political leaders have made those statements and it has become the norm. Jesus never taught us to discriminate and they should lead by example if they are of true faith. What happened to the teaching that "God is Love" and to Love thy neighbor?

Ultimately the information about the case was not complete. It lacked a significant amount of information, so the only thing you could do was speculate. The worst thing an Attorney General could do is speculate and go to the press about it. Some people take things to the extreme and attack the LGTBQ culture without even thinking of the consequences of their actions.

The case that was presented lacked information. Any professional would dig deep for information. You would need to know what was done, what was said, whether was it a verbal issue, was it shaming the child, was it physical, was it both, was it public humiliation? A teacher shaming a child's sexuality would be considered both discrimination and sexual harassment. Under the 14th Amendment, it says that everyone has equal protection under the law. This was argued in the case of Brown vs the Board of education. That case was a starting point to allow black kids to go to public schools and it is used to argue many other cases of discrimination.

In that case, you would want to know what was done. Was the RSO involved? Was the police involved? Was the chain of command in the education system utilized? Was a complaint filed with the superintendent, Local School board, or up the chain to the State Board of Education? Was there a suit filed with the local courts, appealed, and pushed to the appellate court? If it is a clear form of discrimination I would approve of arguing the case in the Supreme Court. But I would also look into each level of the education chain of command to see if there was negligence in their job. If they failed to act, then it is considered negligence. Then there would be charges starting at the state level and it will roll downhill from there. But at any point, in this case, the parents should be encouraged to contact the Attorney General or Ombudsman on this Civil Rights concern.

In my closing state, I got many people riled up. Looked like they were going to riot. I did begin my ending speech by stating that I am the best candidate because of my past experiences. I suggested that when selecting your next Attorney General I ask that you consider who is going to take us forward and who is going to hold us back. Do we want decisions made based on facts or fiction? I argued that if you vote conservative, that guarantees that we will get nothing done, we will be at a standstill for the next decade and it will set us back 50 years behind everyone else. People got riled up because of that. I told them, "that is what is meant to be conservative." I did tell them that I left the Republican party because of misinformation campaigns. And that misinformation campaigns are disrespectful to every Nebraska and that Nebraskans deserve better than what we have today. Misinformation is just a politician feeding you bad information in hopes that you will follow. I then went into a speech on how people view conservatives. Where most people look at them as racists because of the discrimination they have done against the LGBTQ community. They got really riled up about that. I said, "It sounds like you did not like my Comment." "Good, If my statement is wrong, then you need to get off your butt and speak up."

As I walked off the stage some crazy old lady got in my face and asked if I had kids in school and she said that they should not have any freedom of choice and that she is a Christian. After that encounter, I was walking around the back to some of my Libertarian Supporters and I said "was that a shit show or just terrible." Those guys were rolling. I guess my voice was a little loud and everyone in the auditorium heard it. So they all gave me the stink-eye. I might have lost 300 voters, but I gained 3 loyal supporters. I could only hope that some of them might have some sort of realization from my statement. (Bolinger, 2022)

Article Review

An article written by Helen Raleigh on 6 May 2021 in Newsweek called "Woke Racism is a Systemic Problem in America Opinion," argues troubling issues created in the woke movement. Raleigh states that Woke fights racism with racism but hides behind words such as "fact-finding," "equity," "social justice," and "anti-racism." Raleigh argued several issues of inequality, such as when Biden became president he announced that his administration would instruct COVID-related small business loan programs to prioritize minority and female businesses. Congress followed that by creating a special clause to the American Rescue Plan instructing the Secretary of Agriculture to provide debt relief to farmers based on the color of the recipient's skin. (Raleigh, 2021)

An article written by Margaret Reist on 27 February 2022 in the Lincoln Journal called "Lincoln's Transgender Community Predicted it'd be Target of Fairness Ordinance Opponents" argues equal rights of the LGTBQ community. The City of Lincoln passed a city ordinance that allowed equal rights for the LGTBQ community. Later a group collected 18,000 signatures on a petition to reverse the policy. People decided not to fight against that because of the hostility that was created. In June 2022, a group tried to gain support for this policy. They wanted to add to the policy to protect against discrimination based on sexual orientation and gender identity. (Reist. 2022)

Natalie Weiss made a statement that said that "it did not matter what policies are changed or added, it's about transgender bathroom access." (Weiss)

Bolinger: *When I argued for equal rights of LGBTQ in the workplace, the first thing that gets argued is assuming this means allowing men in the women's bathroom."*

Reist explained that this policy adds military and veterans in a protective class and allows a Commission on Human Rights to investigate allegations of discrimination on housing, employment, and public accommodations. (Reist. 2022)

The Nebraska Family Alliance with the help of former Governor Kay Orr was able to get enough signatures for the petition to get the Fairness Ordinance argued as a "transgender bathroom ordinance." (Reist.2022)

An article written by Veronica Barreto in December of 2022 on KLKN ABC news titled "Changes to Lincoln's Equal opportunity code may be on the ballot after all," further reviews the Fairness Ordinance. The reports state that supporters of the policy attempted to amend the Fairness Ordinance. They turned in 11,000 signatures, but the Lancaster County election Commission rejected the petition. The petition followed the City's guidelines. After the petition was sent in, it was rejected. The commissioners said that the petition had to follow State guidelines, not the City's. (Barreto. 2022)

The Nebraska Family Alliance made the following statement: "Governments across the country are trying to push similar policies to threaten America's constitutionally protected freedoms and force destructive gender ideology on society." (Nebraska Family Alliance)

Conclusion:

Many people claim that if the government passes policies to support the LGTGQ culture, it is a violation of the Constitution and infringes on freedom of religion. Freedom of religion means that you can not force someone to believe your religion or your perspective of your religion. Conservatives want one view and only one view to be allowed. That is not freedom of religion. Our forefathers left Europe to run from public and religious persecution and create a country that treats everyone as equal. If this is argued as religious freedom, then all people will have the freedom to interpret their religion their way and should not be forced into accepting another person's perspective. (Bolinger)

In January of 2023, Congressman Smith sent out a message to people on his network feed telling them that he was taking a stand against the violent acts at different centers. Larry Bolinger had decided to write a letter to Congressman Smith, supporting his stance to condemn the violent act and to address the issue of the growing violent acts against the LGTBQ community. The theory is that if he is going to condemn one act of violence, he should condemn the other. The problem with the growing discrimination against the LGTBQ community comes largely from the GOP/media platform. Below is Bolinger's letter to Congressman Smith:

Date: 1/20/2023

To Honorable Congressman Adrian Smith

Scottsbluff District Office
416 Valley View Dr.
Suite 600
Scottsbluff, NE 69361

Dear Congressman Smith:

I am addressing you as a member of the "Nebraska Politics (open Debate)" group. My name is Larry Bolinger and I was a candidate for Nebraska Attorney General in 2022. There has been a growing concern over the past couple of years in the gay or LGTBQ community where there has been increased tension caused by misinformation and discrimination. One of the biggest issues I had to deal with while running for office was discrimination issues. I had run for office many times over the past two decades and I always fought for equal rights, but Conservatives have been pushing to single out and segregate the gay community.

In Lincoln, they attempted to pass the "Fairness Ordinance" to protect gay rights. So that they can not be denied a job or housing because they are gay. This policy passed, then was quickly changed because a religious organization put pressure on the City Council and they changed over the fear of what they would do. An LGTBQ group did try to do a petition to allow the voters to vote on the policy, but lawmakers refused their petition. I do understand your stance because you chose not to support gay marriage. But, the constitution, under the 14th Amendment states that everyone has equal protection under the law. People should not be singled out or segregated because they are gay. There have been similar policies to the Fairness Ordinance presented at the State and Federal levels but have not passed.

The primary argument in the NEGOP and the media to fight against equal rights is that they don't want men in the girl's bathroom. This policy and what is argued about equal rights have nothing to do with bathroom use. This is media and political misinformation that is used to deflect from the actual policy.

In the latest news in Nebraska, the State Legislatures are reviewing a policy LB374. Under that policy, it states that they do not want to allow indoctrination in schools. Indoctrination is a school function. Listening to the radio, TV, religion, and any type of education is indoctrination. Schools are where kids learn social skills. Not allowing indoctrination would mean that conservatives will not be allowed to indoctrinate kids into any religious belief, so there will never be allowed prayer in schools or the moment of silence. If it is done while this policy is in place, schools and teachers could be fined and face a possible loss of a job. This policy will secure keeping religion out of public schools. If this is a policy that is designed to take a jab at the gay community, it would be a violation of the Civil Rights Act of 1964 which ended legally sanctioned discrimination. The policy is just a jab at the gay community. This can be argued in the Supreme Court because there may be violations of Constitutional Law. Take away the jab at the gay community and you would have a legal policy.

The NEGOP has created a significant amount of problems when they utilize religion for political gain. The NEGOP is not a religious organization, they are a political group that is using religion to incite the people and create fear for political gain. There have been many cases of increased hate crimes, assaults, and death threats. I supported equal rights as a candidate for Attorney General and received more than 20 death threats.

It is good to hear that you signed a resolution condemning the vandalism, threats, and destruction that was suffered by numerous pregnancy resource centers. Let's do the same thing against the attacks, discrimination, and threats against the LGBTQ culture.

With tensions increasing at an alarming rate because of discrimination against the gay or LGTBQ community, what policies are you proposing that could help decrease tension?

Larry Bolinger
2022 Candidate for Nebraska Attorney General

Resources:

RESPECT FOR MARRIAGE ACT; Congressional Record Vol. 168, No. 191**Issue and Section:** December 08, 2022 - House (Vol. 168, No. 191)**Page:** H8827 (PDF 401KB)

Conclusion:

Bolinger: "When running for office you may be faced with issues of discrimination. The number one thing you don't want to do is lose your temper as I did in the debate. Stay focused on your agenda. Hold strong convictions against discrimination. The WOKE and Cancel Coultuers have very few legal arguments and both utilize discrimination to fight against discrimination, so they lack any reasonable arguments or reliable sources. The best thing to do is fight specific discrimination issues with what is protected under Constitutional Law and direct infractions of policies. If the President, Congress, or any legal body creates policies that put the priority of one race over the other needs to be argued as discrimination. In that case, you hold the lawmakers accountable for creating policies that support discrimination. If a policy is passed in a Legislative body you would have to argue it as a Constitutional violation in the Supreme Court to have it overturned. If we allow discrimination in our government it becomes an acceptable normal act that causes a much bigger problem. That is why there are such policies as the 14th Amendment that allows equal protection under the law and the Civil Rights Act of 1964 that ended legally sanctioned discrimination. In the 2023 Legislative session for Nebraska, there are a dozen policies being introduced that are policies that support sanctioned discrimination. Each one could face arguments in the Supreme Court if any of those are passed."

If we are fighting for equality, why is our government creating policies based on race? It is becoming an unethical practice. To fight for equal rights, you have to be a little tough-skinned. You treat everyone equally and ensure everyone has the same rights and opportunities. Pander to one or the other or denying one of the other will eventually result in disaster.

The "Fairness Ordinance" policy has created some arguments about racial inequality and claims of the constitutionality of what that means. The reality of it is that everyone is protected by law. Under the 14th Amendment, it states everyone has equal protection under the law. However, the Nebraska Family Alliance argues that supporting the Fairness Ordinance is a violation of the constitution. The NFA is wrong. The Fairness Ordinance assures equal treatment under the law.

The rejection of the policy was an odd issue. At first, the Fairness Ordinance was approved by the City Council. Then the Nebraska Family alliance formed its PAC to fight against the ordinance. They got 18,000 signatures on the petition to put the ordinance on the ballot to vote it out. But the City Council was pressured to vote on it and remove it. When supporters of the Fairness Ordinance collected 11,000 votes on a petition to put the policy on the ballot to vote to get the ordinance back, the County Commissioners rejected the petition saying that they had to go through the State. But, Lincoln is a "Home Rule" town. Meaning, that they can create their own laws, similar to what the State Legislature can do. But, dirty politics do attempt to reject qualified petitions. So, if you know you did it right, you take it to court. Hold those officials accountable for their actions.

Resources

York News-Times. (5 April 2022). Larry Bolinger. https://yorknewstimes.com/news/local/govt-and-politics/elections/larry-bolinger/article_5cdfafb3-db15-5922-a373-fe7350b45c10.html

Raleigh Helen. (6 May 2021). "Woke Racism is a Systemic Problem in America Opinion." Newsweek. https://www.newsweek.com/woke-racism-systemic-problem-america-opinion-1589071

Reist, Margaret. (27 Feb. 2022). *"Lincoln's Transgender Community Predicted it'd be Target of Fairness Ordinance Opponents."* The Lincoln Journal. https://journalstar.com/news/local/govt-and-politics/lincolns-transgender-community-predicted-itd-be-target-of-fairness-ordinance-opponents/article_b712c9b4-10cd-50b0-a176-76beaba9e54b.html

Barreto, Veronica. *(23 December 2022). "changes to Lincoln's Equal Opportunity Code may be on the Ballot after all."* KLKN. https://www.klkntv.com/changes-to-lincolns-equal-opportunity-code-may-be-on-the-ballot-after-all/?utm_medium=social&utm_source=facebook_Channel_8_News_KLKN_TV_Lincoln&fbclid=IwAR2WQE7uGuQ3ymzSOWzK5MJLD26_Y3W9JrBGL1rB8bvF39dmHEWo18ck7tc

Chapter 15

Supporting EPA regulations

2024 campaign for Legislature. Back ground picture is the Bridgeport Pits.

I.   Title

Mead environmental disaster.

II.   State the purpose of the bill.

Claim the Mead environment disaster as a State and National environment disaster emergency.

III.   State who the bill will affect and how the bill will affect them.

This will affect Eastern Nebraska. This will ensure that both the State and Federal governments will take responsibility and get the contaminated water cleaned up in the quickest possible timeframe.

IV.   State what you want to accomplish.

    a) I want a state of emergency declared and a joint effort from the State and Federal governments to clean up the contaminated water.

    b) Improve our water supply. Everyone pays a water fee. That fee is to pay for good, quality, drinkable drinking water. The tap should be as good as or better than bottled water.

    c) End Fracking in Nebraska.

    d) End the contract with Colorado to store their fracking water, unless the water is filtered and the chemicals are separated from the water.

V.   State how you want to accomplish your goal.

I would want this addressed to the Legislature, the Governor, and the State's Attorney General, and I would want our Congressional representatives to address this in the Legislature.

VI.   **Conclusion: This may be the area where you state the consequences of not acting and the benefits of acting to approve the bill.**

    a)   By not acting, the surrounding water will continue to be contaminated. This will destroy more water supplies and land and it will affect the health of everything and everyone in the surrounding area. By not acting, it will be considered negligence. There are many cases of governments allowing contaminated water to go unchecked, and they have always ended up paying for their negligence. This is an emergency and needs to be treated as an important issue. The clean-up cost will most likely be high. But the cost of lives and destroyed waterways and land will cost much more.

    b)   Ending fracking in Nebraska would save Nebraska 54 million barrels of water each year.

One of the many jobs of elected officials is doing what is right for the environment. As a City Council member, you don't want to approve something that would cause harm to the people living in that city. So you weigh the pros and cons of allowing things to happen or stopping those things from happening. That is reviewed at all levels of government. In Nebraska, one of the main topics is contamination in our water supply and the Mead environment disaster. The Mead issue is when an alcohol plant was allowed to use corn that had pesticide on it. That created hundreds of thousands of gallons of water in waste ponds in that area which eventually leaked and contaminated rivers and lakes killing off wildlife and destroying the land. The company went bankrupt, then the State tried going after them to file charges. It is tough to go after a company that already gone bankrupt. What makes things even worse is that the governor at that time in 2012, signed off on allowing that company to use contaminated corn. That makes the State liable. Which means the taxpayers will pay for his poor decision.

Karen made a statement: *"people need to take action and start fighting to get things done."*

My response was:

How about fighting for accountability? We need to address the environmental disaster in Mead. The state Legislature, Governor, and Attorney General have not done their job in getting that cleaned up. You can't kick dirt on it and call it good. One of the Jobs of the Attorney General is upholding EPA regulations. Hilgers and Peterson should be held accountable for failing to uphold EPA regulations and allowing the water and land to be contaminated in that area. X-governor Hienaman signed off on allowing the contaminated seed to be used in that plant and he endorses Hilgars and Pillen. If either one of those two gets in office they will just try and cover up the disaster and the people who are at fault will not be held accountable and the people will suffer from it. Hilgers already is a failure in his duties as a speaker and should not be allowed to carry over that failure to the AttorneyGenerals' office. (Bolinger 4/15/2022)

In volume I of "Politics: Last Act of defiance" I wrote an analysis on environmental issues and the contamination of our waters. It is an issue that I will explore further. The write-up is as follows:

The Results of our Actions: (Environmental Problems)

Bolinger: This is a Thesis I wrote for a college class I took and it will go through the changes in our water supplies and how our supplies have gotten worse over the years despite the millions of dollars that we spend on trying to take contaminants out of it.

There are many environmental issues we face today that have resulted in our actions or inactions. By not fixing our mistakes, our water supply and environment will continue to get worse. Over the years contaminants from the farming industry, Rail Road, oil companies, fracking industries, and many other types of industries or companies have contaminated our drinking water. Knowing this and having not taken action long ago to clean the contaminants up could have prevented a great deal of damage that has destroyed our environment. Continuing to allow these businesses to commit actions that cause so much destruction of our water supply and environment, which our government has knowledge of, and allowing these actions to continue is negligence on their part. Examples of these would be; spraying for insects, pesticide control, oil spills, introducing fracking water into old wells, or diesel leakage.

I am 51 years old. I was born and raised in Nebraska, and I have noticed significant changes in our environment over the years. My main topic is our water supply and how that has changed over the past 5 decades during my time in Nebraska. I believe that if we don't put more focus on cleaning up our water supply, we could be facing dire straits in the years to come.

As a child growing up in the '70s, I did a lot of swimming and fishing. There weren't any major fears of contaminants in our water supply during my youth. So, I spent a lot of time swimming at the pool, and nearby lakes, and I was even talked into swimming in the city's fountain before they had installed a filter system. At that time, it was a moss-filled, nasty mess, but both I and my cousin had a great deal of fearless fun. The only problem that I saw at that time with the water was when it was hot outside. Towards the end of the summer, after a long heat spell, the fish got wormy. Sometimes people who swam in the different lakes late in the summer would get the swimmer's itch. Nothing major, it was just something that happened now and again.

Thirty years ago, we would have never thought that we would have to rely on bottled water for drinking. The water tasted good and we never heard of anyone getting sick from drinking out of the tap or garden hose. The changes in the water contamination started with testing, with the results showing that there were several chemicals and pesticides in our water. Testing of the water started about 15 years ago. Some of those chemicals that were found in our water supply were blamed on farmers. Some people blamed the chemicals getting into our water supply on the Rail Road. We also had issues with e-coli. A report came out claiming that there was a dead dog in the well. The cure for any contaminants has always been chlorine. In the late 1990's we started having e-coli scares, which helped push for investing in water treatment systems.

In 1998, I was recruited into Network 21, which is a branch of the company called Amway. One of their big sales items was a water treatment system. Easy to install, it took out 99% of the contaminants, including e-coli and chlorine. The system was fairly reasonable, but the filter cost about a hundred bucks. It was a pretty standard practice to sell the system at a fair price to gain long-time customers to pay a high price to maintain their system.

Water treatment sales and promotions were on the rise in the 1990s. However, I do not recall any indication or notice from our government that would lead us to have any concern about the contamination levels of our water supplies. When sales were up for residential water filtration systems in the '90s, water testing was not a huge concern until around 2005, when it became a priority to test our water supply. Looking at these dates and theorizing about our government's concern for our drinking supply, it is a wonder as to why this was not a concern for the general public's safety for many years.

Eventually, our city decided to look into a state program to upgrade our wells and build a water treatment plant. Further studies were done on our water supply that indicated that our drinking water was showing above the allowable levels of arsenic. There are also high levels of mercury in different lakes. After the city had committed to a thirty-six million dollar project to update the wells and build a water treatment plant, we still had test results that showed high levels of arsenic, and we still had e-coli outbreaks. I do believe the completion of the water treatment system took place around the year 2009. Around that time, I decided to serve on the City's Planning Commission.

One of the larger projects I remember while serving on the City's Planning Commission is making the decision and approving the building of a three-million-dollar swimming pool. The old swimming pool deteriorated and had a large crack in it. It was leaking hundreds of gallons of chlorinated water into the ground each day. The crack had been there for many years before it was discovered, wasting hundreds of thousands of gallons of water per year. The old swimming pool had leaked through the soil and eventually back into our water drinking supply.

One issue that comes to mind is when the proposal was being presented to the Planning Commission, one of the City Council members stated several times that the old swimming pool was so gross that he wouldn't even allow his dog to walk in it. The city also stated that it would cost almost as much to repair the old swimming pool as it would build a new one. Building a new swimming pool was estimated to cost around three million dollars. After long deliberation, it was approved that a new swimming pool would be built. During the phase of building a new swimming pool, it was discovered that the actual repair cost for the old swimming pool was closer to fifty thousand dollars, not three million. I personally felt very deceived by the City Council when I discovered that they lied about the cost of repairing the old swimming pool. In retrospect, the odds are that we would have eventually approved the new pool anyway because the old one was getting run down and needed extensive repairs. A couple of years later I found out that there wasn't a crack in the pool that was causing a loss of water. The swimming pool water was connected to the sprinkler system to the baseball field and they were losing water through that. Which seems kind of odd. I'm guessing they probably didn't know what they were talking about so they made up theories so they could gain approval for a new pool.

Additionally, even with the water treatment system still in place, there continued to be reports of e-coli outbreaks in our water system, resulting in more chlorine being added to our water supply. Unfortunately for the residents, there was still an issue of high levels of arsenic. I, myself, was sick for two weeks from drinking the tap water. Many people I knew personally were getting sick from drinking the water also. After a while of drinking the city water, I started having esophagus problems and terrible heartburn. Then suddenly the muscle in my esophagus stopped working altogether. Eventually, the stomach acid ate away all my teeth. It was a horrible experience to go through. I began to notice that I wasn't the only one experiencing this side effect. A significant number of people I knew were having similar issues. This is when I stopped drinking the water from the tap. I just wondered how we could spend over thirty-six million dollars on updating the wells and water treatment systems and still have water that is not pure enough to drink. In my opinion, it is odd enough to pay for water to drink in the first place and even more odd to pay for drinking water you cannot safely drink.

The contamination of our water supply has increased significantly. Contamination continues from activities that create the transference of bacteria, contaminants from ethanol plants, and from places that involve fracking and oil pipeline spillages. With the growth of fracking and the expansions of the Keystone pipeline company into Nebraska, we made an existing problem worse. When the Nebraska Legislatures and Governor were promoting the contract between Colorado and Nebraska to store fracking water in the old oil wells, several people opposed this idea. One resident even challenged a Senator to take a drink of the fracking water. If the Senator had thought it was safe to drink the water then the challenge would have been accepted. However, I feel the Senator was fully aware that it was not safe to drink the fracking water. Weeks later, the contract was approved to store fracking water in the old oil wells, and once again, the people's voices were ignored.

There was also a lack of action by our government to clean up contaminants that were created by an ethanol plant in Mead Nebraska. The plant (Alten)was using seeds that had been sprayed with pesticides. The mash was stored outside in a pit. The contaminants leaked into the nearby stream and killed off all the fish destroying the water supply and destroying many people's lands. There were millions of gallons of contaminated water spilled. The company had the neighboring farmers spread the mash over their land to help with adding minerals to the soil. But with the chemicals that were in it, it made the animals sick. It was not until February 2021 that the plant was forced to close. That's more than a decade of contaminants going into our water supply. The state tried to pressure the AltEn to fix their mash-holding areas and they were never fixed well enough to keep the contaminants from getting into the water supply. As of 2021 1.75 million gallons of contaminants have been cleaned. On 12 February 2021, more than four million gallons of pesticide-ridden wastewater had drained into the downstream waterways. After the 3 September 2021 rain there was an overflow of the bladders and more contaminants poured into the waterways. There were roughly 175 million gallons of polluted wastewater being stored. The leaks have killed off wildlife and created inhabitable lakes. Some of the mash was spread over farmland which led to animals getting sick. (NTV News, 2021)

The "Journal State," states that Nebraska created about fifty-four million barrels of wastewater in 2015 through fracking. Some people who support fracking and who have wells that are being used to store fracking water have stated that they were worried about bad publicity. In reading about this, I feel disgusted because that was their only worry. They did not worry about poisoning anyone. They did not worry about ruining our soil or water supply. I wondered why it wasn't more obvious to the general public that fifty-four million barrels of water is a significant amount of water being wasted. If you take that and add what is used to cool down nuclear power plants, it would more than outweigh the total amount of all the irrigation being used for farming. I remember reading a report on water usage in nuclear power plants at roughly the same time. The contract was being discussed to store fracking water from the state of Nebraska clear to the state of Colorado. That report stated that the water being used on cooling nuclear power plants was more than the amount of irrigation. Instead of blaming the shortage of fresh water on fracking and nuclear power plants, irrigation was being blamed for the water shortage. When you think about the water being used to cool nuclear power plants, and then add what is being used for fracking, it is an extremely large misuse of our resources.

Actions or inactions can cause things to become better or worse. I have been affected by the contaminants in our water supplies and so have many others. My fight started after I felt ill for over two weeks from drinking tap water. Even 10 years later, drinking water out of the tap tastes like chalk. My way of fighting against this problem is to attempt to improve what has been done to our environment, by continuously running for office. I ran for the position of Legislature for my district. I have run for City Council three times and for Congress. I am going on my second time this year running for Congress. Part of my platform for campaigning for Congress is on environmental issues and protecting our resources, with a focus on cleaning up our water supplies. I will continue the fight until we clean up the mess we have made. (Bolinger, 2021)

Resources:

Bergin Nicholas, (June 2016), "Nebraska Judge overturns fracking water disposal decision", https://journalstar.com/business/local/nebraska-judge-overturns-fracking-water-disposal-decision/article_48a28d35-935a-56e5-9273-2ef924187f61.html

NTV News. (3 September 2021). "Mead Community rocked by second AltEn spill amid clean up and heavy rains."

https://nebraska.tv/news/local/mead-community-rocked-by-second-alten-spill-amid-clean-up-and-heavy-rains?fbclid=IwAR2gmUorkyWUFbuATK0W5bbFIb8zkBGPo8I-wTY9L_8CZxPxyiy1fbJFoUY

Chapter 16

Endorsing other Candidates

Endorsing other candidates while you, yourself are running for office can backfire on you. Many of your followers might not like the person you endorsed, so they might stop supporting you as a candidate. Let a PAC or Party endorse the candidate, but it is advisable not to personally support a candidate unless the candidate is in your party and nobody else in that party is running against them. During Larry's campaign, the Marijuana Now Party of Nebraska decided to endorse Herbster for Governor. Herbster was a Republican candidate for Governor running against Pillen in the primary. The LMN party endorsed him because Herbster would allow a petition to legalize marijuana to be voted on and Pillen would refuse any petitions to legalize.

Legal Marijuana Now Party of Nebraska endorses Herbster for Governor in the Primary Election

Krystal Gabel, one of the founders of the LMN wrote this:

Legal Marijuana NOW Nebraska supports Charles Herbster for Governor in the Republican Primary. LMN is ready to run an adult-use cannabis petition, for The People and By The People, in Nebraska. Herbster is for a small government and says he won't interfere with the petition process as the Ricketts administration has done for years.

The constant interference over the last 8 years by current Governor Ricketts is the ONLY REASON why Nebraska does not have Legal Cannabis. Electing anyone Ricketts endorses will be another 8 years of nothing being done. Nebraska is ready for full adult-use cannabis laws. Medical Marijuana has become confusing and any law that has been suggested by the unicameral and any former petition has only made the laws around cannabis more complicated and obscure in the state.

LMN stands firmly on the belief that all Marijuana use is medicinal. Full adult-use cannabis will amend our State Constitution so that anyone 21 or older has the right to possess

cannabis in the State of Nebraska. This amendment will cement legalization in our Constitution, making it nearly impossible to remove in the future. The LMN petition will guarantee every adult the right to possess cannabis in Nebraska.
Peace and love, Krystal, National Party Chair of the Legal Marijuana NOW Party. (Gabel, 2022)

Unfortunately, on the same day that we decided to support Herbster for governor, 8 women came forward accusing him of sexual misconduct. The LMN Party decided to continue the support because little evidence was provided. I always try to push to prove guilt rather than create accusations to gain political support. This was presented 3 weeks before the primary, no charges have been filed, so it seems to be political. I do believe in the due process of law. No matter how bad it looks, I have to support due process. Because there is always that chance that it is just made up to grab the governor's seat and I don't mean by pinching his ass.

One strategy to consider is if he wins the primary and those sexual accusations are proven to be true, he will be a far easier opponent to beat in the regular election than Pillen. That would be the best strategic way to flip the state from red to blue.

Argument of Accountability

Nebraska Senator Slama's allegation of Sexual misconduct by Charles Herbster

In 2022 Senator Slama made allegations of sexual misconduct by Charles Herbster who is running for Governor in Nebraska in the 2022 election. The allegations were followed by witnesses of the misconduct and allegations of other women being abused. Most people jumped to the conclusion that Senator Slama's accusations were correct. She gave a compelling heartfelt statement to the Legislature. But, this is a time that is getting close to the primary election. So there are questions concerning the timing of the allegation and if it is being done to oust Herbster's illegibility to run for office.

Bolinger: *"I am running for Attorney General in Nebraska. I switched parties in 2021 from the "Republican party" to the newly formed "Legal Marijuana Now Party." The leaders of the LMN Party announced that the party is supporting Herbster for governor. On that same day, Senator Slama made her speech to the State Legislature accusing Herbster of sexual misconduct. That put me and the Party in an odd position."*

There would be many questions that would need to be answered to the allegations. One would be why there weren't any charges brought up. There is a claim that Slama was too scared to say anything because Herbster is a powerful and wealthy person. But, you have 7 people who claim to have witnessed this newly appointed senator get sexually harassed by an old guy and somebody took pictures and they all failed to protect that young impressionable lady. All 7 of them failed to act and they failed to uphold the integrity of the Legislative body. 7 seasoned senators would not be shy about turning in some old guy for sexual harassment. I would also question why Slama did not tell Ricketts when she had him in her back pocket.

To review accountability you would review who would be accountable, who knew, what was reported, what was the action of the people who knew, and the legislative bodies' actions. 8 people knew. Did they fail ethics violations by not reporting the incident? If it was reported to the legislative body or Speaker, what was done? Were there actions or any type of consideration of action after being reported in 2019? Was it reported to the Governor or Attorney General? What were their actions or did they act? 8 people saw it, many senior senators, someone acted or they all failed to act. There is a long list of accountability. It would be hard to believe all 8 failed to act. If someone did act, then a legal body failed to act.

In this scenario, it is a tough decision to make on how to proceed. As a candidate for Attorney General, I could choose the easy path, which would be to side with Slama and the other 7 or 8 Senators and push to have Herbster ineligible to run for Governor under ethics violations, or I can take the hard path and take an unbiased approach, review the information's, push for more information and look at the different entities and consider what levels of government are accountable and who failed accountability. If I push a legally due process and review accountability I would look like I support sexual misconduct. If I chose to ignore due process, then it would look like negligence.

Addressing sexual misconduct in the workplace or an issue in public office could be handled in different ways. With this case, Senator Slama chose to present the case in an open public meeting on the agenda of the Legislature. That is something that would not happen in a local business. Something like that would be reviewed by someone in Human Resources and they would impose disciplinary tactics. If they fail to act, it could result in charges of discrimination being filed. If someone went public with the accusations they could face penalties of defamation. Whereas Senator Slama would not be accountable for defamation because Herbster is a high-profile person running for Governor. This action happened at an event held by the Legislature. As a Legislature or a person running for Governor, you have to conduct yourself appropriately if you are working or not. If it was an event or business party, very little action would be done as your actions when you are not at work may not have accountability to your job status.

Article Review

MSN reported in April of 2022 that Senator Slama stated that as she was walking to her table at a 2019 Douglas County Republican fundraiser, Charles Herbster reached up her skirt and up her dress. Slama stated that later Herbster grabbed another woman's butt. MSN reports that 7 other women are making similar reports. (MSN,2022)

Herbster claims that the allegations were false. Slama is Governor Ricketts's former campaign secretary and was appointed by Rickets to fill a legislative seat. Ricketts endorses Pillen for governor and Hilberts believes that this is a hatchet job. (MSN, 2022)

An article in the Nebraska Examiner written by Aaron Sanderford on 19 April 2022 wrote that two men and a woman saw Charles Herbster groping women at political events. Seven women accuse Herbster of sexual assault. One of the women said that Herbster cornered her in a private place and tried to forcibly kiss her.

Kelsy McDonald said that her friend said Herbster grabbed her butt at an April 2021 kick-off event in Fremont Nebraska. McDonald said she was groped by another man at that event. So the person who actually was groped by Herbster is not coming forward. The seven people accusing Herbster refuse to be named officially come forward. Edward Boone is one of the witnesses that saw Herbster grabbing a woman's butt who is coming forward. Boone is the only other person who saw Herbster groping a woman. The other two were only told by someone that they were groped and did not actually see it themselves. (Sanderford, 2022)

In a report written by Sara Gentzler on 19 April 2022 in the Omaha World-Herald, it reports that Charles Herbster denies the allegations of sexual misconduct. Herbster blames governor candidate Jim PIllen and Pillen's supporter Governor Pete Ricketts for creating the story to try and gain more support for Pillen. Both Pillen and Ricketts deny the allegation.

An article written by Dan Crisler on 22 April 2022 in the Omaha World-Herald titled "Herbster files defamations lawsuit against Slama over assault allegations" states that Herbster filed a defamation suit in Johnson County District Court. Slama's Attorney denies being served any lawsuit. On 25 April 2022, Slama filed a countersuit against Herbster.

An article written by Bill Kelly on 28 October 2022 in the Nebraska Public Media reports that Slama and Herbster dropped the cases against each other. For several months there were court dates set, but then each court date was postponed to another date. Until 26 October 2022 when they finalized dropping the lawsuit. (Kelly. 2022) I was disappointed to hear that the case was dropped because now it looks like it may have been politically motivated. There were 4 or 5 other women who made similar claims, but everything was dropped. I would think that dropping a sexual assault or sexual misconduct charge would make that person weak. A responsible political leader would have followed through and filed the charges and would have held Herbster accountable. Proper leaders need to push to end sexual harassment or sexual misconduct. It is something you don't back down on or at least should not back down if you want people to consider you an authority figure.

In 2024, Nebrasak Senator Halloran targeted a female colleague by reading a graphic rape description from a book. Senator Halloran replaced the victim's name with Senator Cavanaugh's name. The book that he read was "Lucky" by Alic Sebold. His intent was to gain support for a bill that would hold teachers and librarians criminally responsible for providing reading materials that could be considered obscene material to students K-12. (Beck, 2024) Halloran's actions were a violation of the workplace's sexual harassment policy. He was reprimanded, but not removed from office.

Conclusion:

If you don't stand up against sexual harassment or sexual assault, it will continue to be ignored or have little penalties, or could be considered something normal to do. If you want change, you need to fight for it. Sexual assault and harassment have become part of the norm in the Nebraska Legislature. People who file claims against those who violate the sexual assault and harassment policies are given a slap on the wrist and some get no penalties. In some cases, charges were filed and then dropped, leaving no penalties for illegal actions. If follow through on charges for conduct unbecoming, then and only then will there be viable changes in how women are treated in the workplace in the Legislative body.

Resources:

MSN, (2022) "Julie Slama details allegations against Charles Herbster, who says he plans to sue." https://www.msn.com/en-us/news/crime/julie-slama-details-allegations-against-charles-herbster-who-says-he-plans-to-sue/ar-AAWezhQ

Aaron, Sanderford. (19 April 2022). Three People speak on the record to confirm allegations of groping by Charles Herbster). Nebraska Examiner. https://nebraskaexaminer.com/2022/04/19/three-people-speak-on-the-record-to-confirm-allegations-of-groping-by-charles-herbster/?fbclid=IwAR3NCVrDW5QboRunKc2Ob5cjlfh-LgJcVW2KN17T0NaEoXTTCQ99d2akKeQ

Gentzler, Sara. (19 April 2022). "Herbster digs into denial as campaign prepares lawsuit." Omaha World-Herald. https://omaha.com/news/state-and-regional/govt-and-politics/herbster-digs-into-denial-as-campaign-prepares-lawsuit/article_4d81523a-c00f-11ec-b4eb-9b74e34c2015.html

NTV News. (22 April 2022). *"Gubernatorial candidate Charles Herbster files lawsuit against State Sen. Julie Slama"* https://nebraska.tv/news/local/gubernatorial-candidate-charles-herbster-files-lawsuit-against-state-sen-julie-slama?fbclid=IwAR2om_yO-A0UKixCrKDSLkzJig8qwsq5abbdunwxG0IvHCibP3b_pbI-xR0

Crisler, Dan. (22 April 2022). *"Herbster files defamation lawsuit against Slama over assault Allegations."* Omaha World-Herald. https://omaha.com/news/state-and-regional/govt-and-politics/herbster-files-defamation-lawsuit-against-slama-over-assault-allegations/article_bcd8fbfa-c281-11ec-ab7c-273daa3fbd05.html#:~:text=Herbster%20files%20defamation%20lawsuit%20against%20Slama%20over%20assault,accused%20him%20this%20month%20of%20groping%20them.%20Herbster

Dvorak, Gena. Westhves, Kevin. (25 April 2022). *"Nebraska State Sen. Julie Slama countersuies candidate Herbster."* 6 News. https://www.wowt.com/2022/04/25/nebraska-state-sen-julie-slama-countersues-herbster/

Kelly, Bill. (2022). *"Herbster drops defamation suit; Slama ends sexual battery case."* https://nebraskapublicmedia.org/en/news/news-articles/herbster-drops-defamation-suit-slama-ends-sexual-battery-case/

Beck, Margery. (2024). "Nebraska lawmaker who targeted a colleague during a graphic description of raper reprimanded." https://www.msn.com/en-us/news/us/nebraska-lawmaker-who-targeted-a-colleague-during-a-graphic-description-of-rape-is-reprimanded/ar-BB1l23Y5

Chapter 17

Immigration Policy Inconsistencies

There are some inconsistencies in immigration policies if you review the many reviews of actions that are being taken toward immigrants, asylum seekers, and refugees based on what country they are from. The National Security Council is the office that focuses on national security and foreign policy decision-making. This would include areas of national security, economic, health, and environmental security. "The National Security Council was established by the National Security Act of 1947 amended by the National Security Act Amendments of 1949. Later in 1949, as part of the Reorganization Plan, the Council was placed in the Executive Office of the President." (whitehouse.gov. 2022)

The change or proposed improvement I would make with the National Security Council would focus on security, immigration, refugees, and the process that was created. At one time it was reported we had over 90,000 people waiting for a court date for citizenship. While people were being left in jails and cages for months on end. There are several issues of priority that need to be considered. One is Human Rights, another is if someone is introduced to the US they are protected under Constitutional Rights. Other issues would be safety and security. We need to have control over crossing the border, but we don't want to add unnecessary harm or risks to immigrants. There needs to be a review committee to review the entire process and implement policies to correct the flaws. We need to push for equal treatment for different refugees. Refugees from one country should not be treated any better or worse than refugees from another country.

In the case of refugees from one nation being treated differently from refugees from another country, we can look at Afghanistan and Ukraine refugees. Afghan has to pay a $515 administration fee, need to show proof of vaccination, and they would need an in-person counselor interview. Ukrainian refugees don't have to do that. In this case, the Afghans are being processed as an immigrant and not a refugee. Reviewing the numbers shows 45,000 applications from Afgan for humanity parole, 2,200 were denied, 270 were approved while 4,000 Ukrainian applications were approved. (De Lace, 2022)

A news report by Pete William on 28 April 2022 on ABC News, titled "Supreme Court hints it might let Biden end Trump-era remain in Mexico immigration Policy" shows treatment towards immigrants from South America was discrimination. We have policies in place for South Americans who are seeking asylum to wait in Mexico while their claims are being decided. Each case is decided case-by-case. But they are forced to revert to Mexico because the US doesn't have enough money to detain all the people who cross the border. The US also claims that there is a lack the detention capacity. We have a lack of policy and procedures when many asylum seekers were reported to have been kidnapped, raped, tortured, and assaulted while waiting to get processed. This article says that federal law requires the government to send asylum seekers back to Mexico if there's no room to detain them. If we are out of room, how can we accept refugees from other Nations? If we are out of room, we can not unless there are discrimination policies against South America. (William, 2022) When there are asylum seekers or refugees treated differently depending on where they are from, shows a lack of structure, and consistency in policies and procedures. A lack of structure could negatively impact our National Security and International Relations.

Review:

Bolinger: As a person running for Attorney General in Nebraska, I am limited on what I can do to create change in immigration laws. Nebraska for the most part is not directly impacted. I can try and show support for Attorney Generals in states that are directly implicated. If elected I can make a push for a review committee along with other AGs to help make changes to policies and procedures. But as a candidate, one of the things I can do is educate and present the argument for needed change. In this case, what will happen is an article of submission to several media outlets throughout the state of Nebraska. Since this is an issue that affects all States, this article can go out to media outlets throughout the US which would be roughly 500 media outlets.

Article submitted on 16 May 2022.

Resources:

De Lace, Dan. (29 April 2022). *"Afghans subject to stricter rules than Ukrainian refugees, advocates say."* ABC News. https://www.nbcnews.com/politics/immigration/afghans-subject-stricter-rules-ukrainian-refugees-advocates-say-thousa-rcna26513

William, Pete. (26 April 2022)
"Supreme Court hints it might let Biden end Trump-era 'Remain in Mexico' immigration policy"
ABC News. https://www.nbcnews.com/politics/supreme-court-consider-whether-biden-can-end-trump-era-remain-mexico-p-rcna25409

De Lace, Dan. (29 April 2022). *"Afghans subject to stricter rules than Ukrainian refugees, advocates say."* ABC News. https://www.nbcnews.com/politics/immigration/afghans-subject-stricter-rules-ukrainian-refugees-advocates-say-thousa-rcna26513

William, Pete. (26 April 2022)
"Supreme Court hints it might let Biden end Trump-era 'Remain in Mexico' immigration policy"
ABC News. https://www.nbcnews.com/politics/supreme-court-consider-whether-biden-can-end-trump-era-remain-mexico-p-rcna25409

Chapter 18

Justice Reinvestment Initiative

END THE

SCHOOL TO PRISON

PIPELINE

The "Justice Reinvestment Initiative" is a restructuring of our policy and procedures in our legal system. This would argue the need for law reform. Research has shown that utilizing diversion programs has decreased recidivism by as much as 60% in adults, and 40% in children. With the overpopulation in our correctional facilities, there is a need to get our government educated on statistics and learn what works and what has failed in our legal system. The rest of this chapter is a research analysis on truancy and compares the impact of putting kids into the system or utilizing diversion programs.

Truancy

Juvenile Court vs. Social Service Mediation

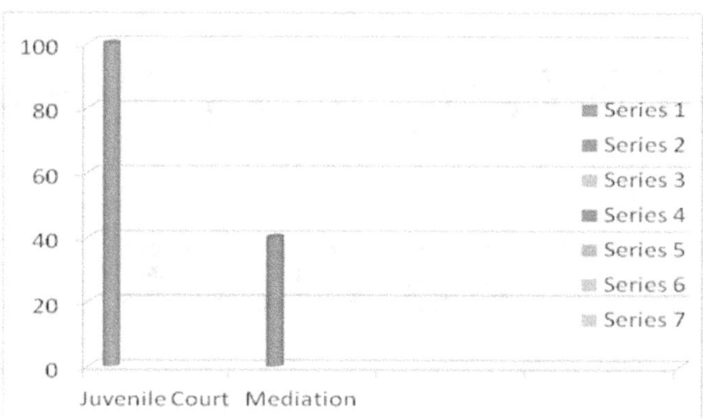

Recidivism Rate

Introduction

Truancy and Juvenile Delinquency have been a concern for many years. But, it is the responsibility of the judicial system to weigh the impact on the child as well as the impact on the community and choose the best course of action. In some cases, research may help with the best choice of action.

I do remember years ago when Governor Heineman of Nebraska reduced grants for youth correctional facilities to put more focus on "at-home responsibility" rather than sending kids away to a correction facility. Putting a kid through a Juvenile Court system because he/she skipped a class does not fix the issue at home. "In May 2013, Nebraska Governor Dave Heineman signed into law Legislative Bill 561, a major reform bill aimed at improving the juvenile justice system in the state. The law shifts the supervision of all juvenile offenders in the community from the Department of Health and Human Services to the Office of Probation Administration in the Nebraska Supreme Court, which places a renewed emphasis on a diversion through community-based programs focused on the rehabilitation of youth involved with the criminal justice system." (The Justice Center, The Council of State Governments). This was a little misguided. What happened is it changed from having mediation through the DHHS to making a push to put more kids going through juvenile courts and fining parents with misdemeanor charges by utilizing the Office of Probation Administration.

The Truancy in Alliance, NE. was a topic of discussion for the BoxButte County Commission and School Board in their agendas in December 2020. There was a write-up in the Times-Herald in December of 2020 titled *"Commissioners Kill Virtual Learning At Slagle Building"* written by Kathryn Kellar that goes over what was discussed in the Commissioners' meeting. In the article, Box Butte County Attorney Curtis wanted to utilize the Slagle building to run classes on Zoom to help the kids meet educational goals. Trying to force kids to use the Slagle building might not meet the needs of the entire community as it might not be easily accessible. To actually support equal rights you have to meet the needs of the entire community.

The County Attorney's options to try and fix the truancy problems were to force the kids to utilize the Slagle building or put the child that skips classes in a juvenile court system and file charges against the parents giving those parents misdemeanor charges that would go on their permanent records. If those are the only options that were considered, our government has failed the people it's supposed to serve. With the issues of the pandemic and the risk factors for the children, parents should have the choice to allow their kids to go to a public school or use online or homeschooling. That should not be the County attorney's decision.

Studies in Sociology and Criminology have shown that rehab and diversion programs have decreased recidivism by more than 40%. A Juvenile Justice system based on penalties is not a rehab program. Social Services, schools, RSO officers, and parents working together is in my opinion a better choice for a better community-based program. By working together you take away the damage that a court system can do to the social development of the child.

Paul Hammel wrote an article in the Omaha World-Herald on 10 March 2021 titled "Nebraska Legislature narrowly advances bill to provide diversion programs for truant kids." The article covers the LB568 bill that is on the state Legislative agenda. The bill would focus on counseling rather than a court for kids who skip school. This bill was introduced by Senator Patty Brook. This bill would remove truancy as a status offense that would require a juvenile court hearing. This would eliminate a juvenile court hearing for truancy and replace it with a concentration on the root causes of absenteeism. Brooks states that the current system contributes to the "school-to-prison" pipeline. She states that 70% of kids who end up in juvenile court will end up in adult court. (Hammel, 2021)

Questions:

- What is the average truancy over the past 10 years?

- What is the recidivism rate of a child that goes through a Juvenile court compared to social services mediation?

- Are homeschooling and Zoom school considered different? Or should they be considered the same?

- What is the stress factor on a child when put through a juvenile court system?

- Is the percentage of children going through a juvenile court system more likely to be a cause that leads to continue breaking the law compared to a child that received help from social service mediation?

- Research has shown that early education improves social skills and that education and higher education reduce criminal activities. Would putting a child in a juvenile court system deter that child from attending school? What is the percentage of dropouts from kids going through a juvenile court or any court system compared to social service mediation?

When the legislature creates laws, it is very important to look at the cause and effects of those laws. The above questions should be considered to see if the actual system is working or failing our children and our communities.

Hypothesis: I hypothesize that kids have a higher dropout rate when pressured through a Juvenile Court system compared to utilizing Social Service Mediation. Research analysis does prove that decreased education increases crime. I also hypothesize that kids who have gone through a Juvenile Court system have a higher percentage of continuing criminal activities into adulthood compared to kids who went through Social Service Mediation. To help give insight and prove the hypothesis I have researched several literature reviews, law reviews, and case reviews and put together a logit regression. I believe the research is important because it can show the impact our current system has had and could give a reason for the need to change.

Literature Review

"Truancy is defined as the habitual engagement in unexcused absence from school." (Zang, Willson) A survey conducted by Zang and Willson from Texas A&M University in 2003 consisted of 230 middle school kids. This survey showed that 30% of the kids deliberately missed school and 10% were often truant. The study showed that parents who spent more time with their children helped improve their cognitive development. Parents who manage their kid's academic achievements are more likely to stay in school. Students in a disorganized, unsafe, or unsupportive environment are at high risk for absenteeism and truancy. (Zang, Willam, 2010)

The study conducted in South Carolina from 1986 to 2006 on Juveniles being referred to the system showed that the average was 14.47 years old, 55% were referred once, 19.0% were referred twice, and 26.1% had three or more referrals.

A cross-tabulation showed that low-income families have a 60% higher likelihood of committing truancy. The study also showed that truancy offenders were referred to the system more often than other offenders, had more probations than other offenders, and were significantly younger than the "other" offenders. 7,195 children incurred a second offense, 1,243 led to a second truancy, and 5,952 conducted other offenses. Studies show that the younger a child was at first referral was more likely to have a second referral. Those with a second referral at an increased age had a greater chance of other offenses. Minority children were at a greater risk for a second truancy compared to other offenses than the majority of children. The 2007 study showed that truancy offenders had more incarcerations and more probation than other offenders. The numbers suggest the need for effective intervention. A major reason for truancy is due to difficulties with school. So kids may use truancy to distance themselves from an environment in which they feel threatened. (Zang, Willam, 2010)

A book written by Paul Sharp and Barry Hancock (1995) called "Juvenile Delinquency Historical, Theoretical and Societal Reactions to Youth" researched the effects of restitution. Restitution has been shown to have some positive impacts on recidivism. None had high recidivism rates that participated in restitution like those that received probation or detention conditions. The effects on recidivism and restitution had 10% fewer crimes but did not receive statistical significance at the .05 level. (Sharp, Hancock, 1995)

A book written by Larry Siegel and Brandon Welsh (2018) called "Juvenile Delinquency. Theory, Practice, and Law" was used in a Juvenile Delinquency class at UNO. Larry Siegal has an MA and Ph.D. from the State University of NY at Albany and was a teacher at Northeastern University, the University of Nebraska at Omaha, Saint Anselm College in New Hampshire, and the University of Massachusetts – Lowell. Brandon Welsh is a professor of criminology at Northeastern University and received his Ph.D. from Cambridge University. In their book, they state that 750,000 youths are arrested each year and those charges range from loitering to murder. Chronic delinquent offenders are recognized as a serious social problem. Looking at social problems you look at the contributing factors to those behaviors which could include abuse, substance abuse, neglect, education, or peer relations. The Office of Juvenile Justice and Delinquency Prevention was created to identify the needs of youths and to find policy initiatives. Their goal is to remove status offenders (which would include truancy) from secured lockups, detention centers, and post-disposition treatment facilities. In the progress that was made to restructure status offenders, the Juvenile Courts worked against that progress by relabeling "status offenders" as "delinquent offenders" to keep them in the system to be able to have control over them. Studies have found that "the effects of the formal processing on status offenders can increase the likelihood that they will get involved in subsequent delinquency." (Siegal, Welsh, 2018) This is a clear cause for reform. Many states have changed from a juvenile court system to a community-based system utilizing community resources and family support centers. Many status offenders have serious emotional problems and may engage in self-destructive behaviors. (Siegal, Welsh, 2018)

An article written by Henry Cordes posted in the Omaha World-Herald on 22 March 2022 argued for prison reform. Cordes argued that more than three dozen states had implemented a wide range of reforms which would include decreasing penalties and conducting enhanced supervision programs. Nebraska Governor Ricketts says reform is being soft on crime. In politics, during an election year, you can not be caught being soft on crime, so some ignore the statistics. In Texas, they had pushed for Drug Courts, and enhanced treatment programs to divert low-level offenders from prisons. That act reduced the prison population enough to be able to shut down 10 prisons and saved the state 2 billion dollars. The reinvestment initiative has been conducted in several States. In each of those states, it has shown a crime reduction. Ricketts, along with 14 other people participated in a justice reinvestment workgroup. Their review showed time served for drug offenses was up 42% and recidivism rates were increasing. Seeing those numbers should be a clear indication that there is a need for change but Ricketts chose not to accept those findings and pushed for more correctional facilities to be built. (Cordes. 2022)

Case Review

State V. Rice. 204 Neb.732,285 N.W.2d 223 (1979) concluded that a violation of the law is not in itself, evidence of neglect under section 43-202 (2)©, R.R.S. 1943. In this case, the State of Nebraska challenged the district court's decision and held that the appellee (Leslie Rice), was not a dependent child and that her parents had not violated Nebraska law in educating their child in a non-accredited, home school, religious-based program. The parents created a non-accredited religious homeschooling program for their child and were modeled and assisted by an accredited private religious school. The court found that the child's academic needs were being met even though the parents were not certified, teachers. The state argued that in not attending a state-certified program, the parents and child were violating the mandatory attendance laws and thus were necessarily in violation of the dependency statute by not providing a state-approved education. The court held that the statute relating to compulsory school attendance and the statute regarding the neglect of children did not pertain to the same subject matter and could not be construed in pari materia. The court held that dependency required a showing of severe parental misconduct that jeopardized the child's well-being, not the mere technical violation of a statute. The court held that the child and the parents were not in violation of the state laws regarding neglected and abused children. It was argued that Neb. Stat.ch.79 does not equate nonattendance with neglect under Neb.Rev.Stat. & 43-202 (2)© and that if it did, it would have said so.

In re Interest of Rice, 204 Neb. 732, 733, 285 N.W.2d 223, 224, 1979 Neb. LEXIS 1180, *1 (Neb. November 13, 1979)

Law review:

"The Juvenile Justice and Delinquency Preventions Act (1974) (JJDPA) is based on a broad consensus that children, youth, and families involved with the juvenile and criminal courts should be guarded by federal standards for care and custody, while also upholding the interests of community safety and the prevention of victimization." (juvjustice.org) The JJDPA provides for a juvenile justice plan with federal funding to improve programs and operations. One of the core requirements is to work on the deinstitutionalization of status offenders and focus on alternatives to placing juveniles into detention facilities and work on removing any racial or ethnic disparities that are in the juvenile justice system. Through the JJDPA they created the "Office of Juvenile Justice and Delinquency Prevention," which creates effective education, training, research, prevention diversion, treatment, and rehabilitation for juveniles. (Juvjustice.org) Which also lead to such programs as the "Runaway Youth Program" and the "National Institute for Juvenile Justice and Delinquency Prevention."

The Nebraska truancy law requires school districts to refer students to their county attorney when the child has been absent for at least 20 days within a school year. This would include kids ages six to eighteen or who have reached the age of sixteen and have withdrawn from school under section 79-202 of the state statute. Nebraska statutes on truancy state that a violation of the law is not, in itself, evidence of neglect under state statute 43-202(2)©, R.R.S. 1943. But Subdivision (3)(a) of sections 43-247 and 79-210 makes a minor child's parents or guardians culpable for the child's truancy. (Nebraska Legislature.gov)

Methods:

I researched the data from the ADA at Berkeley post-election. I ran a "Logit Regression" tabulation between the dependent variable "has ever been stopped and quested by police (v162297," and the independent variables age (v161267), Native (v161310c), Latino v161309), white (v161310a), black (v161310b), and income (v161361x). The logit regression tabulation is done to show if there are increased policing activities based on age, race, or income.

To add additional information to the research I would need to:

- obtain "View Waver" from a judge to get the actual numbers of kids that went to juvenile court and how many returned and second time or more than twice. How many of those kids improve and graduated? How many dropped out of school? How many went to jail as an adult?

- Would need a list of kids that were referred to a social service outlet to mediate truancy between the child, parent, and schools. How many improved and graduated? How many dropped out of school? How many went to jail as an adult?

DATA:

SDA 4.1.2: Logit/Probit Regression

ANES 2016 Time Series

May 11, 2021 (Tue 09:14 AM PDT)

	Variables				
Role	**Name**	**Label**	**Range**	**MD**	**Dataset**
Dependent	**v162297(Recoded)**	POST: FTF CASI/WEB: In past 12 months any family membered stopped/questioned by police	0-1		1
Independent	**v161267**	PRE: Respondent age	18-90		1
Independent	**v161361x**	PRE FTF CASI/WEB: Pre-income summary	1-28		1
Independent	**v161310c**	PRE: R self-identified race - American Indian/Alaska Native mentioned	0-1		1
Independent	**v161310a**	PRE: R self-identified race - White mentioned	0-1		1
Independent	**v161309**	PRE: R: Are you Spanish, Hispanic, or Latino	1-2		1
Independent	**v161310b**	PRE: R self-identified race - Black/African-American mentioned	0-1		1
Weight	**v160101**	Pre-election weight -full sample	.0895-6.8139		1

	Logit Coefficients			Test That Each Coefficient = 0	
	B	**SE(B)**	**Exp(B)**	**T-statistic**	**Probability**
v161267	.015	.002	1.016	6.413	.000
v161361x	.004	.005	1.004	.770	.442
v161310c	-.533	.207	.587	-2.572	.010
v161310a	-.097	.147	.908	-.660	.510
v161309	-.075	.141	.928	-.532	.595
v161310b	-.481	.167	.618	-2.891	.004
Constant	.701	.275	2.017	2.551	.011

Color coding:	<-2.0	<-1.0	<0.0	>0.0	>1.0	>2.0	T

Effect of each variable:	Smaller than average	Larger than average

Log Likelihood = -1,848.190 Pseudo R-sq = .019

The value of the constant term is .701. There is no zero code in the independent variables so we cannot interpret the constant term. The age variable has the strongest T-statistic (closest relationship) to the dependent variable at 6.413. The highest regression coefficient is for people who are Native which is at .-533 and Black with a coefficient of -.481. One unit change in identifying as a Native creates a change in being stopped by police by -.533. Blacks would be at per -.481. Both Native and Black are statistically significant as the probability for Natives is .010, Black is at .004, and age is .000 which is p<.05, two-tailed test. That suggests that there is a high probability that you would be stopped by law enforcement if you are Native, Black, or of a specific age. This would be interpreted as rejecting the null hypothesis as people who stopped and were questioned by police may be influenced by many variables (age, race, income). Based on the Native coefficient of -.533, p< .01, two-tailed test.

Conclusion:

The research showed that white children were in the system for truancy more often compared to black children. But more black children were in the system for other offenses. That could bring into question if white children receive a lesser penalty on average than black children. In the logit regression, it showed that more children that were Natives or Black were stopped by police and questioned than the other variables.

Senator Brooks's assessment said that 70% of kids who are put into the system as a child will repeat criminal activities as an adult, citing there is a much greater decrease in recidivism when we utilize more focus on root causes and counseling.

The impact of social skills starts at a young age. The largest impact on developing social skills comes from the parent. Early childhood development and our school system play an additional role in developing social skills. When a child is taken away from their parents and a regular school system, run through a Juvenile Court and placed into the system, takes away fundamental social skills development. That leads to increased recidivism. When children repeat those offensives, they receive more incarceration rather than pinpointing the specific cause of the problem. Not addressing the issue in many cases leads to continued criminal activities into adulthood. The conclusion to this research is to look at community programs such as utilizing community resources and family support centers. Many status offenders have serious emotional problems and may engage in self-destructive behaviors. The effects of formal processing on status offenders can increase the likelihood that they will get involved in subsequent delinquency."

This research has been used to promote change in our legal system. It has been sent to every Legislature in the State of Nebraska, several law enforcement agencies, county attornies, as well as many media outlets. As of 24 May 2022, very little has been done. No policies or procedures have been changed. When the facts are provided and the people in charge fail to act, that is time to replace those people.

References:

Kathryn Kellar, Alliance Times-Herald
Kellar, Kathryn. (2020). *"Commissioners Kill Virtual Learning At Slagle Building."* Times-Herald. Commissioners Kill Virtual Learning at Slagle Building - Alliance Times-Herald

CSG Justice Center Staff. (2013). *"Nebraska Emphasizes Community-Based Services and Comprehensive Reentry Programming for Youth."*
Nebraska Emphasizes Community-Based Services and Comprehensive Reentry Programming for Youth - CSG Justice Center - CSG Justice Center

Juvjustice.org. *"History of the JJDPA."* Juvenile Justice and Delinquency Prevention Act | CJJ (juvjustice.org)

Nebraska Legislature.gov. *"Nebraska Revised Statute 79-201."* Nebraska Legislature

In re Interest of Rice, 204 Neb. 732, 285 N.W.2d 223, 1979 Neb. LEXIS 1180 (Supreme Court of Nebraska November 13, 1979, Filed). https://advance-lexis-com.leo.lib.unomaha.edu/api/document?collection=cases&id=urn:contentItem:3RXP-6DP0-003D-B2YP-00000-00&context=1516831.

Zhang, Dalum. Willson, Victor. (May 2010*). "Truancy Offenders in the Juvenile Justice System: A multicohort Study."* Texas A&M University.
https://www-jstor-org.leo.lib.unomaha.edu/stable/43153821?Search=yes&resultItemClick=true&searchText=truancy&searchUri=%2Faction%2FdoBasicSearch%3FQuery%3Dtruancy%26sd%3D2010%26ed%3D2021&ab_segments=0%2Fbasic_search_gsv2%2Fcontrol&refreqid=fastly-default%3Af14c142497a850d0acd55769541a3c11&seq=1#metadata_info_tab_contents%20%20%20

Sharp, Paul. Hancock, Barry. (1995). "Juvenile Delinquency Historical, Theoretical and Societal Reactions to Youth." Prentice-Hall, Inc. (pg. 410-421)

Hammel, Paul. (10 March 2021). "Nebraska Legislature narrowly advances bill to provide diversion programs for truant kids." Omaha World-Herald. https://journalstar.com/news/state-and-regional/govt-and-politics/nebraska-legislature-narrowly-advances-bill-to-provide-diversion-programs-for-truant-kids/article_6f719235-48f6-55be-b292-37191b780a12.html?utm_campaign=snd-autopilot&utm_medium=social&utm_source=facebook_&fbclid=IwAR1aHmV9Jl5ZrUjCzrPOFx9UP4IqwxpG6l33MwXek8OZeBfNJCRT3pV8D5A%20%20%20

SDA. Berkeley.edu. ANES (2017) https://sda.berkeley.edu/sdaweb/analysis/;jsessionid=B4DE8B0D1780BC5CC9EF7DD403CF0780?dataset=nes2016

Siegel, Larry. Welsh, Brandon. (2018). "Juvenile Delinquency. Theory, Practice, and Law." Cengage Solution. (pg. 14,15, 29-33.)

Cordes, Henry. (22 March 2022). "lack of conservative buy-in time helped doom Nebraska prison reform efforts." Omaha World-Herald. https://omaha.com/news/state-and-regional/govt-and-politics/lack-of-conservative-buy-in-time-helped-doom-nebraska-prison-reform-efforts/article_d68fb562-d77f-11ec-bfb1-0f41a42db789.html#tncms-source=signup

Letter to the editor

Author: Larry Bolinger
Of Alliance Nebraska
Nebraska Attorney General Candidate

I am writing to you concerning the article written by Henry Cordes on 22 March 2022 titled "Lack of Conservative buy-in time helped doom Nebraska prison reform efforts," in the Omaha World-Herald. My specialty is in Criminology and I felt the article and the research done by Cordes were very accurate. The research that was done was exemplary. It is unfortunate that when facts are provided, politicians fail to act or even acknowledge facts. When elected officials are provided with facts and fail to act shows that they do not meet the skills for an effective 21st-century government. We need to build human capital to improve government performance. Utilizing diversion programs will take a lot of work. Some people in government may be overwhelmed because of the necessary changes to make the program work. That is understandable that they may be overwhelmed. But, that is when you rely on specialists, such as myself, to help with the necessary changes. The problem with the overcrowding in our correctional facilities is that the leadership lacks the skills for an effective 21st-century government. That, and an unwillingness to work have stagnated our progress to the point that we have the highest per capita prison population in the Nation. Law reform is a big undertaking and needs to be done by people willing to work and it needs to be done by people with the education to get the job done right.

Cordes, Henry. (22 March 2022). "lack of conservative buy-in time helped doom Nebraska prison reform efforts." Omaha World-Herald. https://omaha.com/news/state-and-regional/govt-and-politics/lack-of-conservative-buy-in-time-helped-doom-nebraska-prison-reform-efforts/article_d68fb562-d77f-11ec-bfb1-0f41a42db789.html#tncms-source=signup

Chapter 19

Attorney General Restructuring

When you have a failing system, there may be a need for mass restructuring. In Nebraska, as of 2022, we have the largest per capita prison population. It has been reported that while all other states' recidivism rates are going down, Nebraska's recidivism rates are going up. Many Legislative representatives have argued for decreasing penalties and implementing diversion programs. But those requests have been shut down, even after research has been done and information provided to confirm that is the correct course of action. When Nebraska Governor Ricketts takes part in being a member of the research team and then votes against the information, makes you wonder what his agenda really is. Does he want to fix the problem or does he want to continue to pack the prison to gain acceptance to build more prisons? When the majority votes against fixing failed policies, tell me that they do not meet the skills for an effective 21st-Century government.

Bolinger: "There is a clear need to revamp the whole system, which includes building human capital to improve government performance. That means getting people into positions that will act based on facts and not based on political agendas. This would create significant demand for a specialist in several fields of law. It would also put some demand on reviewing my two political books and assigning assistance to specialize in several chapters to help create the needed changes and needed arguments. My primary goal would be to reduce the prison population by 40% by utilizing diversion programs and keeping within the 60% recidivism rate reduction. The opposition to the plans wants more prisons to fix the overpopulation, but more jails do not reduce the recidivism rate. Approving the new correctional facilities would cost taxpayers upward of around 400 million dollars while utilizing diversion programs and law reform with cost time, training, and effort. Utilizing diversion programs could be adding additional training for law enforcement, social workers, drug counselors, and legal staff. This could also mean adding additional costs to expanding counseling practices for both drug and alcohol addiction as well as mental health. My goal would be to keep the cost under 200 million dollars while showing a 60% reduction in recidivism."

The changes that I would work on are:

- Reducing sentences for non-violent offenders
- Diversion programs
- Enhanced drug and mental health treatment
- The expanded drug court system
- Post-release supervision
- Reintegration programs

This would need the support of both legal specialists and policymakers. To make it work well, you will have to have good coordination between law enforcement, human services, public defenders, prosecutors, and judges and have a basic knowledge of what an area can offer to help support diversion programs. It sounds like a big undertaking. Some people can not fathom working that hard or creating that big of a coordinated effort. Those people are the ones we do not need in government. Sometimes the right thing to do may be the most difficult task.

There are many specialists that I would need to push different policies and correct unethical practices. Many that I point out in the two books I wrote on politics. This specialist would cover:

- Realty law
- Native law
- Consumer rights: (Right to Repair)
- Discrimination: (LGTBQ Rights)
  This would also include international laws, such as
    - Convention on Enforced Disappearance.
    - Convention on the Rights of the Child.

- Election policies
- Labor laws
- 14th Amendment specialist (equal protection under the law)
- Environmental specialist for state, federal, and international law. International policies would include such policies as:
    - LOSC: Laws of the Sea Convention.
    - London dumping convention.
- A specialist on the Task Force of 21st Century Community Policing
- Tort violations
- Judicial reviews

That would take 17 specialists with supporting staff that could put the number well over 100 people working on revamping the system. Some of those numbers could come down if utilizing intern programs.

Article Review:

An article written by Henry Cordes posted in the Omaha World-Herald on 22 March 2022 argued for prison reform. Cordes argued that more than three dozen states had implemented a wide range of reforms which would include decreasing penalties and conducting enhanced supervision programs. Nebraska Governor Ricketts says reform is being soft on crime. In politics, during an election year, you can not be caught being soft on crime. In this case, some politicians ignored the statistics. In Texas, they had pushed for Drug Courts and enhanced treatment programs to divert low-level offenders from prisons. That act reduced the prison population enough to be able to shut down 10 prisons and saved the state 2 billion dollars. The reinvestment initiative has been conducted in several States. In each of those states, it has shown a crime reduction. Ricketts, along with 14 other people participated in a justice reinvestment workgroup. Their review showed time served for drug offenses was up 42% and recidivism rates were increasing. Seeing those numbers should be a clear indication that there is a need for change but Ricketts chose not to accept those findings and push for more correctional facilities to be built. (Cordes. 2022)

Rational thinking:

This is a big undertaking. Too big of an undertaking would scare off interests. To be rational about what needs to be done, I would have to break it down into importance and what would be most acceptable. The May 2022 law reform bill that was presented to the Nebraska State Legislature was 58 pages. That bill was turned down. It was too long and it had some controversial policy changes. Breaking it down into several policy change requests could have had better results. Breaking it down and pushing 15 policies and having some of them passed could have created the start of policy changes. For the ones that failed, you do more research, add more information, and prepare a better argument for next time. To be reasonable, I would break it down into 3 different areas. 1) Community Policing: Continue education on the Presidential Task Force on the 21st Century Community Policing. That would mean Law Enforcement officers would review materials, go to seminars, and take some college classes. 2) Environment concerns: make a push for the London Dumping Convention. This would take a research analysis and then it would be handed over to a Congressional representative to present it to Congress. The policy is within our own EPA regulations and will show we are environmentally responsible. A push on this policy would look good in front of environmentalists and could aid in political support 3) Property Rights: change the policy on tax liens so that it doesn't make it so easy to take over someone's property. Current policy allows a 3rd party to pay your land tax if you are late on your payment and then charge you a significant fee to do so. Changing the policy to not allow 3rd party investors until the landowner is 4 years behind on taxes would secure people's property, and it would look good in front of the voters (primarily the working class).

The issue is how to argue these without looking like you are soft on crime or trying to tear down Law Enforcement.

2) **Improve policies in Community Policing and Law:** For over 15 years I have worked on continuing education for law enforcement. Several years ago, the movement of 21st Century Community Policing started due to profiling issues when departments utilized 1980's era community policing. Updating policing tactics and law reform to bring it into the 21st Century has reduced crime by as much as 40% while reducing recidivism by as much as 60%.

3) **Environment Concerns:** One of the Attorney Generals' jobs is to support and understand EPA regulations. There were a lot of policies ignored or overlooked that resulted in the environmental disaster in Mead Nebraska. This issue has been a problem for over 12 years and lacks action. We do need to address policies to protect our livelihood. I would like to see things back to where it was 20 years ago when it was safe to drink water out of the faucet. One small step to start that process of cleaning up our water supplies is to ratify the London Dumping Convention. It is concerning that only a few countries follow policies to clean up our water supplies while others ignore policies. So we end up with some countries spending hundreds of millions of dollars and thousands of man-hours cleaning up after other countries. Improving these efforts can improve our economy, create jobs, and improve our environment.

4) **Property Rights:** What started me in politics back in 2006 was fighting for Property Rights. I was serving on the Planning Commission and the city proposed a policy to claim a part of town as "blighted and substandard" to help landowners retain taxes to put back into their business. This sounded like a good idea so we passed the policy. But, instead of helping the landowners, the City Council claimed eminent domain and forced the sale of those people's properties so that they could sell the property to a Bank. The Abbot Bank wanted that property and the city wanted the old Abbat Bank to create a new municipal building. After everyone was forced to sell their property, the deal failed, and the city was left with an empty lot for the next 15 years. In this case, the city violated section 18 US Code 1001 by lying and misrepresenting the policy and they failed both city and state codes by not properly informing the people of the proposed policy that would affect that area.

- About a decade ago, we had a change in our land tax lien program where 3rd party investors did not have to wait 3 years before buying out someone's taxes. That change resulted in thousands of people losing their property to 3rd party investors. My goal is to change this back to where a 3rd party investor can not buy out someone's taxes until they are 4 years late on taxes. Then the property owner would be given 1 year to pay off the back taxes before a forecloser could start.

The goal is to reduce tax lien foreclosures by 40%. Change a policy that focuses more on helping the working class rather than just supporting the wealthy.

My primary goal is to expand Drug courts and rehab programs. Which will expand diversion programs. The reality of what would take for the entire state could be overwhelming for most. Drug Courts and diversion programs have a good start in Omaha, Nebraska. To move that at a reasonable speed, I would look at copying their efforts to the largest 10 cities in the state. That could be reasonably done. Each area that has made the changes would need research analysis and show improvements to allow continued policy and procedural changes. That could set a good example of how we need to improve across the state. Pushing diversion programs could be looked at as being soft on crime. Being soft on crime could cost an election for someone seeking an Attorney General's position even if the research shows his policies work. How do you promote diversion programs without being looked at as weak on crime? You may consider not necessarily being direct about diversion programs. Instead, push the faults of current policy failures.

Nebraska has the highest per capita prison population with an increasing recidivism rate. We don't just need to be tough on crime, but we also need to be smart on policies. Having the highest per capita prison population shows a failure in policies. This is an indication that we need to change and update our policies and procedures to meet our state's needs.

The next step would be to utilize a bargaining approach to gain support from individuals and organizations that support diversion programs. I looked for support by reviewing articles about the prison overcrowding problem and will contact senators who expressed the importance of law reform. I will also contact organizations that have endorsed law reform programs. I will work with them to create the connections and then work with them to create the policy changes.

Resources:

Cordes, Henry. (22 March 2022). "lack of conservative buy-in time helped doom Nebraska prison reform efforts." Omaha World-Herald. https://omaha.com/news/state-and-regional/govt-and-politics/lack-of-conservative-buy-in-time-helped-doom-nebraska-prison-reform-efforts/article_d68fb562-d77f-11ec-bfb1-0f41a42db789.html#tncms-source=signup

Ch. 20
Managing Human Behaviors in a Campaign

Managing Extremism, human behaviors, and utilizing Creativity to Create a Positive Campaign.

Larry Bolinger was a candidate for Attorney General in Nebraska's 2022 election. He is writing a training manual to help people learn what it takes to run for office as well as help them understand and react to many of the problems they may face. The manual is called "Politics: Last Act of Defiance, Volume II." Larry had run for office several times. He wrote a book called "Politics: Last Act of Defiance, Volume I" that covered his first 15 years in politics running for office. Larry has run for office in the Democrat, Republican, Independent, and Legal Marijuana Now Parties. Running for office in several parties, you see other parties through their eyes. There is an understanding that in each party there are moderates and extremists. This chapter will review extremism, human behaviors, and utilizing creativity to push forward in the campaign.

This chapter points out the many issues revolving around running for office. This will give some insight into what you might go through. In running for office you may have to handle issues of extremism, odd behaviors, and many forms of conflict. You may need to use a fair amount of creativity to keep your campaign running progressively. Running for office, there is a need for creating structure as well as creating a strategic plan but always be prepared for those hiccups in the campaign that do occur. This goes through Larry's introduction as a candidate for Attorney General and reviews his strategic plans and the changes he had to go through to create a successful campaign.

There were several reasons why Larry changed from being a Republican to changing to run as a Legal Marijuana Now Party candidate:

- There is an extreme political bias between the Republican and Democrat parties. It's not just a mere disagreement, it's the push to hate one party over the other. Decisions are made only by party affiliation rather than considering majority constituent opinions. Larry said that he can't be part of that until both parties clean up their act.
-     In Larry's two campaigns for Congress in 2018 and 2020, he supported medical marijuana and legalization. He supported the LMN agenda and they did endorse him. He ran against Mark (who is one of the founders of the LMN Party and he is someone that he ran against for Congress) in the last election, but Larry also supported his platform. The people running the legalization campaign were very focused and were consistent in the work they did. The LMN isn't just about legalization. It is also about helping the communities. Helping the farming communities. Larry pushed to support the "Farm Bill" and the "Prime Act" to help both the farming and ranching businesses as well as the many food programs we have. Larry supported the private and locally owned ranching business over the corporate slaughterhouses. Corporations manipulated the market at the expense of both the ranchers and consumers. The Farmers and Ranchers work hard and the corporate packing plants manipulate the price so the consumer pays more, the corporate retains a higher profit and the farmer and ranchers receive lower rates. Larry also supported the agenda of police reform and law reform. He pushed for law reform for more than 12 years. Larry studied Political Science, Law, and Criminology at UNO. The information on reform is there. It was pushed by both the Obama Administration and the Trump administration. Decreasing the lethal tactics to a more professional tactic has been available for the past decade. The biggest problem in police reform is the refusal to reform at the State and local levels. There are defensive tactics available to use and there are Colleges that teach updated Criminology. But in some cases, lawmakers are scared of law reform because that might mean a loss of control. Studies do show that rehabilitation has a better success rate than imprisonment. But our government has been focused more on filtering money to private corrections facilities for the past 17 years costing the taxpayers $28,000 to 74,000 dollars per inmate. Having a high cost per inmate makes to reason to keep prisoners rather than rehabilitation as more prisoners means more money going to the private or corporate-owned facility at the expense of the taxpayers. Which has given us the prison overpopulation we have today. Rehabilitation reduces recidivism, decreases crime, decreases the prison population, and decreases overall expenses.
-     These issues are not new, they are stagnating issues. Politicians may argue the issue but there is too much political bias to make the changes that are needed to help Nebraskans.

Larry: "From what I've seen from the work of the LMN party, is that when they are focused on a policy they stay consistent in the work they do and they are committed to that policy change, then changes are eventually made. To make the necessary change we need commitment and consistency and not falter under political bias. "

In the campaign, Larry had changed from a Republican to the Legal Marijuana Now party. With that, he had to adjust his platform to meet some of the needs of the party. In July of 2022, he had to adjust his style of campaign again after he claimed Independent and broke away from the Legal Marijuana Now Party. He had to adjust some of his speeches to be more neutral and to stay away from one party over the other to help gain support from all parties. As an Independent, he knew he would have the majority Democrat, Libertarian, and LMN votes, but he needed a large amount of the Republican party vote to win. He had to control and redirect any disruptive impulses and correct conflicting arguments. There was a lot of work and adjustments to the campaign Larry was running. He had drawn the moral line and detailed arguments of how he dealt with extremism and how he adjusted. He saw problems, made changes, and utilized council.

The reason why this chapter is created is to show everyone the aspect of running for office and give some insight on what to expect and give some advice on how to handle problem areas. The manual was created to help with campaign strategies. This chapter will go through issues of conflicts and how to handle conflicts and extremists. If you handle conflicts poorly it could cost you an election. This will help you be better prepared.

The problems this project will solve are how to deal with extremism and when to change your stance or neutralize your stance to decrease conflict. No matter your stance on a policy, someone will try and put you on the spot. No matter your answer, someone will argue that you are wrong. Some people argue just to create conflict and stress. Sometimes it is best to make a statement, then walk away and avoid the argument. People will find fault in anything you do or say. The reason why we have this chapter is to give you ideas on how to handle conflicts and problems situations. Sometimes you just have to have tough skin to ignore the conflict and stay the course. Don't give up. Sometimes you need to get creative.

This section should help give some insight into the behavioral issues someone could face while running for public office and provide a more agreeable reaction to negativity. One of the most challenging jobs in a campaign is staying motivated as well as keeping your staff motivated. You have to stay consistent in promoting important issues and squash things that create a negative impact. Some things are not worth arguing. Make a statement if need be, then move on. Stay on task and on topic. Do not get pulled into propaganda traps. Propaganda traps are very damaging to a campaign especially if you are trying to pull support from each party. Creating an agreeable platform doesn't just come from just the candidates, it also comes from constituents, your staff, and volunteers. If you are addressing their concerns, they will be more motivated to go to work.

In a campaign, it is important to utilize a participative management approach. Utilizing fact-to-face or other means of communication is important. If time, distance, or money is short, online instant messenger or internet group chat have been widely used. Face-to-face interaction helps the development of the campaign and gets people more involved in the process and direction of the campaign. (Benhardt, 202) As an Independent, the focus is staying out of conflicting arguments, don't fall into propaganda pit-falls, and motivating your volunteers to work.

It is best to control and redirect any disruptive impulses and correct conflicting arguments. There was a lot of work and adjustments to the campaign Larry was running. He explains where he had drawn the moral line and detailed arguments of how he dealt with extremism and how he adjusted. He saw problems, made changes, and utilized council. It is important to know your strengths and weaknesses. Then utilize your assets to develop a working team. You cannot expect things to go your way all the time. Things will go astray and you have to adjust. Sometimes that requires some creativity. Sometimes you have to use your council to help create ideas to help with a plan or strategy and then obtain their support to put those ideas into action.

What Larry has found out when dealing with extremists is there is emotional instability and that they may suffer from mood swings and sporadic behaviors. They often have very little flexibility and are not open to more than one interpretation. It creates a nitch development and lack of creativity and growth. Similar behaviors are addressed in Benhardts research listed at the end of the chapter. (Benhardt, pg.66)

Running a campaign, Larry had to recruit and create a network of supporters. Creating a network, had its ups and downs. Most people who were recruited handled responsibility very well. Some were overwhelmed with any type of responsibility. The people who could not handle even the littlest of responsibility possessed a high level of stress and created conflict with others. They wanted their issues handled over everyone else's and wanted all the attention. This caused a problem in the network. Larry said there was one team leader (Karen) who was at a very high stress level that took out her stress on the entire group. She was overwhelmed with personal issues. She lost her parental rights and she was fighting with her ex-boyfriend all the time and trying to get people to defend her. Her ex making a claim to the judge that she was threatening to blow him up did not help her case. She wanted Larry to fight for her parental rights, which the office of the Attorney General does not do. Larry was not a lawyer but had studied law for his Bachelor of Science degree. What she needed was help from a local legal office, which she did have. However, the AG office could review procedures if there were procedural flaws.

Karen would try and get motivated to put out campaign signs, then complain about not being helped and not being trained, and then complain that she wasn't getting help from anyone, then she would say that she has to work on court issues. She was up one minute ready to help, then complaining that nobody was helping. This went off and on every other day for about 6 weeks. She would call Larry every few days and spend hours complaining about her problems. One day a lady was arguing about people who carry guns and claimed that people who own guns support domestic violence. She made the statement because her ex-husband held her at gunpoint 30 years ago. Larry made a statement that he owns a firearm and has a concealed carry permit and is strongly against domestic violence. He also stated that people who have a domestic violence charge cannot buy a firearm. Karen read the statement and spent several hours talking about Larry supporting domestic violence and refusing to sympathize with that woman, and made false claims that Larry was trying to blame the woman for the violent act. That made zero sense. But politics is full of nuts. Karen tried to get the campaign staff to join in. She became a weak link that had to be replaced as she disrupted the entire campaign. Karen put a lot of stress on the campaign and was a destructive force. The networking plan was to create 20 team captains in 20 different counties. That amount of captains or team leaders presented a manageable campaign after the weak link was removed. Being in that leadership position, you do have to have patience and be willing to listen to the people you are working with. In Karen's case, she refused to redirect when she was making false claims about Larry. There were too many individual factors that created too much stress in her life. Larry thought that giving Karen more responsibility would give her focus and a positive outlook to help take away the negative factors in her life or at the least make it so she wasn't focused on just the negative things.

Critical Race Theory: (8/13/2021)

The Critical Race Theory was a topic of interest in the media by many elected officials in the 2020 and 2022 campaigns. Several people who ran for office argued Critical Race Theory regularly. There was controversy no matter if you were for or against CRT. The people who were for CRT pushed the agenda of teaching truth in history. The people who argued against CRT claimed that it taught racism. Larry had studied CRT in Sociology and tried to give an educated response on what CRT was, but trying to give an educated response had negative responses from Conservative Republicans. Conservative Republicans are considered the Extremist or Far Right. Below is an argument Larry had about CRT. His argument was with his opponent for Attorney General in an online FaceBook chat.

Bolinger: My argument with Karen who was a Republican candidate for Attorney General in 2020.

Karen
Your support for CRT would also not align you with the Republican Party.

Bolinger: I support the 1st Amendment and responsible Legislation.

Bolinger: Your statement makes no sense. CRT has never been part of what the Republican Party was in design. I would be very concerned about a person running for Attorney General who is backing speech and expression suppression. You are not backing what is Cons…

Bolinger: you can take a political stance on CRT if you are running for positions such as Governor, Legislature, or School Board. But you cannot as an Attorney General. You have to argue what is legal even if it's against your personal stance. Being an Attorney…

Karen CRT promotes racism. I oppose racism.

Bolinger: You promote a political lie. An Attorney General should not get caught up in spreading political lies. That is how you get petitioned out of office. You have to be legally correct. Taking this political stance would be in poor taste.

Karen I will continue to be a strong opponent of CRT and CSE. The voters can decide what they want to support.

Bolinger: sounds good. I'll be a strong supporter of the Constitution.

After Larry took a stance on CRT, many accused him of supporting Communism, Marxism, and Socialism and were against the US. Some accused him of approving an education system that taught to hate white people. There are some misconceptions about what Marxism is and what CRT is. Marxism is a theory of inequality of social status or social class. Karl Marx argued the inequality of social status and used Capitalism as a tool to argue his theory. He hated Capitalism and supported Communism. He blamed Capitalism for the inequality of treatment between social statuses. He went a little overboard on his theory. There are issues of inequality of social status but he should not have argued on ideology. There are proven issues of inequality of social status and in some cases of inequality by race but when adding ideology creates the issue of overreaching on a philosophy.

"Politicians use CRT as a political tool. The "go-to move" for politicians is to pick a topic and claim it's anti-American or that it supports communism or Marxism. They make accusations that if you don't believe them that you are a Nazi. So in the argument of CRT, they claim all that, and the ones claiming it are the ones who are causing the hate, and misinformation and supporting the anti-American effort by taking away your First Amendment rights. During the Trump administration, the Democrats claimed Republicans were white supremacists supporting systematic racism if they backed Trump or the republican party. During the Biden administration, Republicans claimed the same thing against Biden and anyone who supported CRT through misinformation, propaganda, and slander to create drama and incite people. Similar issues happened during the Obama administration. During Obama, if you supported law enforcement the far Left called you a fascist. The claim is if you don't think their way, then you are a communist, or nazi or you believe in fascism. Spewing hate all the time is a show of ignorance. Sometimes it is just best to be well-educated on a subject and ignore the propaganda in the media. The propaganda politicians create drama to gain support through hate and fear.

In November of 2021, Larry wrote a letter to the editor to give an unbiased and educated response to the argument of Critical Race Theory

Letter to the Editor:

"My objective view of Critical Race Theory as a Chairman and Candidate in the Nebraska LMN Party. The Democrats have their argument and the Republicans have presented theirs. Both parties overreach in their arguments. They both have created misinformation. If they were more direct in their argument the outcome may have been different.

CRT can be a very diverse and expansive argument if you argue CRT as a whole. Democrats and Republicans have argued a small portion of CRT but claimed it as CRT in its entirety. The Republicans have made claims that CRT teaches teachers how to segregate children in their classrooms and that it teaches hatred of people based on their skin color. The Democrats claim that getting rid of CRT is getting rid of the truth in our history. They are both not on the same page. They are not even arguing the same thing but they claim it as CRT. The Republican Party lost its argument at the Nebraska State School Board (board of regents) because it overreached to the argument of CRT. The argument could have been won if they presented a valid argument.

But they tried to penalize the State College by arguing issues that are k-6 grade issues. It was a poorly thought-out argument.

What I suggested is that if the argument was narrowed down and specific, there could be a different outcome to the argument as long as nobody lies. Asking a politician not to lie is like asking a squirrel not to collect nuts. Example: A teacher who segregated kids by race in her classroom should have been penalized. That person and the school should have been penalized. When a teacher discriminated against Natives by putting on a performance that mocked Native Culture, you penalized that teacher for her insensitive racist act.

There are arguments about approved books. Some of those books that were approved for the K – 6 grade have been argued as being sexually explicit. One person made a false claim about the books being pornographic. That was quickly debunked as no proof could be presented. Trying to claim it as CRT failed. If they had selected certain books that were inappropriate there may have been a different result. In Kansas, the school board was reviewing 28 books that may be considered inappropriate for children. That is the correct way to handle an issue. They were direct in their complaint and are reviewing the books.

The argument that the Democrats presented was a bit misleading. They claim that ending CRT is changing history and is a refusal to teach the truth in history. CRT is a theory of race inequality. Teaching about Dr. King, the 1960s riots, how blacks got the right to vote, how women got the riot to vote, WWII, and the Civil War would be tough to teach if you try to leave out racial issues. Nobody is arguing to take those things out of history classes. There are only accusations that the Republican banning of CRT will erase history which is not fact. The argument is about sexually explicit materials and racially motivated materials that are approved for the K-6th grade class. The materials that are in question are fiction books not facts of history. So truth in history is not even in jeopardy and therefore not relevant.

There were questionable accusations that teachers were not allowed to speak at School Board meetings. There were slanderous statements accusing parents of acting like a terrorist or being domestic terrorists. By law, people are allowed to speak at government public hearings. However, some of the issues with parents were reported as threatening board members with physical violence. I expressed my view as a candidate for Attorney General and had my life threatened 4 times as I am a supporter of the 1st Amendment. You can argue the issue as a Constitutional Right to speak at those hearings but they have no right to threaten someone with physical violence as it poses a "clear and present danger."

When the Republicans tried to argue with the University of Lincoln board they presented their argument poorly. They argued against CRT by utilizing false claims. I studied history, the constitution, law, and sociology at UNO that talked about topics that could be theorized as CRT such as; the Jim Crow Laws, fighting for the right to vote, fighting for the right to work, fighting for equal pay and the 1960's race riots.

The extreme Left and extreme Right are cancers of politics that think spewing misinformation is actually politics. Inciting the people and creating fear to argue policies has become a norm in political debate. Overreaching on issues to try and settle for a lesser policy. The argument of CRT is overreaching. It looks like the argument was put together so there would be no winner to the argument to incite the people and gain more publicity. I can only hope that the next generation of politicians will do better." (Larry Bolinger. 2021)

Neutrality View: With conflicting items, sometimes it is best to take a neutral view. In this case, CRT and CSE have been a media topic for some time and it has been a blown-up political spectacle. In this issue, it would have been better to take more of a neutral stance or legal stance. Make sure that you support the people's Rights to address their concerns to the School Boards and that the School Boards and Parents will decide the fate of CRT and CSE. After Larry had made his statement and then tried to educate people about what CRT really is, it took about 4 months to repair the damage by trying to push a neutral view. It is something that would have harmed his campaign if this had happened more toward the regular election. Karen did lose in the primary and Larry worked with some of her staff on some petitions. That helped regain some political support.

In this case, this particular subject was not part of the base platform. The best thing to have done is ignore the extremist agenda and stay focused on what was important. Work with my staff and stay on task, and promote the base platform. Giving an educated response was more damaging than good. As a rule of thumb, stay out of propaganda pitfalls, unless you are backed by one of the major parties. The major parties expect you to support extreme ideals, but as an independent, you cannot take the risk as you are trying to pull votes from each party. So you work on items that can be agreeable to every ideology.

Sometimes when running for office you may need to make major changes. Sometimes a major change might be changing your supporting staff, maybe creating more responsibilities, creating different positions, changing strategies, or changing platforms. In the example below, Larry writes about why he had decided to distance himself away from the Legal Marijuana Now Party of Nebraska after he had won the Primary.

"When running for office, I recommend that you stick to your moral values and hold those accountable for unethical behaviors. The LMN party failed to uphold ethical behavior, so I chose to denounce my involvement with the party to claim Independent." (Larry Bolinger)

Beginning of the End of the LMN Party

Larry was recruited by Mark Elsworth Jr. to run for office in the 2022 election in Nebraska under the Legal Marijuana Now Party ticket. Things went alright until around July of 2022 when there was a disagreement between Larry and the leaders of the LMN party (Mark Elsworth jr. and Krystal Gabel). I'll do the rundown of what happened and why Mark flipped out. Mark and Larry discussed doing a t-shirt fundraiser for Larry's campaign. He started a "SmokeEm" t-shirt fundraiser, Larry presented his t-shirt for a fundraiser that had his name. He was ok with that until he started the promotion. Mark and Krystal flipped out and said that Larry was under-minding their authority and riding on their backs. Out of spite, they forced Larry to take down the website that Larry paid for and built for the Political Party because they were still mad about the t-shirt thing. They, then told Larry that if he didn't smoke dope he could not support stoner rights, and then they told Larry that he should rethink being chairman in the next election. They said that they should pass a policy that only people who smoke weed are allowed to be chairmen. Then Mark wanted to start a "Fuck the Police" campaign and said that the FTP campaign is the base of the LMN party. Larry refused to be part of that campaign. Larry told Mark, Krystal, and the other chairman that it would destroy everyone's campaign and the legitimacy of the party. Larry told Mark that if he wanted to do something like that then put it to a vote and let the chairman vote on it and he refused. Then he did a bunch of cursing, a lot of F-bombs in a private message. He did all that stuff because he was mad about the t-shirt fundraising program and he was mad that Larry created the structure of the LMN political party. Mark and Krystal were forcing Larry out because of that, so he resigned. Mark and Krystal made statements time and time again that they did not want the political party to resemble any type of business. They wanted to be a social area for pot smokers.

What Larry had to do in his stance with the Marijuana Now Party of Nebraska was review the organizational climate and it did not fit his agenda or moral code. It was harming his campaign and his personal values. They refused structure, refused others' input and creativity. He had to go through some creative adjustments. He needed to create work consistency in the campaign, as well as manage staff and manage extremist behavior problems. Changing from one party to the other, Larry gained a different perspective and had to implement changes in strategies. When you are faced with problems, you get creative and come up with solutions to the problems and put those solutions into action.

After Larry's resignation, Mark, Krystal, and the National LMN party stated that they would start a defamation campaign against Larry.

Below is the argument between Larry, Mark, Crystal, and the National office:

Cannabis Rights Party of Nebraska is in Nebraska: *July 19 at 4:43 PM ·*
We are having problems finding good candidates.
Larry Bolinger has left the party on his own Accord.
He claims we ousted him. Which is a complete lie.
The truth is he's never smoked weed and he's an infiltrator and a police informant.
He is running on a complete lie.
We weren't gonna mention it but he's out spreading lies about us.

Larry put out a note on the legalization campaign:

During the election, Larry helped support the petitions to legalize medical marijuana. He participated in several events and obtained several hundred signatures to help the Democrats petition. In July of 2022, the petition for legalizing medical marijuana failed. Shortly after the petition failed Larry lost the support of the Legal Marijuana Now Party. He was the only one from the party that pushed to gain legalization support, so he put out a general message to gain interest.

Larry: *"MARIJUANA: LEGALIZE IT OR NOT.*
What is plan B? If my opponent wins, he will make sure that marijuana will never be legalized. There is a very high chance the Marijuana petition will fail. What is your plan B? If Pillen is voted into as governor, he will veto any Marijuana policies. I started on plan B more than 6 months ago. If I'm not voted into office, you will not see legalization until 2026 or later. I am your only hope for legalization. I need managers, promoters, people that can fundraise, and organizers. I can win, but, I can't do it alone. If legalizing is important to you, then help me get into office. You can send me a message to volunteer or donate. You can also sign up on my website to volunteer or donate. If legalization is a dead issue, then I need to move on to something else."

Marks' response is: *Cannabis Rights Party of Nebraska is in Nebraska. "This guy is a cop and a liar. Please don't volunteer for him. He's a police informant who sits behind the computer all day. It's totally full of himself and using scare tactics. He states he's Nebraska's only hope until 2026. That is a total lie. We will do it this year or in 2024."*

Note: One thing Mark did not want is structure in the Legal Marijuana Now Political Party. He intended to create a social group so people could just sit around and smoke weed. Larry provided structure and was able to work with the other chairman to campaign for his election. They were putting up campaign signs throughout the state and trying to come up with other ideas for his campaign. Mark felt threatened by the structured political party. So he went out of his way to destroy it.

There was a lot that Larry could have done if he wanted to retaliate such as filing charges against Mark and Krystal for their defamation campaign and removing them from their positions under conduct unbecoming. Those two passed agenda items without a vote from the chairman. They violated the prime directive. They violated the 1st Amendment by banning Larry from the political party's Facebook site. But the correct move was to move on to greener pastures, change the platform, recreate his base platform, and distance himself from marijuana legalization.

Creating a platform that would be acceptable to any party

Larry's new base platform (the moderate approach):

- **Improve policies in Community Policing and Law:** For over 15 years I have worked on continuing education for law enforcement. In 2015 the need to change community policy started due to profiling issues when departments utilized 1980's era community policing. Updating policing tactics and law reform to bring it into the 21st Century has reduced crime by as much as 40% while reducing recidivism by as much as 60%.
- **Protect Property Rights:** 2 areas of property rights I will change are; 1) address issues of violations of section 18 US code 1001 to stop unethical government land grabs, 2) change tax liens from 1 month, back to 4 years before a 3rd party investor can buy back-taxes. The goal is to reduce tax lien foreclosures by 40%.
- **Environment Concerns**: One of the Attorney Generals' jobs is to understand EPA regulations and make sure our government follows those guidelines. I will make sure our government is utilizing these policies in the best interest of the people to preserve our health and our land. There were a lot of policies ignored or overlooked that resulted in the environmental disaster in **Mead Nebraska**. The people's voices were ignored when our government approved dumping fracking water into Nebraska. I will put the people's needs first.
- **Establish HHS Oversight Committee:** Protect parental rights by establishing a review committee to oversee HHS cases concerning child placement. There are many complaints of children being taken from parents under false pretense and defamation. A review committee will be created to establish the parents' rights, the child's rights, and welfare, and to review procedural policies.
  - ➤ Parents should not have to fear that their children will be taken away if they ask HHS for help.

> Parents should not have to fear that their child will be taken away when they take their child to the hospital for an injury.
> There are over 400,000 children in foster care. Being poor should never be a reason a child is taken away from their parent.
> Establish reunification procedures.

Larry's base platform is to work on **law reform**, try important cases, and work on programs that **reduce recidivism**. This is a very big job and it is not going to be an easy task. We need to be tough on crime, but smart on reform. *"As a Veteran and Business owner, I know what it takes to get the job done. The improvements I will make will save Nebraskan millions of dollars and open the door to decreasing taxes." (Bolinger)*

In a message on Larry's personal campaign group:
Larry: *"I do expect the National LMN leaders to do something about Marks's defamation campaign. When you do something that jeopardizes a person's life, you can't really just ignore that."*

Message from Krystal Gabel

"Larry knock it off. You left the LMN board chat so we just assumed you left the board. We didn't oust you at all. The only way we can do that is via a vote next April. We even sent you a gift in the mail. The polite thing is too much, however. If you choose them over LMN I can see why you think someone is against you. Because we don't support that as a board I already told you. We support you as a candidate esp since you spent so much of your own money so far. So calm down and run your race. No one is listening to your nonsense. You're just sounding like a clown now."

"I'm not sure what u mean by any of this. I haven't seen you in years. Jeopardy is a TV show. I can't collect medical signatures bc I don't live there anyway. Mark and the party had 7 or 8 events. I thought you were at one of them. Stop being a big baby. You need to just run this race and move on with your life. Write about it in a book if you want. No one will read it anyway. Sorry but not sorry. I'm pretty sure you went off your meds.
This is just nuts and a waste of everyone's time.
No one from the party wants to hear about it. If you want to win go fucking win. Stop making excuses
Taking screenshots is for whiny ass bitches. Share that one all day long
Lol okay, Larry you're harassing me at this point. As the LMN party national chair, I am trying to put you in your place and I'm being honest with you. You're being whiny. No other party leaders would give you any of this kind of time.
You're harassing me now. Remember that when you reply bc I've said out loud that you are not welcome anymore to post on our pages as you have been. Be focused as a candidate or move on.
Stop attacking the party that gave you a primary win. We have a right to talk to you like you're not in the game.
As a woman, I find all of you unbecoming."

Legal Marijuana Now: *"This is Krystal, I'm the national chair."*
Mark*:* Don't be texting Krystal she doesn't want to talk to you anymore

Larry's message to the Legal Marijuana Now MN (National Office)

Larry: *"Who do we file a complaint with when Party members are treating others poorly?"* Basically, the way Mark and Krystal treated me and Leroy (who is running as a candidate for State Auditor)

Note: There should be a national review committee that can review and reprimand them for their actions.

Message from the Legal Marijuana Now MN: *"Ok we'll boot their asses out."*

Larry: *"OK. I have no problem helping the Party out, wherever need be, but for what they did, I couldn't work with them. I mean, for what Mark and Krystal did, I could not work with those two."*

Legal Marijuana Now MN: *"Unfortunately Mark and Krystal run the Nebraska Party because they ran a petition to form the party. The states are separate entities. Up here in Minnesota we have an anti-police message probably that's more anti-police than the Nebraska party. We're looking at your website. You should consider promoting weed more than cops. You sound like you should be running Republican, not anti-police LMN."We want the police disarmed and disbanded. The police made sure the war on drugs was a war on the people. Good luck with your race, hope you finish strong and move on afterward. Stay positive, you'll get your 5 percent for the party ballot access. It's a win. Go get that 5 percent Larry. Don't get up caught up in the bullshit. If you ever come to Minnesota let us know and we will get fucked up.*

Larry: *"I expect 65% voter support. Mark and Krystal's ordeal stopped the momentum for about 3 weeks. I had to repair the damage they caused."*

Legal Marijuana Now MN: *"Man, good for you, 65 percent is impressive, we can't wait to see the results. Don't let Mark and Crystal hold you back. Politics is rough and you must be able to roll with the punches."*

Larry: *"Mark pulled all my LMN support. So I had to replace managers in those areas. I'm working on trying to set up team leaders in at least 20 different counties. September should be filled with meetings in Lincoln and Omaha."*

Legal Marijuana Now MN: *"Ok, well that's awesome, we wish you luck. Smoke a bong on a YouTube video and let everyone know what you will do for them. Make sure marijuana is in every photo of you. Just push marijuana, we get this legal and we'll go after mushrooms and cocaine. Are dabs legal where you are at yet? We got to go, the dispensary is closing soon. Hope you win dude."*

Larry: *"I have the democrat vote and the libertarian vote. That should put me at roughly 170,000 votes. I need to be at 260,000 votes. "*

Legal Marijuana Now MN: "*Doubt it. You want to tax medical patients and use the money for drugs against them. Democrats and Libertarians don't believe in that."*

Larry: *"Drugs that you get at a pharmaceutical company are not taxed?"*

Legal Marijuana Now MN*: "Nope."*

Larry: *"The stuff you wanted me to do for the party would be crazy to do. It would not be responsible. I will not support glorifying drug use in any way, shape, or form. Responsible Legislation for medical marijuana is the only acceptable plan. Marijuana will eventually be legalized in Nebraska. Maybe not this year, or the next year, but it will eventually be legalized. When that happens we need to have the legislature pass responsible policies. To create responsible policies, they would need to gain input from the population and conduct a thorough research analysis to show what works and what doesn't. We cannot have a free-for-all. Political parties glorifying smoking weed rather than supporting its medical needs hinder progress. Glorifying smoking weed would encourage kids to use drugs. That should not be the message we want to send out. That is not a responsible act. Passing such policies should be done with care and consideration of the effects on the States and Communities. If we have a free-for-all, we will end up with an increasing drug addiction problem as bad or worse than the opioid addiction problems we have today. Three growing addiction problems are Opioids, Fentanyl, and Waxing or Liquid THC. A mass addiction to waxing would stop any attempts to legalize recreational use. Kids being hooked on a product that is 99% THC is where you get your Marijuana overdose and death. CBD oil is at .3% THC, one joint average 14% THC, and waxing is between 58% and 99% THC. Many states that have legalized marijuana have a growing number of street pharmacists that lack regulation. Lack of regulation on drugs is how you increase deaths from overdosing because you have misinformation and you get issues with lacing the product. Your regulated pharmacists are a trusted source of trained professionals. But, no pharmacists should be required to sell any particular controlled substance and no physician should be required to prescribe it. There should be strict regulations against street pharmacists with high penalties to help encourage people to utilize trained professionals. Legalizations or no legalization, we will* *still continue to have a drug addiction problem. Drug addiction is a growing problem. Responsible legislation would take a percentage of all Pharmaceutical sales and put that towards drug courts, rehab, and diversion programs. Sending people to prison for drug addiction does not decrease addiction problems, it increases them. Drug Courts and rehab have been shown to reduce the return rate and repeat offenses by 60%. We need to take a portion of those pharmaceutical drug taxes and put that into a diversion program that works and turns our drug problems into a drug solution."*

Larry: *"That is the only stance that I WILL SUPPORT!!!"*

Legal Marijuana Now MN: *"You don't support marijuana. The national and Nebraska parties have both voted for you to drop from the ballot. We are asking you to drop from the ballot asap since you don't really support marijuana."*

Larry: *"NO. End of conversation."*

Legal Marijuana Now MN: *"Ok well we're going to the media next. You don't support marijuana. Why do you still want to run with the party if you don't believe in drug glorification."*

Larry: *"I don't want kids on drugs."*

Legal Marijuana Now MN*: "Then why are you running with our party? You have to be 18 to vote. No kids vote."*

Larry: *"I am running for law reform and diversion programs. When I'm able, I'll change parties."*

Legal Marijuana Now MN: *"We're doing a full media blitz against you starting this weekend. Our party is sick of Republicans getting on our ballots and faking candidacy."*

Larry: *"I ran on the ticket for medical use, law reform, and diversion programs."*

Legal Marijuana Now MN: *"You are not part of our party, you are clearly a Republican. Our party doesn't support taxing medical."*

Larry. *"You don't want to tax, but you want to get kids hooked on drugs."*

Legal Marijuana Now MN: *"We're gonna let all our supporters know that we don't support you and that you are really a conservative Republican."*

Larry: *"Thank You."*

Legal Marijuana Now MN: *"We're gonna start calling voters as well. In your hometown."*

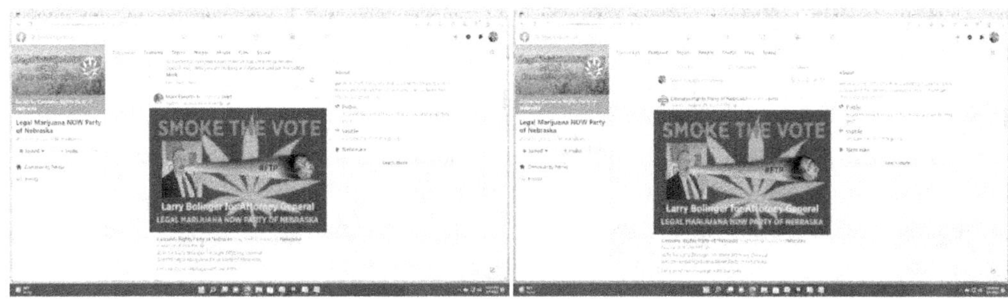

Mark: *"We only support Marijuana Smokers. If you don't support Marijuana and you are on our ballot we will advertise you as a party candidate. You have until the end of this month to drop from our tickets or else the party reserves the right to advertise our ballot. You look like you are still on our ballot. We're gonna be pushing legalization now. That's what our party is about, you're the main candidate so we will be creating pro-Marijuana memes for you regardless if you like Marijuana legalization or not, you are on our ballot."*

Larry: *"As long as it has my approval and is not defamation of my character."*

Mark: *"It's just about weed and you run for the weed party. We don't ask for permission, we just run."*

Larry: *"You are acting negligently and with actual malice."*

Mark: *"Actually that's what you are doing. Saying you support weed and you're running for the weed party is not malicious, you wouldn't have gotten on our ballot if you didn't support the platform. You are attacking our party by not supporting legalization, you need hugs n kisses dude. Political discourse has a very high 1st Amendment Standard. The truth is you are a candidate on our ballot."*

Larry: *"That is easily proven."*

Mark*: "You are on our and our opinion is our truth. I have a real attorney. Sue me and I will take you for everything you own."*

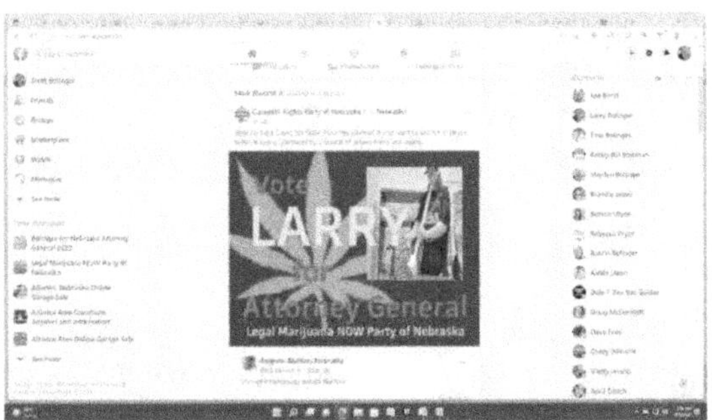

Conclusion of this conversation: Mark would go on every couple of weeks and make wild accusations and threats. Larry refused to respond any longer and stayed focused on his campaign and working with the people in his support group. Except for one act of weakness when he put the LegalMarijuanaNowPartyofNebraska.com website up for sale. He owned the Party's website and had the right to sell it. Marked argued it saying it would be illegal for anyone to use it. It was done just to put a burr under him. This is a good learning experience. Honor your moral values. When your support team is not conducting themselves ethically, you make the call to change. Sometimes changes are needed before you progress. The majority of people will not tolerate unethical behavior in business or in politics.

This change was needed for many reasons. Running for a State office under the Legal Marijuana Now Party would have a very high probability of losing. Almost no chance of winning. That is the hard reality. The leadership was unstable and had zero structure and did not allow others' creativity. When Larry added structure and got people to work, the leadership took that as an insult and stated they did not want a party to run like a business. They stated they just wanted to have a party to conduct socials for smoking pot. Having a blowout and denouncing the Legal Marijuana Now Party was probably the best thing that could have happened. Because Larry had to pull votes from all 4 parties to be competitive. When he resigned, he lost some of his support, so he had to adjust and recruit more support. Leaving the LMN party took away a lot of stress from dealing with unstable support. After leaving the LMN party, Larry lost 4 team leaders. He was able to readjust by recruiting 2 of those LMN chairmen to continue help on his campaign and then had to recruit several more people to make up any losses. Then he had to go through an expenditure to spend a couple of weeks campaigning in one of the largest Cities in the State to help stabilize his campaign.

Dealing with human behaviors is a big part of running for public office or being in public office. You are there to work with the people of that State. Working with people and dealing with problems, behavior problems, and conflict helps you as a person to develop a certain amount of resilience. You learn, adapt, and improve. You improve your social skills, utilize critical thinking to help resolve problems and develop a critical consciousness. (Denhardt. pg. 113)

During Larry's first campaign, he was faced with a significant amount of negativity he explains in one of the questionnaires. The questions asked: "What is something that has been a struggle in your life?" This is his response:

"One of the biggest struggles in my life was when I ran for City Council in 2006 on a platform to protect people's Property Rights. That led to fighting against government corruption, which got me blacklisted in my local government. I was politically targeted and discriminated against, my own government utilized defamation against me, tried running me out of town, and tried micromanaging my business which ruined my contracting business and investments, they tried to blackmail me, extorted money, and committed fraudulent acts against me. Through my campaigns, I found out that the local government was doing similar acts to other residents, and they requested my help to address the many issues they were facing. It took me 6 years of fighting corruption in my town to fix the problem. It resulted in replacing every City Council member, the City Manager, the Police Chief, and the City Clerk. Many people in the community were very thankful that I went to bat for them." (Bolinger)

While fighting against corruption, he was faced with significant ridicule by the community. He also gained support from people facing similar actions. He changed his position of accepting being ridiculed for what he was doing in his fight against corruption to making a change in promoting gratitude for what was accomplished. Helping to make major changes in a local government, to improve a failing economy, and reducing crime. When he initially tried fighting against government corruption he was socially isolated. But by educating the community he eventually gained more and more support. Through community support and education, the local government was improved. By that improvement, it created a positive change for the entire town. Instead of being targeted by the negative few, he focused on the positive outcome. Adjusting his attitude helped in his approach to addressing his agenda. He did seek help in creating that adjustment. Larry ran for office 7 times. He ran as a Republican, Democrat, Independent, and Legal Marijuana Now. He found balance in his campaign when claiming Independent by separating from the LMN Party and gaining council from chairmen of the Independent Party that argued neutrality. This created a common ground between each party, which gained support from each party. It did not resolve every issue, but it did create a common ground of support.

When running for a state-wide election there is a need to understand what it takes in its entirety. To run a successful campaign, there are many actors and it can cost a lot of money to run. Larry spent roughly $4700 in his campaign, while his opponent received more than $400,000 in endorsements. With such a wide gap in campaign funds creates the need to be creative. Larry campaigned in a 3rd party, so he set his strategy to take a neutral stance so that he was able to pull votes from all four parties. He did end up with 30% of the votes, which is a record for 3rd party votes. When Larry switched from Republican to the Legal Marijuana Now Party, he lost many Republican supporters that he had during his previous campaigns for Congress. However, some were loyal and were able to help the campaign in their territories. Each party has extremists, but to pull from each party you stay away from extremist ideology.

That is how Larry was able to keep a fair amount of support from the Republican party. When the LMN Party decided to push extremist ideology, Larry decided to go Independent, he lost some support from the leadership of the LMN Party but retained half the leadership support who continued to help his campaign. Larry denounced the LMN Party because they wanted to push glorification for drug use, support getting children hooked on drugs, they wanted to legalize mushrooms and cocaine and they wanted to start a defund the police campaign. All of which Larry could not support. Larry gained significant support for stepping down and sticking to his moral values.

Throughout most of Larry's campaign, he tried to push to recruit campaign managers which he called the 20/20 plan. That would consist of 20 campaign managers in 20 different Counties. If you are not endorsed by a major party, you will need to recruit your own team. Throughout the campaign he kept his team informed with the regular council, updating the manuals and keeping everyone informed.

Running for office on a limited budget, you have to get creative and use every asset you can think of while training your staff. Things that were done were writing a letter to the editor once a month, utilizing Facebook and Twitter to promote the campaign, signing up on 40 different groups on Facebook to do open recruitments, and then doing some direct recruitment to people who ran for office that did not win the primary. This way, he gained their support and their supporter's support, and he helped them with campaign ideas for the next time they decided to run for office. The team that was recruited saw a complete strategy for running for office, in-depth research analysis to help argue policies, and hiccups in the campaign which created a need for change and reactions to those changes.

In running a party or your own campaign and creating a team, sometimes you have to know when to change. Larry tried building a team for the Legal Marijuana Now Party of Nebraska as well as putting together a team for his political campaign for Attorney General. The closest description of the team he built would be considered a virtual team. Most of the conversations, training, and file transfers were done on Facebook or through email. He was able to create a team to cover the state. The structure was very dynamic. He created an in-depth campaign strategy with several videos and research analysis to aid in training. Where there was slack was a lack of face-to-face interactions and interaction between each team member. This is where he would have needed the most work. Create sub-teams to work with the district leaders. That way they create their own mechanism and manage their own process. (Benhardt. pg. 323)

The team did build trust and they knew their opinions were valued. But he needed to get them to be open with their opinions to argue policies and they needed to work more as partners rather than just working as individuals for their specific district. He needed to recruit and build district leaders, but that needed to lead toward building individual teams in those districts. That way each group can coordinate what needs to be done. The review also showed that more than just the leader needs to be holding the team members accountable. Each team member should be supported in their roles to hold each other accountable. In Larry's campaign team, he was the one who disciplined anyone, and he was the pacesetter to help keep people motivated. Making sure everyone has equal authority and equal stake in the campaign can help them be more involved in the decision-making. When they are more involved in the decision making they value the work that needs to be done.

Larry's original strategy was called a 20/20 plan. That plan consists of recruiting 20 team leaders in 20 different counties. Larry was the only person delegating jobs. That may be considered more of a work group than a team. To expand, Larry would need to work with each team leader and help create a strategy to create individual teams that help plan out campaign strategies in their area. Individual groups for each district could manage their own process and they will get the needed face-to-face time. (Benhardt. Pg. 318) He would want to establish a top management team to help with the platform and develop project teams to strengthen the overall campaign strategy. There will be team-building meetings to help expand the sub-committee base. (Benhardt. Pg. 319) He would have to try and get people more involved so that there is equal sharing of leadership as well as training. From what his staff went through in his campaign for Attorney General, any of them could be an asset for leadership and training. Rather than having open forms, he would have to have specific dates and times for meetings to help get people engaged in the process. He would also need to look at ways to get everyone more involved in keeping each other accountable. When the team isn't being held accountable, work isn't being done, or work is being done by 1 or 2 people and the other 30 are stagnant.

Larry lost the election, but if you are determined to create change, you don't let a loss stop progress. Larry set up a plan of what he would achieve if he won the election and he had a plan set up for if he lost. If he lost, he would focus on lobbying policies, and sign up for an appointed position that the Governor appoints. Selecting the party to change to was determined by who won the governor's seat. A Republican won, so he switched to the Republican Party. Shortly after that, he applied for 6 different appointed positions which included a vacated Senate seat. The next thing to do is work with his campaign staff to review policies that he wanted to lobby. He started with 3 sets of 5 policies to lobby that included research analysis on many of the policies. The sets of lobbied policies are in volume III.

The idea behind that is people will vote for people who have experience, but if you are not in Office you don't have experience. Many of the people that Larry had on his campaign staff will run for office in 2024. Working with Larry to lobby needed policy will help them gain experience and show that they have political experience and are ready for the job. If a policy passes, that's a feather in their hat. Then each person endorses the other to help cross endorsements to help each other gain higher population support.

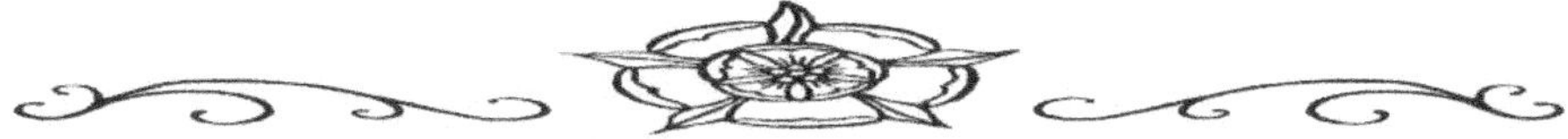

Example of Policies to be Lobbied: *(sent to Legislature 11/17/2022)*

By Larry Bolinger.

Introduction:

I am a veteran and a graduate of the University of Nebraska with a study in Political Science and Criminology. I was a candidate for Legislature in 2012, Congress in 2018 and 2020, and Nebraska Attorney General in 2022. I've addressed more than 50 policies. I feel these 5 are important to review for our Legislature and be presented to Committee to add to the Agenda for Legislature. Listed are 5 policy requests, followed by research analysis to help argue the policies. In 2024, I do plan to run for public office again. I have not yet picked an office to run for yet. I will not represent the LMN Party.

Thank you for your time.

Policy #1

Country of Origin Labeling for all Meats:

 This must include imported cattle that are sent here to be slaughtered, so they can be stamped as a USA product. Products grown in another country, but packaged in the USA should not be allowed to be stamped with a "Made in the USA" stamp.

Policy #2

Milk Policies: Allow raw milk to be sold without being processed. Allow a choice for customers to choose processed or non-processed milk. Some studies show raw milk and processed milk are good and bad for consumption. Let the people have the choice.

Policy #3

Meat Packing Inspectors: There needs to be established 3 types of inspectors:

- State Meat Packing Inspector: To be qualified as a State Inspector the inspector has to be a veterinarian and follow state inspector guidelines.

- USDA Meat Packing Inspector: Follow federal guidelines for USDA Meat Packing Inspector.

- USDA Qualified State Meat Packing Inspector: Follow the USDA guidelines for a USDA Meat Packing Inspector.

Research Analysis Provided

Policy #4

Right to Repair: This will allow people who buy a product to have ownership of that product. Congress passed the "Digital Millennium Copyright Act" in the 1990s which prohibits consumers to work or repair computer programs. These programs are such things as Apple cell phones, Tesla automobiles, and John Deer tractors. This is a copyright policy umbrella as a copyright. But, there is no copy and use. The Attorney General needs to argue that the "digital millennium copyright act" is a consumer rights violation. The state needs to pass the "Right to Repair" policy to allow consumer rights.

Research Analysis Provided

Policy #5

Consumption Tax:

A way to end over-taxation and the large land taxes that many of the Farming and Ranching community receives is with a Consumption or Fairness Tax. This needs further review and consideration.

In Larry's campaign, he did argue many policies. This group of policies would have high support across the state and possibly gain farming and ranching PAC endorsements for 2024. If the 20 or 30 campaign managers that helped with Larry's campaign decided to run for office in 2024, that could be a major endorsement for the entire group, which could create much-needed changes in State policy. There would also be cross endorsements from each people running for office.

Conclusion:

"One of the most challenging aspects of a leadership role running for the Attorney General is to reconcile cultural differences. Parties create propaganda that divides cultures rather than brings cultures together. Many people who run for office lack diversity. Some give up their morals to support political party agendas. One of the most controversial issues I faced was people utilizing Christian values to gain support for discrimination. Defending culture is met with criticism and false allegations. I find that moral leadership had higher values for me than party support. I worked with addressing the needs, interests, and concerns of the people I worked with. The conservative far right spoke out against the LGTBQ community. Many of my supporters were part of the LGTBQ community. Most were supporters of the LGTBQ community and had concerns about discrimination. Arguing for equal rights and against discrimination helped me understand the social standings in different cultures compared to political values. I

may have lost the campaign, but gain the respect of a lot of people who will help me in campaigns in the future." (Bolinger)

The next thing to do is to create a research analysis to argue the social changes caused by internet interactions. My theory is that people are becoming socially-retarded or socially ill-minded from their online interactions. Poor online behaviors give people a false sense of security and they act out in the same manner face-to-face.

A basic theory in politics is to gain power in a campaign, you have to submit to the power of the organization or party. But doing so can create an issue of violating ethics or tainting your moral values.

One of the errors in the campaign is defending a statement. People will support or argue about any subject. Sometimes they argue to rope you into an argument. You have to show some self-control. If you are at a debate, you argue your stance. If you are on an instant messenger, you make a statement and ignore the responses. Don't get defensive when there is negativity. If we make a statement and the information is credible, you don't need to waste your time arguing. What we want to work on is persuasive communication by utilizing credible sources. Do a proper research analysis, cite where you got the information, and give an educated presentation. "When you prepare your message, you start off with the "why" to determine the purpose of the message, and "who" to determine who your audience is and how to approach them about the topic, the "which" to decide which is the best way to present the issues (press release, instant messenger, live event, debate… etc), conduct proper research on the subject. Create a proper speech and know how to address common concerns. Then you figure how you are going to prepare your message and be able to address common concerns." (Benhardt. Pg. 294)

One of the toughest and most argued issues, when Larry ran for Attorney General, was racial and gender diversity. This was in the media a lot. Leaders of different parties talked about this all the time. It is something that has been dramatized, which created more problems with issues of discrimination. To prepare to argue such issues you have to educate yourself on the topic, do a research analysis, know what has been argued, and prepare educated responses. Know and believe in what you are saying.

When presenting a policy we want to understand possible stances between the two major parties. Presenting the policy in an unbiased manner will have a better chance of fitting in their range of acceptance. We want to create a mutual understanding, but if we debate, we keep it civil. Try not to argue your stance. If we argue, we show we lack confidence and we look weak. We create an educated statement. If an issue needs to be argued, we use that as a tool to create an event and motivate people to attend the event. Present a credible presentation and clarify any problems to help gain credibility.

What to do Next

The manual was given out to volunteers that helped Larry's campaign for Attorney General for 2022 to help educate and train staff. The end of the book will cover up until December 31st. Then Larry will go through each chapter and finalize each chapter. He will conduct research analysis when needed. The manual may be released in July 2023 after an announcement to run for Senate. Upon that release, the manual will be published and presented to his campaign manager and volunteers. If Larry chooses to run for Legislature the manual might not be published until January 2024 after the announcements to run. If Larry has major party support, he will most likely run for Senate. If he does not have the major party's support he will run for Legislature as a Republican.

"There are many things I've learned running my campaign and in my studies for my Masters of Public Administration. Learning the importance of creating a structured organization for my campaign. I did recruit to create campaign management teams. But lack some diversity and lacked interaction. There are things I'll need to change to help keep people motivated. Making sure they all have a say in how the campaign is run, and what policies we should be working on to help give value to each individual. There is an importance to managing organizational behaviors to create structure. Creating structure in an organization creates professionalism and competence in leadership skills." (Bolinger)

Business-wise, it may be best to add to the research and update a new edition for volume one and inter it into several literary competitions in January of 2023. Then finish volume II early in 2024 and enter that into several literary competitions along with marketing his campaign for office. If Larry runs for Senate, he would announce that in July of 2023 and then finish volume II in January of 2024 to create more funds to run for office. Then publish volume III in July of 2024 to make a push for the regular election. But, a rough draft will be handed out to campaign staff in January of 2023 to help educate the staff on his strategy and prepare for the next campaign. Larry's campaign staff will receive rough draft updates over every volume to keep them informed and to help aid in setting up a good strategic plan.

If you are running for the Senate or House, you can make that announcement a year or two in advance. This can give you a longer period to market your campaign, gain support, and raise funds. But, in many cases, you may not gain party support unless you are an incumbent or if you win the primary. Utilizing the book to be part of the marketing strategy to both help with creating name recognition and to help with creating more funds spread out on certain dates can help with consistency of funds and marketing.

Outside of the manual's date of release, there is a strategic plan to lobby many of the policies presented in Volumes I and II. This is to focus on specific interest areas such as in law pertaining to victimless crimes, policies concerning the farming and ranching business, policies concerning contractors, and the housing industry. Those policies will be updated and sent out to Legislature by the end of December and then again in January so they can be reviewed and have the policies addressed to the Legislative committees for discussion to be approved to be on the Legislative agenda in the 2024 session. This will help create an experience in policies to help set the strategy for the next campaign.

"I hope to help inspire people to invest in improving their government and communities by assuring their voices will be heard."(Larry Bolinger)

Resources:

Benhardt, Robert. Denhardt, Janet. Aristigueta, Maria. Rawlings, Kelly. (2020). *"Managing Human Behavior in Public and Nonprofit Organization 5th edition."* Sage Publications LTD.

Bolinger, Scott. (2023) *"Politics: Last Act of Defiance. Volume II"*

Bolinger Scott (2021). "Politics: Last Act of Defiance. Volume I" Chapter 17

Macionis, John. (2019). "Social Problems" Pearson. Pg. 15,16

Rice University. (2017). "Introduction to Sociology" pg. 16, 17

Ch.21
Letter to the Editor

This chapter will cover several of the "letters to the editor" and questionairs that Larry Bolinger wrote during his campaign. During a campaign, it is a fair idea to send out a letter to the editor once a month to help gain name recognition. Most letters to the editors are free, but many have a word limit.

The Need For Human Capital To Improve Government Performance

By LARRY BOLINGER

Alliance

I am writing to you concerning the article written by Henry Cordes on 22 March 2022 titled "Lack of Conservative Buy-in Time Helped Doom Nebraska Prison Reform Efforts," in the Omaha World-Herald. My specialty is in Criminology and I felt the article and the research done by Cordes were very accurate. The research that was done was exemplary. It is unfortunate that when facts are provided, politicians fail to act or even acknowledge facts.

When elected officials are provided with facts and fail to act shows that they do not meet the skills for an effective 21st-century government. We need to build human capital to improve government performance. Utilizing diversion programs will take a lot of work. Some people in government may be overwhelmed because of the necessary changes to make the program work. That is understandable that they may be overwhelmed.

But, that is when you rely on specialists, such as myself, to help with the necessary changes. The problem with the overcrowding in our correctional facilities is that the leadership lacks the skills for an effective 21st-century government. That, and an unwillingness to work have stagnated our progress to the point that we have the highest per capita prison population in the Nation. Law reform is a big undertaking and needs to be done by people willing to work and by people with the education to get the job done right.

Reference: Cordes, Henry. (22 March 2022). "lack of conservative buy-in time helped doom Nebraska prison reform efforts." Omaha World-Herald.

Bolinger, Larry (2022). *The need for human capital to improve government performance.* Alliance Times Herald.

Attorney General, "The Peoples Lawyer?"

Author: Larry Bolinger
Attorney General Candidate
Residence: Alliance, Nebraska

It is my understanding that the Attorney General has many jobs and many labels, one of those labels is "The People's Lawyer." You can not be an efficient supporter of the people while supporting policies that support discrimination.

In June 2022 Attorney General Peterson joined several other states to challenge a Supreme Court ruling in Colorado against a business that discriminated against gay people. Peterson wanted to overturn the ruling which would support discrimination. In July 2022, he joined other States to fight against the USDA anti-discrimination policies for schools so that schools can deny food to children who are gay.

A study done by the World Justice Project ranked the US civil justice system 27th, they ranked respect for fundamental Rights 27. The study showed that the US underperformed many countries in protecting the rights of privacy, due process of law, and labor rights. In that area, they ranked 60th. The US ranked 19th out of 99 countries in terms of adherence to the law. When we have several Attorney Generals working together to support lawsuits that support discrimination, I can see why we rank low in those areas.

Equal protection under the law is for everyone. That is in the 14th Amendment. Pretty basic policy. Easy to understand, which should make it easy to follow. That policy does not discriminate due to a person's skin color, religion, or sexual orientation.

A quote I'd like to impose is "The government is to serve and protect the people, not rule over them with an Iron Fist." (Ronomundo).

Letter to the Editor (November 2021):
My review of CRT

My objective view of Critical Race Theory as a Chairman and Candidate in the Nebraska LMN Party. The Democrats have their argument and the Republicans have presented theirs. Both parties overreach in their arguments. They both have created misinformation. If they were more direct in their argument the outcome may have been different.

CRT can be a very diverse and expansive argument if you argue CRT as a whole. Democrats and Republicans have argued a small portion of CRT but claimed it as CRT in its entirety. The Republicans have made claims that CRT teaches teachers how to segregate children in their classrooms and that it teaches hatred of people based on their skin color. The Democrats claim that getting rid of CRT is getting rid of the truth in our history. They are both not on the same page. They are not even arguing the same thing but they claim it as CRT. The Republican Party lost its argument at the Nebraska State School Board (board of regents) because it overreached the argument of CRT. The argument could have been won if they presented a valid argument. But they tried to penalize the State College by arguing issues that are k-6 grade issues. It was a poorly thought-out argument.

What I suggested is that if the argument was narrowed down and specific, there could be a different outcome to the argument as long as nobody lies. Asking a politician not to lie is like asking a squirrel not to collect nuts. There were issues where a teacher segregated kids by race to show them how it felt to be segregated, and there was a news report that showed a teacher mocking Native Culture. A teacher who segregated kids by race in her classroom should have been penalized. That person and the school should have been penalized. When a teacher discriminated against Natives by putting on a performance that mocked Native Culture, you penalized that teacher for her insensitive racist act.

There are arguments about approved books. Some of those books that were approved for the K – 6 grade are sexually explicit. One person made a false claim about the books being pornographic. That was quickly debunked as no proof could be presented. Trying to claim it as CRT failed. If they had selected certain books that were inappropriate there may have been a different result. In Kansas, the school board is reviewing 28 books that may be considered inappropriate for children. That is the correct way to handle an issue. They were direct in their complaint and are reviewing the books.

The argument that the Democrats presented is a bit misleading. They claim that ending CRT is changing history and is a refusal to teach truth in history. CRT is a theory of race inequality. Teaching about Dr. King, the 1960s riots, how blacks got the right to vote, how women got the riot to vote, WWII, and the Civil War would be tough to teach if you try to leave out racial issues. Nobody is arguing to take those things out of history classes. There are only accusations that the Republican banning of CRT will erase history which is not fact. The argument is about sexually explicit materials and racially motivated materials that are approved for the K-6th grade class. The materials that are in question are fiction books not facts of history. So truth in history is not even in jeopardy and therefore not relevant.

There were questionable accusations that parents were not allowed to speak at School Board meetings. There were slanderous statements accusing parents of acting like a terrorist or being domestic terrorists.

By law, people are allowed to speak at government public hearings. However, some of the issues with parents were that some were reported threatening board members with physical violence. I expressed my view as a candidate for Attorney General and had my life threatened 4 times as I am a supporter of the 1st Amendment. You can argue the issue as a Constitutional Right to speak at those hearings but they have no Right to threaten someone with physical violence as it poses a "clear and present danger."

When the Republicans tried to argue with the University of Nebraska board, they presented their argument poorly. They argued against CRT by utilizing false claims. I studied history, the constitution, law, and sociology at UNO that talked about topics that could be theorized as CRT such as; the Jim Crow Laws, fighting for the right to vote, fighting for the right to work, fighting for equal pay and the 1960's race riots.

The elite Left and Right are cancers of politics that think spewing misinformation is actually politics. Inciting the people and creating fear to argue policies has become a norm in political debate. Overreaching on issues to try and settle for a lesser policy. The argument of CRT is overreaching. It looks like the argument was put together so there would be no winner to the argument to incite the people and gain more publicity. I can only hope that the next generation of politicians will do better.

By Larry Bolinger

2022 Attorney General Candidate.

Resources:

Bolinger Scott (2021). "Politics: Last Act of Defiance." Chapter 17

Macionis, John. (2019). "Social Problems" Pearson. Pg. 15,16

Rice University. (2017). "Introduction to Sociology" pg. 16, 17

Norfolk Daily News

Larry Bolinger
Attorney General Candidate for Nebraska
507 Niobrara Avenue
Alliance, NE 69301
www.LarryBolinger.com

2) Background: Larry has been married for 29 years and has 5 kids. He is a Veteran who served in both the US Air Force and Army National Guards. Larry is an Author who wrote and published 17 books and working on his 18th. He earned a Bachelor of Science degree from the University of Nebraska. Majored in Political Science and minored in Criminology, with a concentration in government affairs and civic engagement. Much of the studies were in law, constitutional law, international law, and criminology. He is a student at Bellevue University, earning a Masters in Public Administration. He also ran his own business as a contractor for 20 years.

3) Previous elective office held (if any) or pertinent related experiences:

- Served on the City of Alliance Planning Commission for several years
- 5 years working in corrections which include working in a rehab facility, a troubled youth facility, and as a jailer.
- Chairman for LMN Party of Nebraska District 3
- I helped raise funds for Nebraska Boys Ranch, YMCA, ABATE, and the DAVA for disabled veterans.
- Volunteer on the Activate Alliance Initiative. One of the programs I worked on was to create a bicycle share program for the city of Alliance.
- Gave free rental space for the BBC tower to allow internet access for the local government in Alliance, NE.
- Volunteer In Police Services (VIPS). This organization helps the local law enforcement where needed voluntarily.
- Donated training materials to several police departments and law enforcement academies in several States.
- More than 15 years in politics. Larry ran for City Council, Legislature, and Congress. He has argued for many policies and created positive changes for the community and State. He has argued many issues of civil rights, government overreach, conflicting policies, and government accountability.

4) What are the three most important issues facing the United States and how would you address them?

- **Inflation:** In the past, when there was a recession our government would create a committee to address Federal spending to see why there was a significant increase in inflation and where there can be cuts in spending. In many cases, a significant change in our tax practices was imposed. Today, the big proposal that would create a massive change in our taxing program is the Fairness Tax, which is also called a Consumption Tax. That would need further review and could be the change we need to fix our over-taxation policies. But, that would need to be something that the voters would need to vote on. What happens a lot in government is that they will create an issue to take people out of their comfort zones to force a political agenda. An example would be to triple the gas prices to force people to buy electric cars. If that happened, and there were government representatives who bought stocks in companies that build electric cars, that would be a serious violation of consumer law, insider trading, and stock market manipulation. Something like that would create a very large investigation. Congress has the power of the "Purse." Insider trading has been a problem in Congress for many years. I would pursue ending elected officials' ability to commit insider trading or market manipulation. One of the many jobs that the Attorney General has, is protecting consumer rights.

- **The war in Ukraine:** It is unfortunate that Russia and Ukraine went to war. The aggression started in 2014. In 2019 Ukraine and Russia agreed to a cease-fire, but soon after the treaty was signed, Russia broke the agreement. They broke the cease-fire agreement on a regular base until an actual official declaration of war. Russia had built up its military to 85,000 troops along the eastern border of Ukraine and Crimea and started building strongholds just outside the border. The UN requested to send troops in and do an evaluation but Russia refused to allow them into Ukraine. In the many infractions leading up to the war and the invasion, I would appeal to the General Assembly with multiple charges of war crimes, treaty violations, and genocide. Officially claiming this war as genocide would force UN action, according to international law.

- **Health Care and the World Health Organization:**
The USA is the wealthiest country in the world with the best physicians. But not necessarily the best health programs. I do support improving our health programs. Over the past couple of years, people who rely on VA health and Medicare have seen a decrease in coverage. Veterans are forced to travel 60 to 200 miles to get medical care. We have programs that are supposed to cover your needs and those programs should support your hometown hospitals and family doctors. There are concerns with the World Health Organization. The US gives them $500,000,000 per year. But failed at a massive scale to address the Pandemic. There should be audits done regularly on this program and have every single cent accountable.

5) **Briefly summarize your position on the following issues:**

- **Acts of violence:** Acts of violence should always be addressed to reduce the continuation of violence. Some acts of violence may be jailable offenses and some may not be, but in every case, there should be some form of counseling. An act of violence could be an out-of-control child tearing up their room, punching a wall, fighting with someone else, domestic violence, sexual assaults, to murder. Utilizing city assets to address violent behaviors may decrease violent behavior later in life. A proper rehab and counseling program for people who have committed violent crimes or violent behaviors reduces the probability of reoffending after release from prison. There have been many cases where there was a Domestic Violent act, the person went to jail, was released, and re-offended. In most cases, there was no rehab and nothing addressing anger issues. Without addressing the underlying issue, the anger problem remains and the victim will be at risk.

  Act of violence in our school system needs to be addressed. The many reports over the years show a need to improve. Security and protocols need to be improved. Proper restraint and de-escalation tactics need to be taught and the RSO should be considered both an Officer and Councilor versed in diversion programs. Over the past couple of years, there has been "active shooter" training, but it has been taught in a limited number of schools. It is a serious issue that we need to expand on. I would add to the needed training and evaluate and improve school security systems.

- **Federal spending/U.S. debt:** When there is an extreme inflation problem like we have now there is a need to have a review committee and address the overspending in Congress and present a solution. Congress has the power of the purse. I would expect our Congressional representatives to come up with a plan to reduce the debt and get this inflation under control.

- **Federal farm policy:**

  I do have a fair amount of experience in the farming and ranching business that dates back many years ago. I had been a ranch hand for a couple of years back in the 1980s. In the 1990s, I helped out with many brandings in the 2000s, worked at the Nebraska Boys Ranch. The NBR was a youth corrections facility with a working ranch. I worked with a network marketing group that sold surfactants to farmers and ranchers. In 2018 and 2020 I ran for Congress in Nebraska Dist. 3 which is a very large farming and ranching district. There was a very big concern about policies in the agricultural industries. While on the campaign, I talked to several farmers and ranchers and listened to their concerns. I also reached out to a couple of farming interest groups who expressed their concern over some of the policies. The members of the interest group requested to remain anonymous so they would not endure any political backlash for any of their statements. That is something that understood quite well because I had endured a fair amount of political backlash running for office. Problems that were presented were policy changes in the Packers and Stockyard Act and the Prime Act.

  Some of the things that I would want to do are to approve "the Prime Act, have mandatory country of origin labeling, and stop importing foreign beef" to help secure proper trade, and quit collecting the beef checkoff from cattle producers. Fix the mislabeling and implement a policy that must include imported cattle that are sent here to be slaughtered so they can be stamped as a USA product. If it's not grown in the US then it is not a US product. I would insist that there be a complete investigation of the 4 largest meatpacking plants in the US, with money being returned to the ranchers who have been ripped off for years from the monopoly they have created. The government needs to support the smaller meat packers and farmers so they can sell directly to the consumer. We need to restore ownership of the American farmlands, oil rights, and companies to Americans. (Be sure to grandfather in purchases for the past 20 years)."

Did the government overreach on the Packers and Stockyard Act and the Wholesome Meal Act? Did those policies interfere with the ranching business's ability to operate profitably?

The 2020 pandemic had created a bottleneck in the meat processing business where processing plants were slaughtering pigs and throwing them away and the dairy farmers were pouring out and destroying milk. The bottleneck had shown that there is a flaw in our system. It has many serious flaws that should not be ignored.

There was an article in the Times-Herald on 5 May 2020 written by Elise Balin in which Governor Pete Ricketts made a statement that Nebraska could not follow Wyoming in the revised "Food Freedom Act." The Food Freedom Act would allow meat producers to directly sell to consumers within the state by bypassing USDA meat inspections. According to the Governor, the Nebraska State statute says meat has to be inspected by the USDA. However, the Wyoming Department of Agriculture Public Information Officer said that they can conduct sales in the State without inspections but transferring out of State would need a USDA inspection. But by federal law, the meat would need to be inspected by a USDA-approved inspector, not necessarily a USDA inspector. So you could have a state inspector that is USDA certified. The Wyoming and Nebraska governors both missed the boat on that one.

Governor Rickets made the excuse that Wyoming has state inspectors while Nebraska only uses the USDA. So Nebraska cannot get around utilizing other inspectors. However, he could have made an executive order to show leniency or add a policy to allow state inspectors. He also says that the meat lockers are already over capacity and that workers are working as hard as they can. He expressed the importance of the inspections as they should reduce the possibility of selling or processing contaminated meat.

Governor Rickets could have allowed the use of the Food Freedom Act by creating an executive order and then authorizing several state inspectors to do the work of the USDA inspectors. I'm not sure why Governor Rickets thinks we have to use the USDA. Would it be because of federal funds that are spent on inspections? It is a very big risk we face when the system is slowed down. During a time when Governor Rickets was refusing to bend on this issue, he put people's jobs and homes at risk. If the main argument is of safety concerns, then what we would need is a guideline to follow. There should not be any difference between a federal inspector to a state inspector, except on who cuts their paychecks.

There are three questions of concern: Why is there a policy that restricts state and federal inspections that are controlled by the USDA? Does that interfere with the separation of federal and state governance? Was the policy created to enrich large corporations that are in the processing business? I remember that about 20 years ago people were skeptical about allowing corporate processing plants in our area. Now, I can see why allowing corporate processing may have been a bad idea. Creates an understanding of which policies were the major factors in why beef sales were so badly managed during the 2020 pandemic. Stores were running low on meat, but ranchers were not allowed to sell directly to the stores and restaurants. During that time issues were getting the meat processed.

When I talked to Senator Brewer about the issues of meat processing he said that "if the small town locker could be inspected, they can sell meat retail to the public. As it is, they are using the custom-exempt slaughtering rule and the ownership of the animal doesn't change hands. The Rancher has to find buyers and sell beef instead of selling cattle. If the locker could sell meat to the public we could ease the bottleneck and move a lot more heads through these local butchers and expand this market for ranchers, and bring back a little prosperity to these struggling little towns. " (Brewer) He was also trying to gain support for his bill LR 380 which he says will help with trade across borders. But without the changes in the federal policy there could be difficulties in passing the policy, or if it is passed, would the USDA or federal government allow cross-state sales? I had suggested that he needs to make a push on our congressmen to support the Prime Act to help ensure the success of his policy. I did talk to Congressman Smith who is the Nebraska Congressman for District 3 about the policy issues. I had requested that he support Senator Brewer's bill and that he needed to support the Prime Act. Smith's stance is that everything is going fine. Stores were running out of meat, the retail price for meat increased from $25 a role of meat to $80 a roll, ranchers were getting less for their product and the corporate slaughterhouses manipulated the prices to get a higher price, and international trade was at a crawl, and the product was being destroyed because it was not allowed direct sales. But Smith says everything is going alright. In 2021 Brewer introduced a bill that allowed state inspectors, but by federal law, it would not allow state-to-state sales or international sales. I addressed this flaw to the Legislature with a proposal to fix this flaw.

I do support the "Farm Bill." Policymakers have been trying to cut funding from the Farm Bill for years but I believe that cuts in the farm bill would affect funds for the conservation stewardship programs, rural business, and cooperative services which would also include the rural micro-entrepreneur assistant program. So with that reduction, we are slowing down programs that help expand and educate people about farming operations. By reducing the food programs such as SNAP, we reduce the farming customer base and expansion programs.

I would continue to push to support policies that allow the sales of unprocessed milk, the "Right to Repair" policy to protect farmers' and ranchers' consumer rights, the Farm Bill, and I will continue to push for state and USDA-qualified state meat inspectors to help set a new direction to allow direct sales and free enterprise.

- Immigration

There are many areas of immigration that need to be addressed. It is a security concern when undocumented immigrants come into the country and a National security violation if undocumented immigrants are transported from one state to the next. There should be a review to consider finishing the wall with input from state and local representatives. Most of the time the US puts pressure on Mexico to address the immigration problem. But that is also what the media pushes. The issue should be addressed to the "South America Union of States." Much of the immigration is because of destabilized areas such as Cuba, Honduras, and Venezuela. The lawlessness and human trafficking in those areas are high and there needs to be a coordinated effort to stabilize the area. We have been focusing too much on the Middle East when we should have been helping our Neighbors.

DACA and Dreamers: The ongoing battle of DACA/Dreamers is one's interpretation of constitutional law which may differ from one person to the next. In most cases, a DACA/Dreamer would qualify for citizenship under constitutional law. Many DACA and Dreamers have been in the states for more than 20 years. Many were born and raised in the US and know no other language than English. It would be inhumane to transport these people to a country they have never been to.

Immigrant Veterans: We have policies that fast-track citizenship for immigrants who served in our military. A couple of years ago our government tried to get rid of this program and leave our veterans high and dry. I will argue to support fast-tracking our veterans.

- **Health care reform**

The US has the best doctors in the world, but a health care system that is flawed. We should not try to get rid of it, but we should always try to improve our system. Switzerland and Italy have the best healthcare system in the world and it would be in our best interest to evaluate what they are doing and try and create a better system based on that. We also need to get back to being allowed to use a family doctor. VA health won't allow using the family doctor.

- **Taxes**

Taxes and inflation have been out of control for many years. I would want to see more audits on large expenses to make sure all our tax money is accounted for. If we want to take charge of our taxes, we need to make sure it is being used in the way in which it is intended to be used. I will not let fraudulent spending practices have a free pass.

- **Global military issues**

I would want to address the issue of Iraq requesting that the US military leave Iraq. By international law, when a country no longer wants or needs our help and requests the US to leave, we have to leave. The president at that time refused to pull out US military forces because Iraq owes the US a large sum of money. The Iraqi government could file charges against the US for not following international law which would cost taxpayers a significant amount of money. We need to make sure all our troops are out of Iraq and Syria and then add troops to Litnia. Litnia proposed to allow a new US base there. Litnia has been a strategic stronghold since WWII. Having a US military presence there would deter any attempted aggression in the Baltic Nations. That has been presented to our Congressional representatives several times.

The UN needs to start doing its job as a neutral presence in several countries such as Iraq, Afghanistan, Cuba, Honduras, and Argentina. In some areas the US may have a conflict of interest. we need to utilize the UN to help stabilize democracy and ensure human rights are being followed. Russia has had a foothold in Cuba and Argentina since the "Bay of Pigs." That needs to change because it continues to destabilize the area. Stabilizing the South American countries could be a combined effort between the US, the UN, and the South American Union of States.

The Taliban can not be the recognized government of Afghanistan until they establish a stabilized democracy and a Constitution. The UN will need to have consistent reviews of its progress. Shira Law is not a form of Constitution that supports individual rights and will never be considered an approved form of law. As a destabilized country, Afghanistan can no longer be considered part of the UN.

6) Any Additional information you'd like voters to know:

I see many of the problems not being addressed in this office. We are not addressing issues of mental illness in our prison system. For the past decade, we have been using our prison system to address drug addiction and mental illness. In many cases, someone with mental illness has an addiction problem. Our prison system has been a revolving door for people with mental illness. When that happens the person with mental illness loses their support system and when they are released from prison they are homeless. This has significantly increased our homelessness in Nebraska. We have the highest per capita prison overpopulation in the nation with no plan to fix the ongoing problems. We are 20 years behind everyone else in law reform. I see the need for change. I will provide the necessary law reform and the expansion of diversion programs. Diversion programs have proven to reduce repeat offending by 60% and it has reduced crime by 40% according to studies in 20 states."

I understand what people need because I have worked hard to get where I am today. Nothing was handed down to me. I can make things better because I have been part of the working class all my life and know and understand the struggles.

I am a Veteran and graduate of the University of Nebraska and have the education to bring our legal system into the 21st Century.

In my 2 decades of campaigns, I always represented the needs of the people, I was always consistent in doing that, and will continue to do that as the next Attorney General.

My base platform is law reform and utilizing diversion programs to reduce recidivism in our prison system. I will be addressing mental illness in our prison system, addressing overreaching penalties, conducting law reform, trying essential cases, and expanding diversion programs to reduce recidivism. Develop a specialized team to represent the people properly to help address and protect issues of Consumer Rights, Human Rights, Parental Rights, Defamation, Discrimination, environmental regulations, and individual Amendments. My priority is to make sure the people are properly represented.

The Attorney General should never choose party politics over what is actual law. If they choose party politics over the law, it is a derelict of duty and they should be removed from office in a vote of "No Confidence." If Congress or the President presents a policy that violates Constitutional Law or Nebraska interests, it would be grounds to argue as one of the Attorney Generals' jobs is State interests. I do claim myself as an "Independent." I have campaign managers and support from each party. Everyone is treated equally no matter party affiliation. It is a very unique campaign when you have managers and support from all 4 parties. That doesn't happen very often.

The AG argues what is Constitutionally correct, and should never be politically motivated.

Questionaire by Peru University

Larry Bolinger
2022 Nebraska Attorney General Candidate
www.LarryBolinger.com
LB@LarryBolinger.com

- **What is your stance on free tuition?**
    - College is a big expense and investment. I would like to see expanded education. Adding free tuition will help with preparing someone who is graduating to start a new business or be a first home buyer which can improve both our economy and housing markets.
    - I found it very odd that the Nebraska Attorney General would support a lawsuit to reject student aid. Claiming that helping people is government overreach. Usually, over-taxation, over-penalizing, shutting down businesses, and the government taking away from people is an overreach. Forgiving debt or student aid is not an overreach. If that were the case we would have to claim every bank bailout, business loan bailout, or PPP loan as an overreach.

- **What is your stance on the legalization of marijuana?**

    - I have a firm stance to approve medical marijuana. Arguments by the Institute of Medicine were presented to Congress in 1997 and 2006 showing scientific proof that Marijuana has a medical need. Therefore debunking it as a Schedule 1. But Congress denied scientific proof and continues to support mislabeling this item which is a violation of Section 18, US code 1001. By law, the Schedule will have to change. I sent information about this last year to our Legislature and nothing was done.
    - There are some concerns about penalizing and false penalties concerning laws that target victimless crimes. Some of those policies are about drugs.

I would argue penalties for Marijuana possession as related to being falsely labeled as a Schedule 1 drug. Schedule 1 drug is defined as a drug that does not have a medical purpose. It is also looked at from its addictive nature. This has been knowingly labeled wrong for decades. Marijuana has been used for medical purposes for years. Marijuana was used to treat neuralgia, tetanus, typhus, tonsillitis, dysentery, insanity, excessive ministration, and uterine bleeding. It was used as a useful drug until the creation of the Marijuana Tax Act of 1937. How can something have medical use until the government creates a tax?

The Narcotic Control Act of 1951 created the drug classification and labeled Marijuana as a Schedule 1 drug. A Schedule 1 drug is said to have a high potential for abuse, no medical use, and is not safe even under medical supervision.

In 1997, the Institute of Medicine (IOM) conducted a study of marijuana's medical use. Their findings were that it is a safe effective medicine and patients should have access.

In a political arena, one could argue that any drug offense pertaining to Marijuana could push for record expungement. The IOM proved that it does have medical value but the government refused its findings. That is putting politics over science. This could be argued under The United States Code Title 18 1001 and the Federal Rules of Civil Procedure 9(b). Title 18, United States Code, Section 1001 makes it a crime to 1) knowingly and willfully; 2) make any materially false, fictitious, or fraudulent statement or representation; 3) in any matter within the jurisdiction of the executive, legislative or judicial branch of the United States.

In 1971 Marijuana was argued classified again as a Schedule 1 drug because they claimed there was no acceptable medical use and there was a high potential for abuse. But in the 1990's it was used to help treat chronic pain, glaucoma, Alzheimer's, Parkinson's, epilepsy, and other medical needs. As of 2022, 36 States allow medical marijuana. More than half of the States in the US agree that Marijuana has a medical purpose. I would like to see Marijuana change from a Schedule 1 drug to a Schedule 5.

Current Schedule List:
The drugs and the different Schedules:
- Schedule 1: marijuana, heroin, LSD, ecstasy, and magic mushrooms
- Schedule 2: cocaine, meth, oxycodone, Adderall, Ritalin, and Vicodin
- Schedule 3: Tylenol with codeine, ketamine, anabolic steroids, and testosterone
- Schedule 4: Xanax, Soma, Darvocet, Valium, and Ambien
- Schedule 5: Robitussin AC, Lomotil, Motofen, Lyrica, and Parepectolin

Marijuana fits more in line with Schedule 5. More states approving medical use results in more demand to reclassify marijuana. The only reason to deny changing the classification can only be from a political agenda.

What I would like to see is:
5. Change the Schedule of marijuana to fit what is medically proven.
6. Since the Institute of Medicine proved that Marijuana has medical use in 1997, I would want to see all records of possession expunged from 1997 to date.
7. I would also want the government to pay back any fines or inconvenience.
8. I would want an investigation into pharmaceutical enrichment practices and any government official who received funds from pharmaceutical companies in violation of the Enrichment Act. This could require a regression research analysis that analyses the pharmaceutical companies that donate to elected officials and the elected official's fight to refuse the legalization of marijuana.

Imagine a pharmaceutical company endorsing a candidate to ignore what is medically proven to put more people in prison. Those prison systems are privately owned making those businesses 28k to 74k per person per year depending on what state you live in. To keep the money flowing the pharmaceutical and privately owned correction facilities continue to endorse elected officials to debunk Medical Marijuana at the expense of the people creating an overcrowding problem in our correctional facilities. Keeping people in prison makes someone a lot of money. Keeping people in prison from false labeling is criminal. Of course, this is all just "Theory."

The cost of repaying the false penalties for possession would be an extremely large sum of money. But hundreds of thousands of people were labeled criminals, many of whom were placed in prison because our government purposely mislabeled Marijuana. What price do we put on lives that were destroyed because of this mislabeling issue? How many jobs were lost, refusal of employment, misdemeanor charges, felony charges, false incarcerations, and/or refusal of housing? The cost would be staggering

- **What is your stance on abortion?**
  - The worse legislation that has ever been allowed is when our representatives allowed a man to tell a woman what she can do with her body. It is a clear violation of medical privacy. We do not want a system where abortions were banned and we are back in the 1970s when back alley abortions were done and many young women died. We should not be moving backward, we should be progressing and moving forward.

- **What is your stance on gun control?**
  - My position on the 2nd Amendment as well as any other Amendment will be a bit different than the AG that is educated in Criminal Law. My opponent is educated in Criminal Law as well. While I'm educated in Constitutional Law. My interest in the AG position is making sure they argue what is Constitutionally correct and not what is Party motivated.

    I do support Senator Brewers' conceal carry bill and I do support the stand-your-ground laws.

    I think concealed carry permits were a good idea at the time, but it made officers act inappropriately if someone is carrying. I have a concealed carry permit and an FFL. I've been pulled over, handed the officer my permit, and got the shakedown because of that.

- **What is your stance on vaccines?**
  - I believe in freedom of choice and that includes vaccines. I believe the government has the responsibility of educating the public about vaccines and the importance of getting the shot, but they should never be in a position to force vaccines. Forcing to show vaccine cards could be considered a violation of medical privacy.

- **What is your stance on the border crisis?**
  - There are many areas of immigration that need to be addressed. It is a security concern when undocumented immigrants come into the country and a National security violation if undocumented immigrants are transported from one state to the next. There should be a review to consider finishing the wall with input from

- **What will you do to lower gas prices?**
  - As an AG, there is not a whole lot I can do about gas prices. I could look over the contract and our obligations to the Keystone pipeline. One of my concerns is making sure that if the pipeline starts up again that they follow State and EPA environmental regulations, adhere to the Army Corps of Engineers recommendations, and are held accountable for all contaminants. Protecting our land, property Rights, and water is my priority. Keystone could be encouraged to build a reserve where they stopped production. That would save more than 1000 miles in transportation.
- **Peru State College has a large population of Criminal Justice students and works closely with the Tecumseh State Correctional Institution. What are your thoughts on Law Enforcement and do you have any ideas for reform both within police departments and the prison system?**
  - I do believe that we should continue educating on 21st-century community policing and there should be more education opportunities. We do need to start moving out of the 1980s era community policing and into the 21st Century Community Policing. Officers do need to be well-trained in de-escalation tactics as well as defense and restraint tactics. I have over 30 years of experience in self-defense and wrote a book on "defense and restraints." I would expect that book to be used. I have studied a few de-escalation and defense programs and they lack technique. I would want more education opportunities and expand on approved trainers and training facilities.
  - Reform isn't just to educate law enforcement or our prison system. Reform would need to be done in the office of the Attorney General. The AG is a public advocate and part of the job is child support enforcement, consumer protection,

antitrust law, arguing policies, and environmental laws, representing the state, and implementing civil suits on behalf of the state. There are over 100 lawyers, clerks, and assistants that work with the AG and the worse thing that office could do is have only Criminal Lawyers representing the people. Too many criminal lawyers will create focus on creating compounding penalties that could be considered an overreaching penalty system that would violate the 8th Amendment. The AG's primary focus should always be on what is Constitutionally Correct. I would need to recruit a staff that could argue people's Rights and Civil Liberties. I would need staff that is well educated in Consumer Rights, Human Rights, Parental Rights, Defamation, Discrimination, Environmental Regulations, and individual Amendment. My priority is to make sure the people are properly represented. I have an education in Constitutional Law, International Law, and Criminology, but the office of the AG is not a one-person job. Recruiting the right people for the job may have to be done by recruiting directly from law schools.

o Nebraska has the highest per capita prison overpopulation with an increasing recidivism rate. Many things could increase criminal activities, such as mass immigration or a crashing economy. When you have an incident that increases criminal activity it will eventually go back down and plateau. When we have been at an all-time
high for more than 5 years, that is not a single incident. That is a failure in policy, process, and leadership.

Acts of violence: Acts of violence should always be addressed to reduce the continuation of violence. Some acts of violence may be jailable offenses and some may not be, but in every case, there should be some form of counseling. An act of violence could be an out-of-control child tearing up their room, punching a wall, fighting with someone else, domestic violence, sexual assaults, to murder. Utilizing city assets to address violent behaviors may decrease violent behavior later in life. A proper rehab and counseling program for people that have committed violent crimes or violent behaviors reduces the probability of reoffending after release from prison. There have been many cases where there was a Domestic Violent act, the person went to jail, was released, and re-offend. In most cases, there was no rehab and nothing addressing anger issues. Without addressing the underlying issue, the anger problem remains and the victim will be at risk.

Act of violence in our school system needs to be addressed. The many reports over the years show a need to improve. Security and protocols need to be improved. Proper restraint and de-escalation tactics need to be taught and the RSO should be considered both an Officer and Councilor versed in diversion programs. Over the past couple of years, there has been "active shooter" training, but it has been taught in a limited number of schools. It is a serious issue that we need to expand on. I would add to the needed training and evaluate and improve school security systems.

- Drug addiction and mental illness need to be addressed in our prison system. Sometimes drug addiction and mental illness come hand in hand. Our prisons are not equipt to handle addictions and mental illness, but for the past decade, they have been a revolving door for addicts and mental illness. There have been several cases where psych meds are mishandled that put people in a vegetative position for weeks or months. When someone that has a mental illness is sent to jail, they lose their support system. When they are released from jail, they have nowhere to go, so they become homeless. Utilizing our prison systems to handle drug addiction and mental illness has created a significant increase in homelessness in the state.
- We need to use more diversion programs to help reduce recidivism. Nebraska repeat offender percentages are going up. Utilizing diversion programs has been shown to decrease recidivism. Diversion programs would be such things as Drug Courts, medication, rehab, intense supervision, community services …etc.
- I would push to end truancy as a Status Offense. For the past decade, our legal system has pushed to get kids into the system and put them through Juvenile Courts, and fine parents with misdemeanor charges when their child misbehaves. Research has shown that putting kids through the system increases the likelihood of them repeating the offense or conducting other criminal acts. Putting a kid in the system has been proven to harm their social development. Research does show that utilizing diversion programs for teenagers has decreased recidivism by 40%.
- When you have a failing system, there may be a need for mass restructuring. In Nebraska, as of 2022, we have the largest per capita prison population. It has been reported that while all other states' recidivism rates are going down, Nebraska's recidivism rates are going up. Many Legislative representatives have argued for decreasing penalties and implementing diversion programs. But those requests have been shut down, even after research has been done and information provided to confirm that is the correct course of action. When Nebraska Governor Ricketts takes part in being a member of the research team and then votes against the information, makes you wonder what his agenda really is. Does he want to fix the problem or does he want to continue to pack the prison to gain acceptance to build more prisons? When the majority votes against fixing failed policies, tells me that they do not meet the skills for an effective 21st-Century government. There is a clear need to revamp the whole system, which includes building human capital to improve government performance. That means getting people into positions that will act based on facts and not based on political agendas. This would create significant demand for a specialist in several fields of law. It would also put some demand on reviewing my two political books and assigning assistance to specialize in several chapters to help create the needed changes and needed arguments. My primary goal would be to reduce the prison population by 40% by utilizing diversion programs and keeping within the 60% recidivism rate reduction. The opposition to the plan wants more prisons to fix the

overpopulation, but more jails do not reduce the recidivism rate. Approving the new correctional facilities would cost taxpayers upward of around 400 million dollars while utilizing diversion programs and law reform will cost time, training, and effort. Utilizing diversion programs could be adding additional training for law enforcement, social workers, drug counselors, and legal staff. This could also mean adding additional costs to expanding counseling practices for both drug and alcohol addiction as well as mental health. My goal would be to keep the cost to a minimum while showing a 60% reduction in recidivism.

The changes that I would work on are:

- Reducing sentences for non-violent offenders
- Diversion programs
- Enhanced drug and mental health treatment
- The expanded drug court system
- Post-release supervision
- Reintegration programs

This would need the support of both legal specialists and policymakers. To make it work well, you will have to have good coordination between law enforcement, human services, public defenders, prosecutors, and judges and have a basic knowledge of what an area can offer to help support diversion programs. It sounds like a big undertaking. Some people can not fathom working that hard or creating that big of a coordinated effort. Those people are the ones we do not need in government. Sometimes the right thing to do may be the most difficult task.

There are many specialists that I would need to push different policies and correct unethical practices. Many that I point out in the two books I wrote on politics. This specialist would cover:

- Realty law
- Native law
- Consumer rights: (Right to Repair)
- Discrimination: (LGTBQ Rights)
  This would also include international laws, such as
    - ➢ Convention on Enforced Disappearance.
    - ➢ Convention on the Rights of the Child.

- Election policies
- Labor laws
- 14th Amendment specialist (equal protection under the law)
- Environmental specialist for state, federal, and international law. International policies would include such policies as:
    - ➢ LOSC: Laws of the Sea Convention.

> ➤ London dumping convention.
- A specialist on the Task Force of 21st Century Community Policing
- Tort violations
- Judicial reviews

That would take 17 specialists with supporting staff that could put the number well over 100 people working on revamping the system. Some of those numbers could come down if utilizing intern programs.

Conclusion: The Attorney General's job is a very demanding position. One of the most demanding jobs in government. Bringing our legal system into the 21st Century will be a big job and will take a coordinated effort by qualified staff with a focus on properly representing the people. With my work ethic, work history, dedication, and education, I feel that I'm the most qualified to get the job done.

Chapter 22

<u>Nebraska Attorney General Campaign Budgeting</u>

In a campaign, there can be a significant amount of money being donated, spent, and allocated through the course of the election cycle. Smaller campaigns such as the local School Board or City Council may not have a significant expense. But running for a State or Federal office could have a very large budget to work with. Running for a state office, such as Attorney General would require a strategic promotional campaign throughout the State.

Larry Bolinger has run for several public office positions, such as City Council, State Legislature, and Congress. In July 2021, he announced his official campaign to run for Attorney General. This chapter will cover why there is a need to set a budget. It will cover the changes that were made from a fluctuating budgeting system to something more stable. This example shows a conservative budgeting system for someone running for a State office that is on a low budget. The total cost for Bolinger's campaigns was roughly $4700, and he got more than 188,000 votes.

Larry Bolinger wrote a book called "Politics: Last Act of Defiance. In that book, he goes through the campaigns that he ran between 2006 and 2020. His new book "Politics: Last Act of Defiance" volume II will go through his campaign for Attorney General. There will be nominal groups so there is a continuous dialog with supporters and staff so that they can work together on campaign strategies. The budgeting strategy would be more in line with a top-down budget or centralized budgeting approach. Larry keeps track of all the expenses, creates the budget, and project projections, and presents the budget to staff for discussion. He also updates the Secretary of States Accountability and Disclosure department during their periodic due dates. There may be adjustments to meet the budget which will result in setting priorities. They will set out what needs to be done but adjust to what can be done and create a functional budget with goals to achieve. If there are large donations, there would be a need to hire a treasurer to take charge of accounting and to keep the Accountability and Disclosure account updated. With an accountant, there would still be a need to run a nominal group to discuss the best strategies on how to utilize the funds for the campaign.

Most of Larry's book is on strategies for the campaign, arguments, and research analysis. But, one big part of the campaign in a big race like a state or federal race is setting your budget and goals. Create a flexible budget if you are on a small budget. The budget will show the expenses and a projection of what needs to be done, and what can be done. So we do what can be done, and try and do fundraising activities to be able to budget for what needs to be done to win the statewide election.

What has been started in creating a necessary cost or running cost? Analyze what is needed to keep the campaign afloat. Set a budget for obtaining the materials to do the appropriate job in your marketing plan. Then set a budget and strategy for how to get the materials dispersed. If you end up with a higher budget, then you can add a wider marketing base. Such as adding advertisements in the newspapers, radio, texting programs, and bulk mail. Budget your short and long-term plans. What you need to be done now, is create the calendar of events and set the goal of raising funds to get to those events. If you can't get to events, what would you need to do to get a representative there? So in distance events, you try and get Larry there, but recruit staff and support groups to that area just in case he can't go. If he can't go but is able to have representatives there, he would have to budget to get the materials and information they need to properly run a booth. That could include buying signs, hand-out materials, and a booth fee. So, in your budget, you may be dipping into the material budget, the postal budget, and advertising budget categories, unless you create a special project category just for the event and set a budget for that specific event and draw from your reserve funds.

Budgeting for the campaign for the most part can be a stable process that stays within a specific budget plan, but you have to be prepared for a flexible budget. Unexpected expenses will occur. Unexpected endorsements may happen as well. If that happens you can add it to your marketing plan. A management team may drop out, which could cause you to make a trip to help train new management. If you get a large donation, you could create a reserve fund for unexpected events. For example, Larry disagreed with the leader of the LMN Party. The leader of the LMN Party wanted to start a defamation campaign against law enforcement and wanted to glorify drug use. Larry refused to support that. By refusing to support the LMN Party agenda he was forced out of the Party. That left him short 3 campaign managers. That ends up in a loss of volunteers and a large expense if he has to travel and do the work they were going to do or recruit new people and get them trained.

Up until July, there was a pretty sporadic budget. Nothing was consistent. There were goals and then there were expenses when there was money. August through to the election in November there are reoccurring funds each month, and a lump sum of cash. With a regular cash flow, we can show a set budget for the next three months to assure a certain amount is going to different items such as postal services, media, travel, and material costs. With a lump sum of cash and reoccurring funds, you can set a stable budget and have consistency in expenses. Having consistency in your budget will create consistency in marketing your campaign.

In a campaign, there can be a significant amount of money being donated, spent, and allocated through the course of the election cycle. Smaller campaigns such as the local School Board or City Council may not have a significant expense. But running for a State or Federal office could have a very large budget to work with. Running for a state office, such as Attorney General would require a strategic marketing campaign throughout the State. You would have to gather the funds, create the budget, and be consistent in your efforts.

Larry Bolinger has run for several public office positions, such as City Council, State Legislature, and Congress, and now he is running for Attorney General.

There is a big difference in how a business is run or how a campaign is run compared to the plan at the beginning of Larry's campaign to put his finances into form. You'll see what happens when you don't have a budget and just spend money on the campaign whenever you happen to get funds and compare it to creating a budget and having consistency in expenses. Having consistency in your budget will help with maintaining a minimal marketing strategy each month. It will also present the information needed to review to help with the decision to create better performance within your management team. When running for public office, you have to have your name marketed in a consistent manner. Most people get elected by name recognition. Seeing their name over and over again.

Larry's campaign for Attorney General has been his biggest campaign expense and largest coordinated effort when compared to his other campaigns. Tracking the funds and reviewing performance can create a better strategy for the next campaign. If Larry loses the election for Attorney General he will run for the Legislature in 2024 unless the incumbent for the Senate or House retires. In 2024 the Legislative district Senator is terming out. Running for office in that district would be on common grounds and would pose a very favorable chance of being elected to office. Part of the strategy is to budget and make sure that the Legislative district has good marketing coverage. An AG position is a State-wide position and a Legislature is just one district. But, if Larry plans on running for Legislature in 2024, he will have to make a special effort to cover that district.

This manual will provide a standard outline of a budget, what failed, and what worked. This will provide a base budget platform for the next campaign. It will show what is needed as a minimum monthly budget. The difference would be the territory coverage. A much smaller territory to cover with the same budget should present a far better outcome. Creating a budget and staying consistent with that budget for a year would be significant in a campaign. That would create a consistent marketing strategy that would help the primary function of a marketing campaign, which is creating name recognition.

Another issue to look at is fundraising. You can start a budget with what you put up front as out-of-pocket. Or if you are donating to your campaign monthly out of your pocket. In campaigns for office, you may need to have fundraising events. Which could mean creating a fundraising coordinator position. They review each fundraising activity, perform variance analysis, and utilize what works. The party Larry was affiliated with conducted a shirt sale which brought in $50 in donations. In his campaign for office, he needs $400,000 to keep up with his opponent. The shirts that were being sold promoted the Party's agenda, which was to legalize marijuana. The shirts served no value towards name recognition. If there is no name recognition, then we can assume an unfavorable variance when compared to asking for donations and receiving $100 and then spending $95 on business cards, and distributing 4000 cards. T-shirts with name recognition would have value. T-shirts with no name recognition have little value to the campaign. Performance reviews can help evaluate what is going on to help improve the campaign.

The base campaign strategy is to have 20 campaign managers in 20 different counties. While you are trying to establish that, you recruit people to help those 20 managers. If you have 5 people helping in each of the 20 areas, that would give you good coverage in those counties to conduct door-knocking, hand out flyers, do cold calls, conduct fundraisers, and put out campaign signs. To obtain that many volunteers, you have to market your campaign, which is marketing your name to gain interest. Then set your base budget, which will consist of material costs, travel costs, shipping, and reserve funds. In this campaign, Larry is taking college courses that support the office that he is running for. So there will be a category for education expenses. The education is paid with a student loan, so that would be counted as borrowed money. When dealing with the Accountability and Disclosure Committee, you have to keep track of the donations you get, the in-kind contributions, and loans if you borrowed money. If you spend your own money on your campaign and claim it, it could be claimed as a deduction on your taxes as a business expense, but it is also income when considering your filing with the Accountability and Disclosure Committee. It is a odd procedure when you spend your own money because it's a deduction, but also, income.

Budget

Travel	**$100**
Shipping	$100
Material	$100
Reserve Fund	$1200

The above budget was set in August. There is $300 being donated to the campaign each month. This will be the budget for August, September, and October. The Novembers budget will be for Advertisement only. The $300 per month donation will go towards advertisement in November.

Several people play key roles in Larry's campaign. Larry has to recruit, manage and coordinate his campaign strategies. When more people volunteer, he designates positions. His goal is the 20/20 plan. Which is to recruit 20 managers in 20 different counties. That creates 20 key actors that have the role of coordinating a campaign strategy in those specific counties. Those actors help with fundraising and marketing the name. Each supporter, campaign manager, endorser, or general volunteer is a stakeholder in the campaign. Many people help a campaign to be able to support and advance policies. Some help out to gain support in the next election cycle in hopes they gain endorsements. Most people want something out of the campaign. It could be that they want to see the policies you are supporting get passed. Some want their own policies passed and think you can help if they support you. Each manager and Larry can play big parts in where the focus or control should be. Each campaign manager knows more about their county and what their county needs than any other manager. So if there is a greater need for support in one county over the other, the focus will be directed in that area. If there is a lack of support in a key city, there will be a strategy to help out more in that area. The two biggest cities in Nebraska are Omaha and Lincoln. In a state-wide election, if you win those two cities, you win the election. So that creates an important need to set a special budget just for that area.

Change in control can be looked at in two different ways. Bolinger controls his campaign and makes the ultimate decision on what needs to be done. But, bad decisions will cause a loss of support. So a majority could sway control if Bolinger considers what is best to gain majority votes and support.

The timing of releasing the accounting and budget plan along with the manual would have to consider the strategy for the next step for possible future campaigns. Releasing an accounting analysis would have to be done on specific dates that are created by the Accountability and Disclosure Committee. But the manual for the Attorney General Campaign may be released depending on if the election goes well, or to help the next election or re-election.

Bolinger's applied project for budgeting and accounting for his campaign for Attorney General will have specific dates where there will need to be accounting updates by loading information to the Nebraska Accountability and Disclosure Committee website. The first report is done in May or after there have been more than $5000 in donations or expenses. After you received and or spend more than $5000, you have 10 days to file with the Accountability and Disclosure Committee. Then you have set timelines to do updates to your account on the Accountability and Disclosure website. 10 May is the primary, but 14 June is the end of the primary election update period. The next filing dates are 4

October, 25 October, and 7th of November. December 31st is the end of the general election period. 17 January 2023 is when all general election candidates with the committee's due date. This would also be a date to dissolve any and all candidate committees and finalize your year-end statement.

After the end of the election and the updated information is loaded to the A&D website, there will be a projected timeframe that the "Politics: Last Act of Defiance Volume II" manual will be finished and published. The projected time to finish would be 1 March 2023. The book launch date may not be until July 2023 as part of a prelaunch for the 2024 elections or may be used to help with name recognition for the 2026 re-election campaign. If the manual is used to help with the re-election campaign in 2026, the launch of the book might not be until January 2025.

The financial management of the campaign would need to be done regularly with monthly financial reports for each month so you can compare each month's inflow and outflow of funds. You would have a budget report, an expense report, and a statement of revenue. Campaigns are short-term expenses that you keep track of for 6 to 18 months so you don't have a year-to-year comparison. You have to compare how your campaign is going month to month. After the end of the year is done, you do a final year-end statement to sum up all inflow and outflow of cash.

Expense report: This is what Bolinger started with. This is recording all expenses, but in this format, it would make it hard to set a budget because there is no formal format, and nothing is categorized.

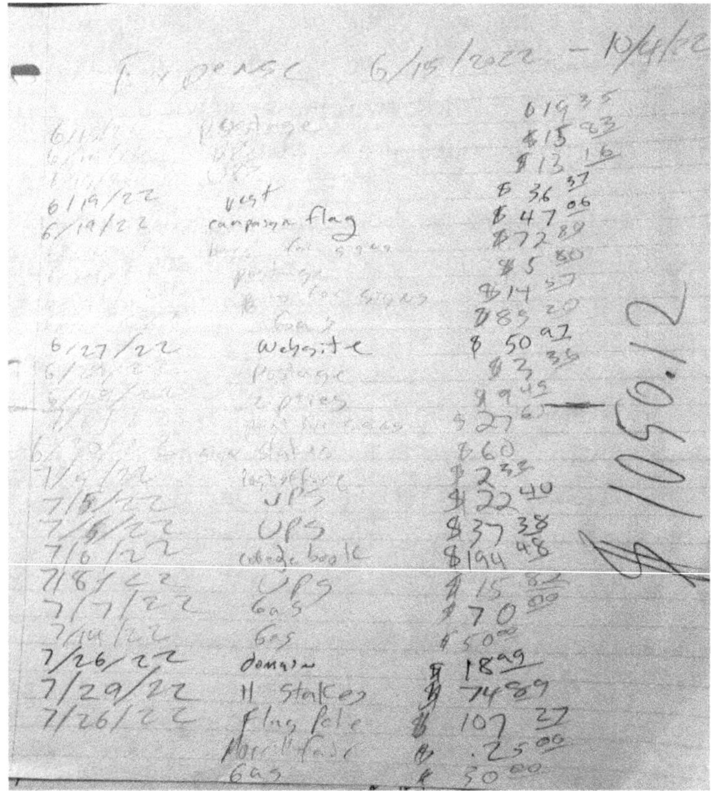

In the below Expense report, the expense is categorized and easy to follow. You know where your cash outflow is going, you can calculate an average cost and set a budget to create some control over where the money is going.

Larry Bolinger Campaign for Attorney General
2022 Expense Report

	Material cost	Shipping cost	Travel	Advertisement	education	used reserve funds
April	$ 4.59	$ 27.20	$ 135.65	$ 52.14	$ 3,987.79	
	$ 65.54	$ 23.20				
total	$ 70.13	$ 50.40	$ 135.65	$ 52.14	$ 3,987.79	$ 308.32

Month	Material cost	Shipping cost	Travel	Advertisement		
May	$ 8.68	$ 15.35	$ 60.26	$ 50.00		
	$ 266.59	$ 9.90		$ 35.00		
	$ 95.00	$ 3.75		$ 100.00		
	$ 31.01	$ 11.60				
	$ 64.17	$ 23.20				
	$ 78.07	$ 11.53				
	$ 6.25	$ 46.40				
	$ 460.58					
Total	$ 1,010.35	$ 121.73	$ 60.26	$ 185.00		$ 1,377.34

Month	Material cost	Shipping cost	Travel	Advertisement		
June	$ 33.10	$ 13.19	$ 85.20	$ 50.97		
	$ 144.44	$ 16.95				
	$ 85.58	$ 19.35				
	$ 18.00	$ 15.83				

	$ 204.14	$ 13.16				
	$ 288.88	$ 5.80				
	$ 36.37	$ 3.36				
	$ 47.06					
	$ 72.80					
	$ 14.57					
	$ 9.49					
Total	**$ 954.43**	**$ 87.64**	**$ 85.20**	**$ 50.97**		**$ 1,178.24**

July	$ 27.61	$ 2.32	$ 70.00	$ 18.99	$ 194.48	
	$ 60.00	$ 22.40	$ 50.00	$ 25.00		
	$ 74.89	$ 37.38	$ 30.00			
	$ 107.27	$ 15.82				
	$ 439.50					
Total	**$ 709.27**	**$ 77.92**	**$ 150.00**	**$ 43.99**		**$ 981.18**

August	$ 53.47	$ 16.95	$ 30.00			
	$ 13.18	$ 12.53				
	$ 64.19	$ 11.40				
		$ 32.15				
		$ 15.20				
Total	**$ 130.84**	**$ 88.23**	**$ 30.00**			**$ 249.07**

September			$ 79.23			
			$ 54.00			

10-day campaign in Omaha and Lincoln	$ 48.10	$ 40.00	$ 116.25			

October							
November							

Larry Bolinger for Attorney General Budget

budget $ 100.00 $ 100.00 $ 100.00 $ 100.00

	Material cost	Shipping cost	Travel	Advertisement	reserve funds or defered inflow of resources	Colledge	Discursed Funds Borrowed funds	Discursed Funds Fiduciary Funds	in Kind Donations	Donations	10 day campaign in Omaha and Lincoln
April	$ 70.13	$ 50.40	$ 135.55	$ 52.14	$ 2,856.00	$ 3,387.79	$ 6,761.00	$ 2,851.00		$ 5.00	
May	$ 1,010.35	$ 121.73	$ 50.26	$ 185.00	$ 2,647.58					$ 100.00	
June	$ 554.43	$ 87.64	$ 35.20	$ 50.96	$ 1,230.34					$ 10.00	
July	$ 709.27	$ 77.92	$ 150.00	$ 43.99	$ 122.10				$ 859.08	$ 20.00	
August					$ 1,400.00	$ 4,225.01	$ 5,625.01	$ 2,535.99		$ 20.00	
September											
October											
November											
Total	$ 2,744.18	$ 337.69	$ 431.11	$ 332.09		$ 8,212.80	$ 12,385.01		$ 859.08	$ 155.00	

Statement of Revenues

	General funds	debit	project fund	Running costs	total funds
Revenue					
in kind docations	$ 859.08				$ 859.08
donations	$ 155.00				$ 155.00
Total revenue	$ 1,014.08				$ 1,014.08
Debt services					
borrowed money		$ 12,386.01			$ 12,386.01
Total borrowed Money		$ 12,386.01			$ 12,386.01
Expenditures					
material cost				$ 2,744.18	$ 2,744.18
shipping cost				$ 337.69	$ 337.69
travel advertisment				$ 431.11	$ 431.11
Total Expenditures				$ 3,512.98	$ 3,512.98
Project Fund					
lincoln/omaha campaign			$ 1,200.00		$ 1,200.00
Total Project fund			$ 1,200.00		$ 1,200.00
Transfer In		$ 12,386.01			
Transfer out	$ 12,057.87				$ 12,057.87
Net change in fund balances	$ 2,478.21	$ 1,278.21			$ 1,200.00
fund Ballace - beginning	$ 158.00				$ 158.00
Fund Balance - ending	$ 2,636.21	$ 1,200.00	$ 1,200.00	$ -	$ 236.21

When you file your information with the Accountability and Disclosure statement the areas you would focus on would be: donations, in-kind donations which are your out-of-pocket, expenses, and borrowed funds. In this financial statement, there are no assets. There is nothing that would be liquidated, and there will be no leftover cash, but there will be debt which is considered a liability or debt burden.

Any business, a government ran project or even a campaign will need a strategic plan to achieve its goals. In Bolinger's campaign, he had to change from just recording expenses to creating a budget for each month until election day. Then he had to put together an expense report that laid out where all the outflow of cash was going. It is important to separate your expenses by category to help create some format and control in your accounting practices. After creating the budget and expense report he moved on to create a statement of revenue for a more professional review of expenses.

Studying financial management and having to comply with the States Accountability and Disclosure Committee, creates the understanding of why you need to set your goals, create your budget, and put everything into a financial statement form. That way you can see where the money is going. You can see all your inflow and outflow of money and you can create an accurate budget plan. It is important to have accurate information so that you know the condition of your business. In this case, it would show the condition of the campaign.

When Larry first started his campaign, he would spend money when he received it and wrote down all the outflow of funds. There was no budget plan. After setting up a budget plan he was able to see flaws in expenses and was able to adjust so that there were consistencies in each expense category. One of the major flaws was that he wasn't spending enough on advertisements. Usually, if you are under budget, that means you are saving money, which is considered a good thing. But in a campaign, you win by name recognition. This means you can not be slacked on advertisements.

In this campaign, there are no liquidated assets. The materials that are in the budget are for signs and sign stakes. All materials are disbursed and considered an expense with no return. The Loan amount is greater than in-kind donations. The total debt is a long-term debt with payments of $260 per month for 15 years. The risk factor in this adventure is high as there is significant debt (liability), with very low cash inflow, no inventory, and no assets.

The next step in this would be to conduct a year-end financial statement to close out the year and prepare to file taxes. If there are any donations given between now and election day could change the amount of cash flow and add to the budget. Any leftover cash after the election would have a portion donated to a non-profit organization, some cash could be used to help fund lobbying for a bill, and some funds could be saved for the next campaign or endorse someone else's campaign for the 2024 election period.

Reference:

Finkler, Steven. Smith, Daniel. Calabrese, Thad. (2020) *"Financial Management for Public, Health, and Not-For=Profit Organizations."* 6 Edition. Sage Publications

Bolinger, Scott. (2022) "Politics: Last Act of Defiance"

Bolinger, Scott. (2022) "Politics: Last Act of Defiance." Volume II.

Willoughby, Katherine. (2014). *"Public Budgeting in Context: Structure, Law, Reform, and Results."*

Conclusion

Nebraska Attorney General Election Results

‹ See all Nebraska state results

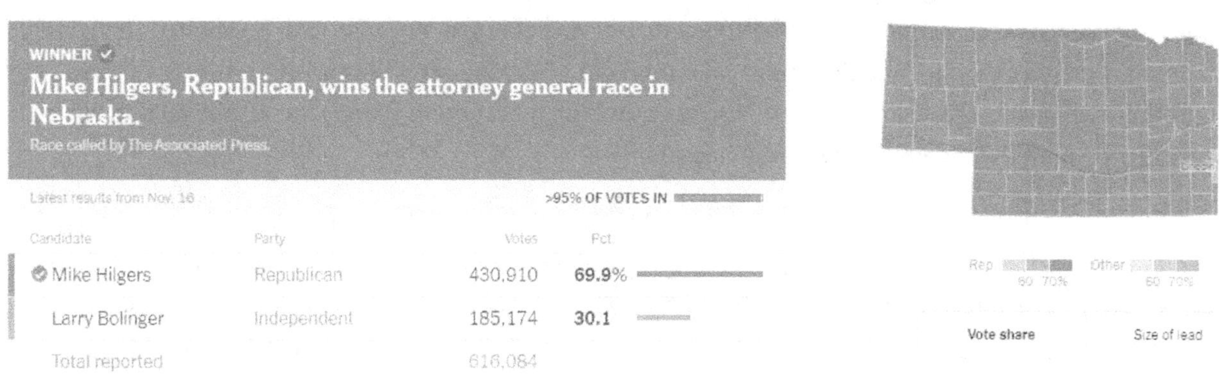

I've run for City Council, Legislature, and Congress. This year I am running for Attorney General. That is the political position that you should push for accountability. The Attorney General's position should be the authority of accountability. You can point out several areas where the legislature has lacked accountability. There are many issues where there were needed actions and issues where they refused to act. Many issues can be shown that the legislature had failed to follow policy and procedures. They need to be called out when they fail to act or when their actions were wrong.

When developing a platform for campaigning for office, you have to create your base platform. After you have your base platform completed, you'll need to have an in-depth research analysis to help educate yourself on the topics and to have ready materials to help educate your volunteers and campaign managers. This manual will help give others an idea of how to create a training manual for their run for office.

In my campaign for Attorney General, I am running against someone who already has over $400,000 in endorsements. While I'm at $250. So keeping people informed and creating a strategy to recruit leaders for different areas of the state needs to be a well-coordinated effort. How to win an election against big money will take a lot of work. To beet big money, you have to have a good strategy and stay consistent and persistent. You have to have name recognition. That takes coordinated effort throughout the state.

In running for office for the LMN party, I have to draw from the Democratic and Republican voters. That means supporting some of their platforms as long as they don't conflict with my platform and limit conflict between the Democrats and Republicans. Focus the support on what may be acceptable to each party. There is a time frame where you can go extreme. But, only a few months before an election is not that time.

To gain Republican support, the LMN party supported Herbert for Governor as he was the only Republican candidate that would support a petition to legalize medical marijuana, but he did not make it past the primary. To gain more support from Democrats I pushed policies that fought discrimination against LGBTQ and helped support their petition to legalize medical marijuana and to create a commission for medical marijuana. This would put me in a position where I would not have good enough Republican support. One option for gaining Republican support is to help out with petitions to support gun initiatives. I would need to be tactful so it doesn't conflict with LMN or Democrat platforms. I chose to push the "Stand Your Ground" petition as I can argue that in a way that both parties would favor. I pushed the legalization petition for several months and it looks like they have enough signatures to get on the ballot as of 17 June 2022. Now, I can switch and push for the "Stand Your Ground" petition.

The way I argue the "Stand Your Ground" policy is that everyone has the right to defend themselves. In today's legal system if some attacks you and you defend yourself, you can be in consent of fighting and be charged with assault along with the person that initiated the attack. The bad side of the argument is that people will assume that the "Stand Your Ground" policy is pushed by white supremacists and would give people more rights to shoot people. This should be argued for defense purposes only and is not to be used as an excuse to shoot someone.

My next step in my campaign is to assure 20 campaign managers across the state. While I expand my management team I'll have to go on the road and put up campaign signs along the highways to help gain name recognition. This will be done in my region and then in each area where I have a campaign manager. At the same time, I will make a push for the "Stand Your Ground" policy. I will have to set up several forums, meet and greets, and signing events. I will also need to recruit roughly 100 petitioners as I have 3 weeks to obtain 20,000 votes. If I secure the 20,000 votes it could help secure a significant amount of Republican voters. While I'm doing that, I will push my agenda, which will be pushing this manual.

State of Nebraska
At an election held on the 10th day of May, 2022
Larry Bolinger
was nominated for the office of
Attorney General
as the
Legal Marijuana NOW Nominee
for the term of 4 years.
Given at Lincoln, Nebraska
this 6th day of June, 2022.
Governor
Secretary of State

Posted in the Ballot News in January of 2023.

Legal Marijuana Now Candidate in 2022 Polled Highest Share of Vote in a Statewide Nebraska Race for a Non-Major Party Nominee Since 1936

Posted on January 24, 2023, by Richard Winger

In November 2022, the Legal Marijuana Now Party nominee for Nebraska Attorney General, Larry Bolinger, polled 30.27% in a two-person race. That was the highest percentage for a statewide Nebraska candidate running outside the two major parties since 1936 when independent George Norris was re-elected to the U.S. Senate with 43.82% of the vote.

<u>Random Quotes</u>

If you are out canvassing an area, knocking on doors, and putting out signs or flyers and you have to break wind, do that along the sidewalk path. If you do that while you are at the door, the door acts as a vacuum and sucks in the fart. You will most likely lose that vote.

One of the failers in today's society is the development of online social media which created the ever-popular online warrior. People who think they are tough by saying and doing whatever they want online. Political debates are changed from arguing about policies to personal attacks. This has created "ScialRetardation" in social skills as people face to face interaction is conducted in the same manner as their online performances and they believe they are untouchable and have no consequences. A threat to me online can be handled much differently than a threat in person as I am a veteran with 30 years of experience in KickBoxing.

2022 is the days of the internet warriors where people can say whatever they want without consequences and then try and do that face to face and don't understand why they got punched. This is the time of social retardation.

Everyone has that spark of genius. What creates success or failure depends on if the person acts on that spark.

Books authored by Scott Bolinger
Politics: Last Act of Defiance Volume I
Politics: Last Act of Defiance Volume I (Second Edition)
Politics: Last Act of Defiance Volume II
Politics: Last Act of Defiance Volume III
WarriorRage KickBoxing Volume I
WarriorRage KickBoxing Volume II
WarriorRage KickBoxing Master Edition
Bolinger KickBoxing
Bolinger Boxing (Four Levels of Boxing)
Stretching by Scott Bolinger
Weight Lifting by Scott Bolinger
Boxing Level 1 by Scott Bolinger
Boxing Level 2 by Scott Bolinger
Boxing Level 3 and 4 by Scott Bolinger
National Self-Defense Solutions
Officials Training Book For Combat Sports
Property Management by Scott Bolinger
Barker Family History

Email: LB@LarryBolinger.com
Website: www.ScottBolinger.website
Published 2024